MOORESTOWN LIBRARY

3 2030 00000 8622

W9-AKN-607

OVERSIZED

158011

LAD 6/2005

Moorestown Library
Moorestown, New Jersey
08057

THE AMERICAN EXPERIENCE IN VIETNAM

THE AMERICAN EXPERIENCE IN VIETNAM

CLARK DOUGAN   STEPHEN WEISS

AND THE EDITORS OF BOSTON PUBLISHING COMPANY

PICTURES SELECTED BY KATHLEEN A. REIDY

W·W·NORTON & COMPANY   NEW YORK LONDON

BOSTON PUBLISHING COMPANY   BOSTON

In the Mekong Delta in early 1962, South Vietnamese marines in search of the Viet-cong fan out from an American helicopter

959.704g
Dou

BOSTON PUBLISHING COMPANY

Publisher: Robert George
Editor-in-Chief: Robert Manning
Managing Editor: Paul Dreyfus
Marketing Director: Jeanne Gibson
Design Director: Lisa Bogle
Picture Editor: Wendy Johnson
Senior Editor: Samuel Lipsman
Senior Writer: Denis Kennedy
Research Assistant: Michael Hathaway
Picture Researchers: Jennifer Atkins, Lauren Chapin
Assistant Designer: Sherry Fatla
Design Assistants: Emily Betsch, Lynne Weygint
Business Staff: Anna Cheshire, Amy Pelletier, Amy Wilson

Frontispiece:
A Marine wades through a stream just south of the demilitarized zone, 1966.

The text of this book was composed in Goudy Old Style
by Waldman Graphics, Inc.
Color separations by Colotone
Manufactured by W. A. Krueger Company

Printed in the United States of America

First Edition

Copyright © 1988 by Boston Publishing Company, Inc. All rights
reserved. No part of this publication may be reproduced or transmitted
in any form or by any means, electronic or mechanical, including
photocopy, recording, or any information storage and retrieval system,
without permission in writing from the publisher.

Library of Congress Catalog Card Number: 88-70320

ISBN: 0-393-02598-5

W·W·Norton & Company, Inc.,
500 Fifth Avenue, New York, New York 10110
W·W·Norton & Company, Ltd,
37 Great Russell Street, London WC1B 3NU

10 9 8 7 6 5 4 3 2 1

CONTENTS

158011

A phosphorus bomb dropped by an A–1E Skyraider falls on a village in the central highlands, 1966.

THE ROOTS
OF INVOLVEMENT

In Bien Hoa, South Vietnam, on a hot July night in the summer of 1959, Americans did not worry too much about death.

Absorbed in the first reel of an old movie, the six advisers did not hear the shadowy, black-clad figures who crept out of the darkness surrounding their mess hall. They did not see them ready a French submachine gun in the rear window or push two rifle muzzles through the pantry screens. They did not realize anything was wrong at all until someone turned on the lights to change the reel.

Suddenly, automatic-weapons fire exploded through the room. The high-caliber shells slammed into the startled Americans, spinning one man around and knocking two others from their seats before the lights snapped off and the gunmen fled. Behind them in the bloody confusion lay Captain Howard Boston. Badly wounded, he would survive. But for Major Dale Buis and Master Sergeant Chester Ovnand the night would go on forever.

The deaths of the two Americans were both tragic and bitterly ironic. On September 2, 1945, other U.S. Army officers had stood on a reviewing stand in Hanoi and listened to a band playing the "Star-Spangled Banner." President Franklin Roosevelt's opposition to French colonialism in Indochina and U.S. collaboration with the Nationalist Vietminh army of Ho Chi Minh during World War II seemed to promise a lasting friendship between the two peoples. As Ho proclaimed his country's freedom in words borrowed directly from the American Declaration of Independence and U.S. aircraft flew overhead in salute, it was unthinkable that fourteen years later Americans and Vietnamese would be dying at each others hands.

But the death of Roosevelt and the onset of the Cold War left a new American president facing larger problems than Vietnamese independence. Alarmed by the threat of Soviet expansionism, determined to maintain cordial relations with a key European partner, and persuaded that Ho Chi Minh was a creature of Moscow, Harry Truman did

In May 1954 near Hanoi, a woman mourns her husband, a victim of the French Indochina War.

not oppose the restoration of French sovereignty in Indochina. When war broke out between France and Vietnam in 1946, the United States adopted a decidedly pro-French "neutrality," declining requests for direct military aid but providing France with sufficient economic assistance that Paris was able to fund the war out of its own pocket.

The French had little success in subduing the Vietminh. But Indochina remained a peripheral issue for the Truman administration until 1949, when the fall of Nationalist China precipitated a crucial change in U.S. strategy. Fearing that another Communist success would have "critical psychological, political, and economic consequences" for the Western alliance, Truman abandoned American neutrality and committed the United States to a French victory. In early 1950 a U.S. Military Assistance Advisory Group (MAAG) arrived in Vietnam to funnel military aid to France's expeditionary army. By 1952 the United States was paying more than one-third of the cost of the war.

Truman's Indochina policy was adopted in its entirety by President Dwight Eisenhower, who believed his predecessor had erred only in allowing France too much leeway. Using more than $1 billion of increased funding as leverage, Washington insisted the French make greater efforts to win Nationalist support and adopt a more aggressive strategy. But nothing could arrest the steady deterioration of the military situation. In March 1954, the Vietminh surrounded 12,000 French troops at Dien Bien Phu. When France requested American help, Eisenhower warned that the loss of Indochina would set off a chain reaction felling other nations in the region "like a row of dominoes." But the administration was not prepared to act alone and found no support in Congress for intervention. On May 7, after a fifty-five-day siege, the French garrison at Dien Bien Phu finally surrendered.

Attention immediately shifted to Geneva, where an East-West conference had just begun to discuss the Indochina problem. Buoyed by their victory, the Vietminh demanded an immediate withdrawal of foreign troops and a comprehensive political settlement. But China and the Soviet Union persuaded Ho Chi Minh to accept temporary partition of Vietnam at the seventeenth par-

allel with elections to reunify the country in two years. Meanwhile, the United States prepared to take over the defense of Laos, Cambodia, and the nascent state of South Vietnam, which few observers expected to survive the year.

The new nation's leader was widely respected as an experienced administrator and ardent Nationalist. But Ngo Dinh Diem faced a devastated economy, a lack of trained civil servants, hundreds of thousands of refugees, and dozens of armed sects hostile to his government. With U.S. help and a stubborn persistence all his own, Diem not only survived but triumphed. In September 1955, in a declaration that reflected both his internal strength and the backing of his American patrons, he denounced the Geneva accords and refused to participate in the reunification elections scheduled for the following year.

Once Diem had consolidated his regime, Washington launched an experiment in nation-building that took on the atmosphere of a crusade. From 1955 to 1961 the United States provided South Vietnam with more than $2 billion in aid. Along with the flood of American money came American engineers, doctors, agriculturalists, social scientists, military advisers, and public administrators to rebuild the South Vietnamese armed forces, reshape the South Vietnamese economy, and reorganize the South Vietnamese government. By the late 1950s more than 1,500 Americans were building roads, planting crops, training bureaucrats, and dispensing medicine all across South Vietnam under the supervision of the largest U.S. Mission anywhere in the world.

U.S. officials called it a "miracle," but their rhetoric outstripped reality. Although the United States was spending $85 million a year on training and equipment, the Army of the Republic of (South) Vietnam (ARVN) suffered from serious manpower shortages and command deficiencies. Although American aid prevented economic collapse and gilded life in Saigon, little was spent on industrial development or used to improve the living conditions of the rural peasants who constituted 90 percent of the population. And although American advisers clothed South Vietnam in the trappings of democracy, Diem presided over a ruthless, authoritarian regime that steadily alienated popular support for his government.

Diem lost ground particularly in the countryside, where his suppression of traditional village government and an ineffectual land-reform program created a receptive audience for revolutionary alternatives. In 1957 Vietminh cadres who remained in the South after partition resumed political agitation in the villages, their efforts soon escalating into a systematic campaign of terror and assassination against local government officials. In January 1959, North Vietnam formally endorsed the resumption of armed struggle in the South and soon after began constructing the network of roads and trails that would become the Ho Chi Minh Trail. Over this route, Hanoi sent weapons and advisers to assist the insurgents who, in December 1960, coalesced under the banner of the National Liberation Front. By the time John Kennedy took office at the beginning of 1961, the military situation had become critical.

Along with the immediate crisis, the young American president had inherited a national commitment. By insisting on the vital importance of Southeast Asia to America's security, Presidents Truman and Eisenhower had made it virtually impossible to retreat from the region. Moreover, Soviet threats to blockade Berlin and the failure of an American-sponsored invasion of Cuba made it imperative in Kennedy's mind that the United States demonstrate its resolve in Vietnam. At the same time, the experience of the Korean War made him deeply reluctant to deploy American troops on the Asian mainland. Nor would their presence alone guarantee victory. The survival of the Diem government depended ultimately on its willingness to address the social and economic needs of South Vietnam's peasant majority, something it had so far refused to do. Yet without a credible threat of withdrawal, Washington had no leverage to enforce its demands for reform.

Confident of his ability to maintain control of U.S. involvement and unwilling to accept the costs of pulling out, Kennedy opted for a middle course between retreat and direct military intervention. Warding off pressure to introduce combat troops, the president substantially increased the amount of U.S. aid and the number of American advisers. Any consideration of a larger U.S. military presence depended on evidence from Saigon that the government intended to put its house in order.

The influx of American men and weapons took the Vietcong by surprise, but the continuing disabilities of the South Vietnamese army enabled the insurgents to regain the initiative. Washington's attempts to change the direction of the Saigon government also met with failure. Diem instituted token economic reforms to appease the Americans while simultaneously enacting new measures of political repression. The inevitable crisis erupted in the summer of 1963 when militant Buddhists challenged the government with massive street demonstrations and fiery self-immolations. After months of upheaval a group of South Vietnamese army generals began preparations that culminated on November 1 with the overthrow of the Diem government. During the coup Diem and his brother Ngo Dinh Nhu were assassinated.

Although Washington had approved Diem's removal, his murder shocked Kennedy and brought to the surface the president's growing doubts about the course he had taken. When he assumed office there were 875 U.S. servicemen in Vietnam. Now there were more than 16,000. Since 1961, millions of dollars had been spent and 109 Americans had lost their lives. Yet the United States was further than ever from its goal of a secure and independent South Vietnam. In mid-November the president ordered a "complete and very profound review" of American policy in Vietnam. Whether or not Kennedy could have reversed a momentum of involvement nearly two decades in the making, he never got the chance. One week later John F. Kennedy was dead.

Following page. *A peasant plows his paddy in the Red River Delta as a French convoy stalls because of a Vietminh ambush ahead on May 25, 1954, two weeks after the French surrender at Dien Bien Phu. The picture was among the last taken by war photographer Robert Capa, who within hours of taking this picture became the first American correspondent killed covering fighting in Indochina.*

policy advisers—men like Secretary of State Dean Rusk and Secretary of Defense Robert McNamara—who had their own stake in South Vietnam's survival.

Compounding matters was the sense of crisis enveloping Southeast Asia at the end of 1963. In Indonesia, the mercurial Sukarno had gone from flirtation with Peking to open war against the pro-Western government of Malaysia. In Cambodia, Prince Norodom Sihanouk had renounced American aid and called for an international conference to guarantee his nation's neutrality. The same theme was trumpeted by French president Charles de Gaulle who challenged American influence in southern Asia with a proposal for the neutralization of South Vietnam.

Meanwhile, the military junta that took power in Saigon was able neither to fill the political vacuum left by Diem's death nor to cope with the upsurge of fighting that wracked the countryside. On December 21, Robert McNamara returned to Washington after a brief inspection tour with a grim report of political turmoil, administrative paralysis, and military reverses at every hand. Unless the situation was stabilized immediately, warned the secretary of defense, the fate of South Vietnam would be "neutralization at best and more likely a Communist-controlled state."

Concerned for his own political standing and the credibility of America around the world, determined to show his critics he could deal with the crisis he had inherited, Johnson responded by vigorously affirming his government's intention of resisting communism in Southeast Asia. He expressed his resolve in terms of American responsibilities around the world. "Our strength imposes on us an obligation to assure that this type of aggression does not succeed," Johnson wrote in February 1964. Neutralization was unworkable, withdrawal unthinkable.

For all that, the new president proceeded with restraint during his first year in office. One reason for the measured pace was Johnson's reluctance to employ American military power on a large scale so far from home. No more than Kennedy or Eisenhower did he relish the prospect of U.S. troops engaged in battle on the Asian mainland. Nor was Johnson certain how the Soviets or Chinese would react to the appearance of American combat forces in the region. Moreover, American assumption of responsibility for the war might seriously undercut South Vietnam's will to defend itself.

Even more important were the potential domestic repercussions of greater U.S. involvement in Southeast Asia. Any significant American escalation would endanger the administration's legislative program and jeopardize Johnson's bid for election in November. Johnson was not only unwilling to let this happen, he saw no reason for it. Preoccupied with establishing his leadership and taking advantage of the moment to push major civil rights and antipoverty bills through Congress, the president balanced commitment with caution, putting off difficult decisions for as long as possible.

Thus, for all the upheavals of the previous six months, the spring of 1964 witnessed little apparent change in the course of U.S. policy. After a review of the options available to him, Johnson authorized the deployment of additional U.S. military advisers and an enlargement of the economic assistance package to Saigon. The emphasis, however, remained squarely on the South Vietnamese, with new plans for an increase in the size of the ARVN, intensification of the pacification program, and stepped-up military operations against the Vietcong. "The only thing I know to do," Johnson told Senator William Fulbright in March, "is more of the same and do it more efficiently and effectively."

Yet, hidden from public view were important changes that, like the heightened rhetoric of U.S. commitment, contained a momentum of their own. Concerned over reports of increased infiltration of men and supplies flowing south, the administration approved a program of clandestine operations into Laos and North Vietnam. Pressed by McNamara for concrete steps to counter the continuing military decline on the ground, the president authorized contingency planning for retaliatory air strikes north of the DMZ. Determined to demonstrate American resolve, Johnson privately warned Hanoi that continued support for the insurgency could bring the "greatest devastation" to North Vietnam. Taken as a whole, these measures revealed a fundamental shift in perspective, a growing belief in Washington that direct action against North Vietnam could somehow achieve what U.S. policy had failed to accomplish in the South.

In an act that shocked the world, Buddhist monk Quang Duc immolates himself on a Saigon street on June 11, 1963, to protest President Ngo Dinh Diem's persecution of Buddhists.

For the time being the counterinsurgency war in the South continued, with the United States more deeply involved than ever. Over the next nine months the number of American military advisers increased from 16,000 to 23,000, among them naval officers working with the fledgling Vietnamese navy and nearly 100 U.S. Air Force pilots flying combat-support missions for ARVN offensives as well as training Vietnamese pilots. The army was also becoming increasingly engaged in the shooting war. By the end of 1964 American Special Forces Civilian Irregular Defense Group (CIDG) teams had established forty-four camps throughout South Vietnam. Many of them were located along the Laotian border, enabling the Green Berets and their montagnard allies to monitor traffic along the Ho Chi Minh Trail

but also making them more vulnerable to Communist attack. From 1960 through 1962, 32 U.S. military personnel lost their lives in South Vietnam. During 1963 that figure climbed to 77, and in 1964, deaths from hostile action totaled 137. If the numbers were still low, the trend was disquieting.

But U.S. servicemen were not the only Americans struggling to contain the Communist guerrillas. In the late spring Frank Scotton, a junior field operator with the United States Information Service, unveiled the first People's Special Forces group—six-man teams of armed Vietnamese civilians trained to fight local insurgent bands on their own terms. By August the program had been taken over by the Central Intelligence Agency (CIA), which also provided arms and funding for Viet-

Special Forces soldiers fire flares and tracer bullets to test the readiness of local montagnard CIDG troops for battle.

namese Counter-Terror Teams and sponsored Radio Freedom, a 10,000-watt station based in Hue that sent propaganda broadcasts to North Vietnam.

Alongside these "public" activities was an expanding program of U.S.-directed covert operations. Some were run by the U.S. Military Assistance Command, Vietnam (MACV), such as Project Leaping Lena, which sent eight-man squads of Vietnamese commandos on long-range reconnaissance patrols into Laos, or Project Delta, in which ten-man "Hunter-Killer Teams" made up of American and Vietnamese Special Forces soldiers penetrated enemy-controlled territory within South Vietnam. The most dramatic covert activities, however, were carried out by the innocuously named Studies and Observation Group (SOG), a highly classified unit controlled directly by the Pentagon. SOG teams entered Cambodia, Laos, and even North Vietnam to gather intelligence on enemy activities, snatch prisoners for interrogation, and interdict infiltration. SOG also sent Vietnamese PT boats against North Vietnamese coastal installations in a series of raids code named Operation 34–Alpha.

Unfortunately, neither the dispatch of additional advisers, the expansion of covert operations, nor an increase of $125 million in aid were able to arrest the steady decline of Saigon's military and political fortunes. The junta that had deposed Diem was itself overthrown two months later by a group of younger officers under the leadership of General Nguyen Khanh. Although Washington lent Khanh vocal public support, the new government was no more successful than its predecessor in extending its authority into the countryside. A U.S. report issued on April 1 estimated that the Vietcong controlled between 40 and 60 percent of the rural population. Even in areas Saigon could claim as its own a lack of trained officials, bureaucratic lethargy, insufficient resources, pervasive corruption, and the sometimes brutal behavior of government soldiers undermined the new pacification program and prevented the implementation of ambitious development plans drafted by the Americans.

Although Khanh proved inept at rallying public support, his main problem was the steadily worsening military situation. In December 1963, as Vietcong units roamed at will over large sections of the South Vietnamese countryside, the central committee of the Vietnamese Communist party met in Hanoi to approve a new strategy for the southern insurgency. Hoping to discourage the United States and bring down the Saigon government, North Vietnam funneled increasing amounts of war materiel to its southern allies, who began to take to the field armed with mortars, machine guns, and recoilless rifles.

A wave of terrorist attacks hit the American colony in Saigon, but the main thrust of the new campaign was to destroy Saigon's strategic reserves already weakened by spiraling desertion rates. Striking repeatedly at isolated posts, the Vietcong lured ARVN units from their bases into carefully concealed ambushes. By late summer much of South Vietnam's military reserves had been annihilated, the territory held by Saigon fragmented into small enclaves, and the nation's confidence virtually spent. Public demonstrations against the government multiplied on Saigon's streets, while an attempted coup d'état from within was aborted only when U.S. officials warned off the conspirators. Maxwell Taylor, who succeeded Henry Cabot Lodge as American ambassador in midsummer, estimated that the Khanh government had no more than "a 50–50 chance of lasting out the year."

Unable to solve the problems that surrounded him, Khanh called upon his countrymen to "March North," a cry echoed immediately by General Nguyen Cao Ky. The flamboyant young commander of the Vietnamese air force publicly announced that his pilots had already been training for just such a mission. "We are ready," Ky told the press, resplendent in a black flight suit and lavender scarf. "We could go this afternoon. I cannot assure that all of North Vietnam would be destroyed, but Hanoi would certainly be destroyed." Although Taylor privately reprimanded both South Vietnamese leaders for their provocative remarks, many Washington officials had by this time come to much the same point of view.

Indeed, pressure for direct U.S. military action against the North was coming at Johnson from all directions. As early as January the Joint Chiefs of Staff had urged the president to "take bolder actions which may embody greater risks." Deploring the self-imposed restrictions under which the war was being fought, the generals recommended the commitment of U.S. combat forces to South Vietnam, an invasion of Laos to hinder infiltration, and the bombing of key targets in North Vietnam. In March, the interagency Vietnam Working Group, chaired by the State Department's Robert Johnson, endorsed the JCS recommendations, suggesting in particular a blockade of Haiphong Harbor and air strikes against military training camps, transportation arteries, and petroleum storage facilities. Although Secretary of Defense McNamara rejected escalation for the time being, he persuaded the president to authorize planning for a bombing campaign against the North. By June, as the situation in Vietnam worsened, both outgoing Ambassador Lodge and the newly appointed commander of MACV, General William C. Westmoreland, were calling for vigorous American military action to bolster South Vietnamese morale. Chief among their proposals were air strikes against Laos or North Vietnam.

Those in Washington who dissented from the new administration's emerging policy were few and far between. Among them was Roger Hilsman, assistant secretary of state for Far Eastern affairs. A veteran of the Kennedy years and a proponent of patient counterinsurgency, Hilsman had cautioned in early 1963 against "over-Americanization" of the war, arguing that Vietnam required "as much political and civic action" as military effort. Charged by Johnson with disloyalty and pressured to resign, Hilsman warned in a letter to Secretary of State Rusk that "significant action against North Vietnam that is taken before we demonstrate success in our counterinsurgency program will be interpreted by the Communists as an act of desperation, and will, therefore, not be effective in persuading the North Vietnamese to cease and desist." Operations against North Vietnam, he concluded, "may at a certain stage be a useful *supplement* to an effective counterinsurgency program, but cannot be an effective *substitute*."

Subsequent events would vindicate Hilsman's insistence on the priority of political over military solutions to the Vietnamese problem and his judgment of Hanoi's tenacity. However, frustration over Saigon's inability to put its own house in order, the existence of a major

unused air capability, and President Johnson's reluctance to risk American ground combat units had fashioned a growing consensus within the administration for the application of air power against North Vietnam. By midsummer, planning for a program of "graduated overt pressure" against the North was well advanced, along with drafts of a Congressional resolution supporting U.S. policy in Southeast Asia and providing authorization to the president for whatever military action he might deem necessary. In Johnson's mind such a resolution was simply "part of the normal contingency planning effort. I continued to hope that we could keep our role in Vietnam limited." Events in the Gulf of Tonkin in August, however, suggested that within the administration the momentum toward full military involvement was almost irresistible.

Among the covert operations approved by the president during the spring were electronic surveillance missions code named DeSoto and conducted by U.S. destroyers off the coast of North Vietnam. These patrols had gone on for several months without incident when, on the night of August 2, the U.S.S. *Maddox* was attacked by three North Vietnamese PT boats near the island of Hon Me in the Gulf of Tonkin. After a twenty-minute engagement the *Maddox* drove off the attackers with the help of four jet fighters from the aircraft carrier U.S.S. *Ticonderoga.* Assuming that the North Vietnamese had confused the *Maddox* with an unrelated 34–A raid against Hon Me two days earlier, Johnson declined to retaliate. Lest his restraint be misinterpreted by Hanoi, however, the president ordered the patrols to continue with the addition of a second destroyer, the U.S.S. *Turner Joy,* the provision of air cover, and explicit authorization to respond with force to any attack in international waters.

On the night of August 4, as the two ships plowed through heavy seas sixty miles from the North Vietnamese mainland, the *Maddox* radioed that the destroyers were under attack by North Vietnamese gunboats. In fact, on an "inky black night" one seaman described as "darker than the hubs of Hell," no one aboard either ship actually saw the enemy craft, firing their guns instead at sonar and radar contacts of questionable reliability. After a brief engagement, the destroyers reported they had repulsed the North Vietnamese without sustaining any casualties or damage. But several hours later the commander of the *Maddox* reassessed the situation, indicating that "freak weather effects" as well as an "overeager" sonarman may have accounted for the apparent torpedo attacks and enemy contacts. Emphasizing that there had been "no actual visual sightings," he concluded that the entire action "left many doubts" and suggested a complete evaluation before any further action was taken.

By the time these second thoughts reached Washington, however, Johnson had already decided on a swift retaliatory strike. Discounting the uncertainty of the men on the scene in favor of North Vietnamese radio intercepts that appeared to confirm an engagement and relying on assurances by Admiral U.S. Grant Sharp, commander-in-chief, Pacific Fleet (CINCPAC), that "the ambush was bona fide," Secretary of Defense McNamara recommended that the air raids go ahead. At 11:37 P.M. on the evening of August 4, some thirteen hours after the first reports reached Washington, Johnson went on television to inform the American people that U.S. jets were already in the air. The carrier-launched attacks, code named Pierce Arrow, struck patrol boat bases and oil storage depots at Quang Khe, Vinh, Phuoc Loi, Hon Gai, and the Lach Chao Estuary, sinking twenty-five PT boats and destroying an estimated 10 percent of North Vietnam's total petroleum storage capacity.

The following day the president submitted to Congress a resolution authorizing him to take "all necessary measures to repel any armed attacks against the forces of the United States and to prevent further aggression." Asserting that the peace and security of the region were "vital" to the national interest, the measure further committed the U.S., "as the president determines, to take all necessary steps, including the use of armed force, to assist any member or protocol state of the Southeast Asia Collective Defense Treaty requesting assistance in defense of its freedom." On August 7, after less than ten hours of debate, Congress delivered the mandate the president wanted. Although Alaska's Ernest Gruening attacked the resolution as a "predated declaration of

war," and Senator Wayne Morse of Oregon warned his colleagues they were circumventing the Constitution, the Senate overrode their objections by a vote of 88–2. The margin in the House was 466–0.

The events in the Tonkin Gulf proved to be a watershed of vast proportions. By seizing the opportunity afforded him, Johnson won a resounding Congressional endorsement for his policies. His firm but restrained handling of the crisis earned him broad popular support, neutralized the hawkish Republican presidential nominee, Senator Barry Goldwater, and paved the way for his overwhelming electoral victory in November. Yet, in time, both he and the nation would pay a heavy price for his victory.

The Southeast Asia Resolution raised the level of U.S. commitment, linked American prestige more firmly than ever with the fate of South Vietnam, and virtually compelled Washington to respond to future North Vietnamese provocations. The air attacks themselves had shattered the barrier against taking the war to the North, making further escalation of the conflict that much easier. And if the administration had punished the North Vietnamese, America had also paid a price. Antiaircraft fire during the raids brought down two U.S. aircraft and damaged two more. One of the pilots ditched his plane in the ocean and died. The other, Lieutenant Everett Alvarez of San Jose, California, became the first American pilot taken prisoner by the North Vietnamese. Although Alvarez would languish in a Hanoi prison for the next eight years, he was not alone. The United States, too, had become a hostage of the war.

During the fall of 1964, however, political considerations of various sorts enforced restraint. With the presidential election fast approaching, Johnson emphasized his desire to limit American involvement. "We seek no wider war," he declared repeatedly, assuring campaign audiences that American boys would not be sent to do the fighting that Asian boys should be doing for themselves. In South Vietnam, meanwhile, a clumsy attempt by Khanh to seize dictatorial power provoked violent antigovernment riots that drove the general from Saigon while warring Buddhist and Catholic mobs rampaged

A photograph taken from aboard the U.S.S. Maddox *shows one of the three North Vietnamese torpedo boats that attacked the American destroyer in the Gulf of Tonkin on August 2, 1964.*

through the streets. Khanh returned to power a week later, but the fragility of his government seemed to Washington to preclude any military initiatives against North Vietnam.

Nonetheless, the pressure on Johnson to expand the war mounted steadily. In mid-September, with both the air force and Marine Corps urging extended air attacks against the North, Ambassador Taylor reported to the president that sharp increases in hard-core Vietcong strength had reduced the area of government control in the South to no more than 30 percent of the country. Two weeks later that figure shrank even further following an uprising of montagnard tribes in the central highlands. When the Vietcong attacked the U.S. air base at Bien Hoa on November 1, killing four Americans and damaging five aircraft, Johnson ordered a wholesale pol-

icy review. By the end of the month a consensus had emerged on the need for what Taylor described as a "carefully orchestrated" air campaign against North Vietnam, a conviction hardened by the bombing of a U.S. bachelor officers' billet in Saigon on December 25 that left two Americans dead and fifty-eight wounded. With bellicose statements issuing from Moscow and Peking and Sukarno pulling Indonesia out of the United Nations, the need for decisive U.S. action in the region seemed compelling.

More than anything else, however, what propelled the United States toward war in the spring of 1965 was the continued disintegration of the Saigon government and the threatened defeat of the South Vietnamese army at the hands of the Vietcong. Combined with reports that North Vietnamese regular units had entered the

The remains of a U.S. Air Force Canberra bomber litter the tarmac of Bien Hoa airfield following a Vietcong mortar attack on November 1, 1964.

country, the political instability that had once been the principal obstacle to escalation now became the most persuasive argument for it. Without the psychological shot in the arm that a strike against the North would provide, argued Johnson's advisers, no anti-Communist South Vietnamese government could survive.

On February 6, Vietcong units attacked U.S. installations at Pleiku, handing the administration the opportunity it sought. "We have kept our guns over the mantel and our shells in the cupboard for a long time now," exclaimed an angry President Johnson. "I can't ask American soldiers out there to continue to fight with one hand behind their backs." One day after the Pleiku attacks, U.S. planes struck North Vietnamese targets in Operation Flaming Dart. When the Communists struck an American enlisted men's quarters in Qui Nhon on February 10, Johnson ordered an even heavier series of bombing raids. "They woke us up in the middle of the night, and we woke them up in the middle of the night," said a grim-faced president. "They did it again and we did it again." But the time for "tit-for-tat" reprisals had ended. On February 13, convinced that Hanoi was "moving in for the kill," Johnson approved a program of graduated, sustained air attacks against North Vietnam code named Rolling Thunder.

After a series of delays the operation finally got under way on March 2 when U.S. Air Force fighter-bombers struck an ammunition depot at Xom Bang, thirty-five miles north of the DMZ. In keeping with Johnson's desire for a "limited air action," the second Rolling Thunder mission did not take place for nearly two weeks. But the meager results of these first strikes, plus pressure from the Joint Chiefs for more substantial blows and ominous reports of a worsening military situation within South Vietnam, induced the president to authorize an expanded effort against North Vietnamese lines of communication as far north as the twentieth parallel. During April, American and South Vietnamese pilots flew a total of 3,600 sorties in what had become a sustained bombing campaign.

The initiation of regular air operations against North Vietnam produced a concomitant deployment of ground forces to the South. Fearing Vietcong retaliation, General Westmoreland requested two Marine infantry bat-

talions to defend the vital U.S. air base at Da Nang. Although a staunch advocate of bombing, Maxwell Taylor expressed grave reservations about the dispatch of ground forces, questioning the suitability of American combat troops for an Asian guerrilla war and the difficulty of "holding the line" once the first step had been taken. Despite Taylor's warnings, Washington went ahead. Preoccupied with the first stages of the air campaign against the North, the administration treated Westmoreland's request as a minor detail, a "one-shot affair to meet a specific situation." On the morning of March 8, the first wave of the 9th Marine Expeditionary Brigade splashed ashore near Da Nang and took up positions on the edge of the sprawling air base.

For Westmoreland and the Joint Chiefs, however, the deployment of the Marines was only the first stage in a troop buildup of much vaster proportions. Having come to the conclusion by mid-March that the only way for the United States to avert disaster in South Vietnam was "to put our own finger in the dike," the MACV commander recommended the commitment of two U.S. Army divisions. Westmoreland also proposed that American troops not be limited to defensive coastal enclaves, as Taylor wanted, but engage in offensive operations against enemy units in the central highlands.

Although frustrated by the limited results of the bombing campaign and angry over a VC attack on the U.S. Embassy in Saigon on March 29, Johnson was still reluctant to become too deeply embroiled in the ground war. He was concerned, however, that a lack of decisive action might precipitate the long-feared South Vietnamese collapse. Johnson forged a compromise between Taylor and the Joint Chiefs formalized in a national security action memorandum dated April 6. The new policy called for a continuation of the bombing campaign against the North, the deployment of two additional Marine combat battalions to South Vietnam, and an increase of some 20,000 men in U.S. military support forces. Although the new troops would continue to be confined to enclaves around major U.S. bases, the pres-

Nguyen Cao Ky (right), South Vietnam's flamboyant air vice marshal, chats with fellow officers before leading his country's first air strike over North Vietnam, February 1965.

ident also approved a "change of mission" for all Marine battalions deployed to Vietnam, permitting offensive operations within fifty miles of their base areas. Three weeks later, under continued prodding from Westmoreland and the Joint Chiefs, Johnson approved the deployment of nine more battalions, bringing total U.S. troop strength in Vietnam to 82,000 men.

The full implications of these decisions, which marked a major step toward large-scale involvement in the ground war, were carefully concealed from the public. During the deliberations that produced the new policy directives Johnson told reporters, "I know of no far-reaching strategy that is being suggested or promulgated." When the Marines' new mission was accidentally mentioned in a government press release two months later the administration issued a heated denial, opening a "credibility gap" that would torment Johnson for the remainder of his presidency. The obvious expansion of the war, however, was enough to provoke vocal protest, including a march on Washington that attracted 12,000 college students. Johnson attempted to disarm his critics by sending spokesmen to university campuses and authorizing a five-day bombing pause in early May. The temporary halt produced no response from Hanoi but did help the administration push through Congress a $700-million appropriation to support military operations in Vietnam.

To the president's dismay, however, neither the new deployments nor the additional funding were enough to reverse the deteriorating military situation. At the end of May the Vietcong launched their spring-summer offensive with regiment-size attacks in Quang Ngai Province that within a week had killed more than 1,000 of the government's best troops. In mid-June the offensive moved into War Zone C northwest of Saigon where tactical ineptitude and a lack of leadership contributed to the savage mauling of still more South Vietnamese units. By the end of the month MACV estimated that five ARVN regiments and nine separate battalions had been rendered "combat ineffective" as a result of the fighting. The new American commitment also seemed

After a successful landing, Marines of the 9th Expeditionary Brigade rest on Da Nang's Red Beach Two on March 8, 1965.

Focus: Training

On July 28, 1965, as a Communist offensive threatened to split South Vietnam in two, President Lyndon Johnson told the American people that their sons and daughters were going to war. "We did not choose to be the guardians at the gate, but there is no one else," declared the president. "We will stand in Vietnam."

Ordering the immediate deployment of the 1st Cavalry Division and a doubling of draft calls, Johnson asked Congressional authorization for a 340,000-man increase in all U.S. armed forces. His request initiated the largest military buildup in U.S. peacetime history. Six months after the president's announcement the number of U.S. military personnel in South Vietnam had jumped from 81,000 to 250,000. Within two years that figure almost doubled. Some of the increase came from volunteers, but the majority of those sent to Vietnam flowed through some 4,000 draft boards that by December 1965 were already processing more than 40,000 men a month.

To handle the sudden demand for fighting men, the air force, navy, and Marines all increased their training facilities. But the president's call to arms had the greatest impact on the army. Ordered by the Pentagon to create three new 7,500-man infantry brigades and more than 700 smaller units, the army expanded half a dozen bases and opened new facilities all around the country. By the end of the year six army basic-training centers—Fort Ord, California; Fort Dix, New Jersey; Fort Jackson, South Carolina; Fort Polk, Louisiana; Fort Gordon, Georgia; and Fort Leonard Wood, Missouri—were teaching nearly 13,000 recruits how to fight and survive in the jungles of Southeast Asia.

Whether they signed DD Form 4—ENLISTMENT CONTRACT: ARMED FORCES OF THE UNITED STATES—or received a letter headed "Greetings," the beginnings were all the same. A bus or a train took them to a place like Marine boot camp at Parris Island, South Carolina, or one of the many army training centers, the lively young men growing strangely silent as they neared their destination. "There was no conversation now, no sound but the mechanical grate and whine of the bus itself," remembered one recruit years later. "Nervous anticipation—raw fear of the unknown—made thought impossible." Then the bus stopped, the train coasted to a halt, and the doors folded open on a new world.

At some reception centers the new arrivals were met by brass bands. The next greeting they received was apt to be a good deal less friendly. It usually came from a large man in a wide-brimmed, forest-ranger hat whose title was drill sergeant, whose face was scowling, and whose voice carried unmistakable conviction when it growled, "You're all mine now!" The routine of the next few days varied from place to place but everywhere included orientation lectures, haircuts, shots, more lectures, blood tests, forms to fill out, talks by chaplains and Red Cross representatives, more orientation sessions, fingerprinting, TB tests, form letters to write home, and a small reference booklet that covered everything a soldier needed to know, including "Pay due a serviceman at time of death." Along the way the new recruits were issued boots, uniforms, field gear, rifles, and bedding. They learned how to salute, how to hold a cotton ball for their blood test, and how to make a bed to military specifications.

In the mid-1960s the army was undergoing a renaissance in the ranks led by army chief of staff General Harold K. Johnson. Convinced that modern warfare required a modern soldier, Johnson wanted his men to think for themselves. "You can't just stand there and yell 'Hurry it up,' " he once admonished a drill instructor. "The American soldier has to be led, not pushed."

The Marines remained wedded to an older tradition, however. Like thousands of others, W.D. Ehrhart's first sight of a Marine drill instructor was unforgettable, as he recounted in *Vietnam-Perkasie: A Combat Marine Memoir.* "The DI who got on that bus was eight-and-a-half-feet tall. And he was ugly. Standing there with his hands on his hips, he looked like a cross between Paul Bunyan, Babe the Blue Ox, and Godzilla." The ear-shattering bellow that came from his mouth, recalled the suddenly terrified recruit, sounded like the voice of God. " 'There's four columns of yellow footprints painted on the deck in front of those steps over there,' roared the DI. 'When I give the word, you filthy pigs have three seconds to get outta this bus and plant yourself on one of those sets of yellow footprints. You will not talk. You will keep your head and eyes front at all times. You will do everything you're told instantly, and you will do nothing else. I'll kill the first cocksucker that fucks it up. You scuzzy shitbirds are *mine*, ladies! And I don't like you. Now, MOVE! *Do it! Do it!*' "

Not that the much larger number of men welcomed into the army had it easy. Despite such novelties as automatic dishwashers and potato-peeling machines in K.P., their training was in many ways tougher than ever. Compared to the eight to twelve weeks of military instruction given during World War II, soldiers heading to Vietnam underwent a minimum of four months of training divided into basic and advanced courses, some of it on subjects unimaginable only a decade earlier.

Once initial processing was completed, the new recruits were divided into 250-man companies and shipped off to basic-training centers. Over the next eight weeks the army provided them with 352 hours of instruction. Some of it took place in classrooms where instructors lectured on military courtesy and sanitation. But the trainees spent most of the time preparing their minds and bodies for war.

Crawling out of their bunks at 5:15 or 5:30 in the morning, they filled the days with calisthenics, close-order drill, and marching, always marching, whether they were Marines or army soldiers. "Whenever I think back to those days at Basic School," wrote former Marine Philip Caputo, "the recollection that first comes to mind is always the same: a double file of green-clad men, bent beneath their packs, are tramping down a dirt road. A remorseless sun is beating down. Raised by our boots, a cloud of red dust powders the trees alongside the road, making them look sickly and ashen. The dust clings to our uniforms, runs in muddy streaks down our sweating faces. There is the rattle of rifle slings and bayonet scabbards, the clattering of mess kits bouncing in our haversacks. Our heads ache from the weight of steel helmets, and the cry 'Close it up, keep your interval, close it up' is echoing up and down the long column."

When they dropped their packs the young recruits were introduced to their rifles. "A soldier's weapon is his best friend," intoned the instructors who made sure their charges not only could shoot their rifles but also knew how to take them apart and put them back together again. There were classes in grenade throwing and hand-to-hand combat, pugil-stick fights and bayonet training. There were exercises in mock combat with real bullets whizzing a few inches over a man's head as he crawled through the mud. Near the end of basic the men were taken out on bivouac to learn how to live in the field and eat C-rations.

Through it all the veterans with the stripes on their sleeves tried to teach the new recruits how to get back in one piece from "the boonies." Never stand in groups, or one incoming round could get you all. Do not give or return salutes—Charlie likes to shoot the officers. When you hear a loud noise, hit the deck, do not try to run for a bunker. Sleep as close to the ground as you can, under the ground if possible. And the one rule that summarized all the rules for survival in a war zone: "Keep your ass down."

Slowly, steadily, the regimen of training began to change the former civilians: It toughened them physically, disciplined their reactions, and taught them the reality of interdependence and the necessity of teamwork. Those who failed any portion of the course "recycled" that segment until they got it right. When everything worked, a group of individuals became a machine that theoretically would respond as a single unit in the face of danger. Finally, after passing the army's exhaustive Physical Combat Proficiency Test, recruits graduated from basic training.

After a well-deserved leave, army recruits went on to Advanced Individual Training (AIT). There they learned additional skills based on their aptitudes and interests. Some received further training as clerks or cooks, typists or truck drivers. Others underwent a nine-week course in one of a variety of combat arms specialties. These ranged from artillery to tanks to helicopters but also included the most basic specialty of all—infantry tactics.

AIT was designed in part to refine skills first mastered in basic training. Already exposed to living in the open, future infantrymen now learned how to sterilize water, self-treat wounds, select food for jungle survival, and prevent malaria or treat it if necessary. Since the Vietcong would not stand around with bull's-eyes painted on their uniforms, Vietnam-bound foot soldiers were taught "instant reaction" and "quick kill" techniques. They learned to shoot at sound and movement without consciously aiming, practicing on multiple targets that popped up at random from behind bushes and trees. Meanwhile, the aggressive psychology necessary for war was fostered through everything from luridly painted signs shouting "Bong the Cong" to hard-bitten instructors grimly reminding the young trainees, "The essence of combat is to kill!"

The primary goal of AIT, however, was to give novice soldiers the experience of Vietnam before they had to face the real thing. To do so, the army constructed replicas of VC hamlets—"staffed" with "enemy" soldiers and complete in detail down to the last tunnel and punji stick—then set combat "problems" for the trainees to deal with. Particular attention was devoted to patrolling and ambush and counterambush techniques, along with the intricacies of camouflage. As an officer lectured one class in methods used by the VC to conceal themselves, a hidden soldier carrying a machine gun jumped from a hole only a few feet in front of the startled recruits.

Once acclimated to the "enemy" environment, the men were taught the nuances of counterinsurgency warfare in Vietnam. They discovered the need for the buddy system—one man walking down a trail with his eyes glued to the ground in search of trip wires while his buddy kept a lookout for snipers. They learned how to detect enemy booby traps and place claymore mines, how to set ambushes and establish listening posts outside night defensive perimeters, how to jump from hovering helicopters into "hot" LZs and flush enemy guerrillas into predesignated "killing zones." Much of the time the recruits learned by making mistakes. At Fort Riley, Kansas, all vehicles and personnel in the training sector were subject to ambush by "aggressor" forces at any hour. At Fort Sill, Oklahoma, veteran trainers gave Vietnam-bound soldiers a taste of what it would mean if they were captured, while at Fort Gordon, Georgia, trainees attacking the fortified village of "Vinh Hoa" found the enemy had escaped through a maze of tunnels.

At the end of AIT the recruits were considered qualified for combat, and many soon found themselves in Vietnam. But some men chose to extend their training into more exotic specialties. There was airborne, where men "slept four and five hours a night and then got up and ran everywhere," remembered one parachutist. "Everything—home, letters, concerns, friends—everything faded under the weight of exhaustion" until the rigors of practice jumps from 250-foot towers and the fear of their first real jumps made them forget how tired they were. Then there was Ranger training, where the schedule made airborne look like a piece of cake: 3:30 A.M. wake-ups, twelve-minute-mile runs with 100-pound field packs, perilous descents down ice-covered cliffs, low-level night parachute jumps into impenetrable cypress swamps.

There was a limit to what even the most realistic instruction could accomplish, of course. "No training could convey the reality of war or the reality of Vietnam," insisted one former platoon leader, and newcomers to Vietnam fresh from "The World" were routinely advised to forget everything they had already learned. If there was no substitute for war, however, the training had hardly been wasted.

The long weeks of preparation gave young men the endurance they would need to hump mile after mile in searing, mind-numbing heat. It taught them how to read a map, how to fire a mortar, and what to do when someone shot at them. Their training nurtured pride in themselves and loyalty to their comrades. Equally important, it transformed the way they looked at the world around them. Landscape was no longer scenery, it was terrain. The little man in the black pajamas was no longer quaint, he was the enemy. They might not be finished with their military education, but the new recruits had come a long way. "When they leave here," said a training officer at Fort Polk's AIT center, "they are ready to fight."

"You're all mine now!" A drill sergeant at Fort Knox, Kentucky, welcomes a group of army recruits.

Above. *At the army's training center in Fort Dix, New Jersey, an inductee loses some of the trappings of civilian life.*

Right, clockwise from top left. *Boys become soldiers: uniform measurement at Fort Dix; being fitted for boots, Fort Knox; trying on a garrison hat; the receiving end of an inoculation gun.*

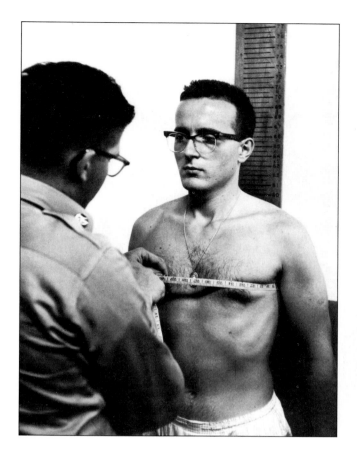
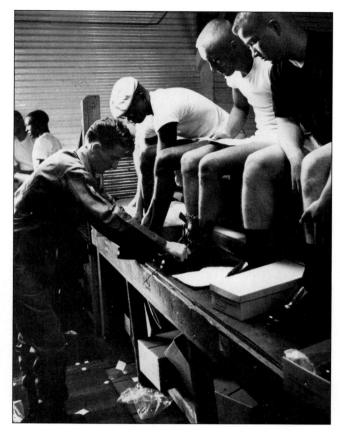
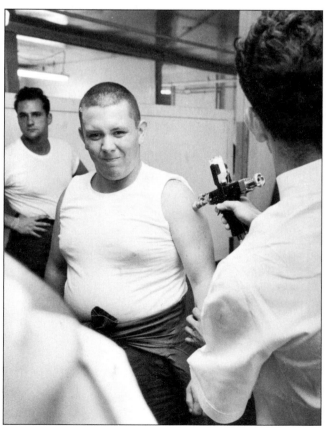

Recruits receive pugil-stick training, which prepares them for bayonet fighting.

New soldiers learned how to throw grenades from four positions: standing, kneeling, crouching, and supine. Here men at Fort Polk, Louisiana, await their instructor's command to hurl their grenades.

Witness: Morris Udall

President Lyndon Johnson once said of the Gulf of Tonkin Resolution that it was "like grandma's nightshirt—you could fit everything under it," and the number of American men and amount of U.S. dollars committed to the war by mid-1965 proved this was no boast. It is hard to know whether such grandiose military plans were in the minds of the U.S. senators and congressmen who nearly unanimously approved the measure on August 7, 1964. Yet it was not without trepidation that the Congress voted it into law, as Congressman Morris K. Udall of Arizona, then in his second term, remembers.

On August 7, 1964, in response to a plea by the president and the leadership of both parties, the House of Representatives passed House Joint Resolution 1145, ironically entitled "A Resolution to Promote the Maintenance of International Peace and Security in Southeast Asia." It is better known as the Gulf of Tonkin Resolution.

The vote was a badly needed mandate for Lyndon Johnson, endorsing his decision to launch U.S. carrier planes to hit targets in North Vietnam following reported attacks on American warships. Passage of the resolution gave the president the authority to conduct foreign policy without the Congress. It was a historic and tragic occasion. It was, in fact, wholly unnecessary, the product of an America that "had never lost a war" and a foreign policy that was built on the now questionable thesis, "Support the president; he knows more than we do."

With this vote, the United States began a tortured and calamitous period in which the government and the military would be subjected to tests of competency and integrity that they would not and could not pass. On that day in 1964, the Congress of the United States did not see what horrors were about to come. Nor did I. Less than a year later I voiced my misgivings over the direction of the war in a newsletter to my Arizona constituents, but I still was willing to give the president the benefit of the doubt.

"The fact is," I wrote, "that the president of the United States, unlike the rulers of China and the Soviet Union, has to operate in a fishbowl. When we demand that he explain his every move, and preferably in advance, we make his position increasingly difficult in relation to these other participants in the world struggle. The president may not always be right . . . but he is our president, and he deserves our loyalty and our support."

In 1967 I would withdraw that support and be accused of disloyalty by the White House. More on that later.

The hows and whys of the Tonkin resolution and the ensuing catastrophe have been the subjects of books, films, television series, and elections. I will not attempt to shed more light on the abstract issues, but I can tell something of the state of mind of the Congress and why it voted for H. J. Res. 1145.

First of all, it is important to remember that the members of the 88th Congress were still heavily influenced by their own experiences of World War II. The signing of the Japanese surrender had taken place less than twenty years prior to the attack by North Vietnamese patrol boats in the Tonkin Gulf. Like me, most of the members of the House and Senate had served in the armed forces during that war. They had grown up, fought fascism, and were elected during a period of total and uncomplaining fealty to the president. During World War II the Congress abdicated its role to an extremely popular and powerful Franklin Delano Roosevelt. That abdication continued through the Korean War years and the Cold War era of Truman and Eisenhower, the Berlin crisis, the Cuban missile crisis, and the deteriorating situation in Southeast Asia during the Kennedy-Johnson years to August of 1964.

On August 3 and 4 the cloakrooms of the U.S. House of Representatives, normally scenes of gossip and rumor, literally buzzed with news of the foolhardy attack by small gunboats of the North Vietnamese navy on the American destroyer Maddox. The next day bemusement turned to anger as other naval units of the United States reportedly came under hostile fire in the Gulf of Tonkin.

This was, of course, an election year. And in an election year events can often be magnified by political rhetoric and bombast. My Arizona colleague Barry Goldwater, for example, was urging massive retaliation after the initial attack on the Maddox. President Johnson, not anyone's idea of a dove, ordered air strikes on the North Vietnamese mainland, but this did not calm down the hawks. To cover his political base, LBJ wanted a show of support from the entire Congress, something short of a formal declaration of war, to give him a mandate for his unilateral military response.

The floor debate in the House, as I recall it, was marked by thunderous condemnation of the North Vietnamese. The stronger the language, the heartier the cheers from Democrats and Republicans alike. Sitting in the back of the House, I could not imagine the House in higher dudgeon at the news of the sinking of the Maine in Havana Bay or the attack on Pearl Harbor.

Leaders from the Democrats and Republicans joined to urge quick action on the resolution. Carl Albert, then Democratic majority leader of the House, urged against partisan debate and quoted President Johnson in a speech made at Syracuse University after the initial attack: "Let not friend needlessly fear nor foe vainly hope that this is a nation divided in this election year. Our free election, our full and free debate are America's strength, not America's weakness."

The majority leader had nothing to fear. His Republican counterpart, Charles Halleck of Indiana, took to the floor and advised his colleagues that the White House had called the Congressional leadership to a special briefing on the crisis. Though the retaliatory attack had been ordered without Congressional advice and consent, Halleck said he agreed with this decision and he supported "this resolution as a clear indication on the part of the Congress of our determination to be a united people in the face of any threats to our liberty."

The debate continued, with senior members of the House citing the need to be unified in opposition to the threat to American warships. The right-wingers, such as H. R. Gross of Iowa and John Ashbrook of Ohio, lustily bashed the United Nations and the secretary of state for, respectively, "token opposition to the halting of the Communist world conspiracy" and "the no-win vacillating course of events which our State Department has followed."

As the debate continued, few words of caution or moderation were heard until shortly before the vote. A clutch of liberals huddled in the rear of the chamber listening to the righteous and fiery rhetoric in support of the resolution. A few of us worried aloud to each other about setting an unhappy precedent allowing the president to use all force necessary to protect American lives without our knowing anything other than what the Pentagon and the White House were feeding us.

Finally, Henry Reuss, a scholarly lawyer from Milwaukee, took to the floor. Allowing that he would support the resolution, Henry said he was "somewhat in the position of the proprietor of the saloon whose bartender calls him on the intercom to ask:

'Is Casey good for a drink?'
'Has he had it?'
'He has.'
'He is.' "

That pretty much summed up the situation that had befallen us.

One of the last speakers before the roll-call vote was Congressman George Brown, a Californian and an outspoken critic of the administration's policy in Southeast Asia, who nonetheless was going to vote for the resolution. He spoke for many of us when he said, "I am of the very firm conviction that the peace and freedom which this country is dedicated to achieve in South Vietnam will not be attained by the gradual escalation of this unfortunate war."

In listening to George's speech, I was chilled by the accuracy of his warning: "As long as the Communist forces, seeking to gain control of South Vietnam, can continually replenish and strengthen their guerrilla units from the mass of unhappy peasants in this land and can arm these units with American weapons seized from the frequently cooperative government forces—there is no victory possible."

In those days the House had no electronic voting device. We had the roll called name by name. I sat quietly listening to the vote on the resolution. "Abbitt." "Aye." "Burton." "Aye." "Dingell." "Aye." On it went without a single dissenting vote. As my name was called, I answered in the affirmative, but not without a sense of foreboding. Though I was not happy with the way things were going in Southeast Asia, I had trust in my president and in our military leaders.

The casualties increased, the corruption of the South Vietnamese government and military was further exposed, and the dissent from the nation rose. I increasingly doubted our policy and the mandate the Congress had given President Johnson with the Tonkin resolution.

In October 1967, it was time to face reality. I chose to speak to a large gathering in Tucson, Arizona, my hometown. The audience was made up of the business establishment. It was not entirely receptive to my remarks.

"Tonight," I said, "I want to talk about war and peace, about presidents, dominoes, commitments, and mistakes. . . . I have thought with increasing dismay and doubt as the limited involvement I support has grown into a very large Asian land war with a half-million American troops scattered in jungles and hamlets, fighting an enemy who is everywhere and nowhere, seeking to save a country which apparently does not want to be saved, with casualties mounting and no end in sight.

"Many of the wise old heads in Congress say privately that the best politics in this situation is to remain silent, to fuzz your views, to await developments.

"But I have come here tonight to say as plainly and simply as I can that I was wrong . . . and I firmly believe President Johnson's advisers are wrong today."

I went on to outline a proposal to withdraw American troops, to continue to fund the Vietnamese but only after ensuring reforms and political stability. I said that we were wrong to continue bombing the North and increasing the American presence in the South. Because

my brother Stew was secretary of the interior in President Johnson's cabinet, my remarks got more attention than usually is given a rather junior member of the House. LBJ, of course, was enraged, unable to understand why a loyal Democrat was questioning his policies. I now wonder: If only more of us had questioned them earlier, would he have been spared the pain and frustration that marked the final year of his presidency?

I have often thought about Lyndon Johnson's personal tragedy. I really think he felt he was right and that he was on the correct course. Later, I contrasted LBJ's more forthright efforts to end the war with Richard Nixon's phantom "secret plan" to end the war in Vietnam. Nixon's secret plan was an escalation of the war that cost tens of thousands of American lives and resulted in disaster for the United States and South Vietnam. Nixon, like LBJ, used the Tonkin resolution to justify his escalation and the killing.

Yes, we who voted for the Tonkin resolution were wrong. We were desperately wrong. More than 52,000 American lives were lost. We set in motion forces that destroyed a nation's trust in those who govern and respect for our military institutions. A decade later we had deserted hundreds of thousands of South Vietnamese to an uncertain fate. We had lost the war.

Our Vietnam tragedy had forever changed the way the administration and the Congress conduct foreign policy. I doubt that there ever again will be that kind of mindless obeisance to a president. The Congress and the nation will rally around our president in times of grave national crisis, but it will not be like it used to be. That may be the only good to have come from passage of the Gulf of Tonkin Resolution.

Focus: ARVN and Its Advisers

After the departure of French troops in April 1956, the United States Military Assistance Advisory Group (MAAG) assumed full responsibility for rebuilding the South Vietnamese army. Over the next four years, as the U.S. provided equipment, streamlined command arrangements, and conducted training programs, MAAG slowly increased its advisory corps from 350 to nearly 700. The outbreak of armed insurgency and the arrival of a new administration in Washington, however, rapidly transformed this relatively low-key effort into a sizable commitment. Alarmed by the deteriorating prospects of the Diem government, President Kennedy sharply increased all forms of military assistance to Saigon. At the end of 1961 MAAG strength stood at 2,067. Twelve months later there were more than 11,000 U.S. military personnel in Vietnam. Among them were several thousand American soldiers acting as advisers to every level of the Vietnamese army. Working with their Vietnamese counterparts, the advisers reviewed intelligence reports, helped plan operations, set up communications, and arranged for supplies.

Getting used to Vietnam was tough enough—the strange language, the alien culture, the ripe smell of *nuoc nam* fish sauce (which the Vietnamese seemed to pour on everything they ate), the mind-numbing heat. But the job itself was even more demanding, especially at the lower levels where advisers accompanied the ARVN into the field to coordinate artillery and air support and assure medical assistance. Although they had no command authority, the Americans were sometimes forced to take upon themselves the burden of leadership when faltering soldiers threatened to panic.

To the Vietnamese they made a striking picture, these tall, confident Americans. Striding through the bush in their sweat-soaked uniforms and faded green baseball caps, carrying World War II carbines in their hands and .45-caliber pistols strapped to their sides, the advisers were the combat pioneers of the American enterprise in Vietnam, the handful of men who blazed the path that thousands would soon follow.

Many of the new advisers who arrived in-country as part of the buildup of the American assistance program in 1962 were assigned to the 7th ARVN Division, whose troops patrolled the watery world of the Mekong Delta. A vast, shimmering plain stretching south from Saigon to the Ca Mau Peninsula, the delta was 26,000 square miles of rich, alluvial rice lands crisscrossed by irrigation canals and the tributaries of the Mekong River. The region had been under the influence of the Vietminh since before World War II. Their Vietcong successors operated out of the hundreds of villages that clustered along the canal banks and from bases concealed in the impenetrable swamps and thick forests that dotted the coast. Hunting them down, discovered one adviser, was "like trying to identify tears in a bucket of water." After three years of mounting violence, the contest in the delta between the Communists and the ARVN was not being won by the government troops.

Like their adversaries, the vast majority of ARVN soldiers grew up in rural villages, the sons of peasant farmers. Like their opponents they had little if any formal education, and like the guerrillas they would serve for the duration or until they were no longer able to fight. Unlike the Vietcong, however, they were usually assigned to a unit far from home. Although some wives followed their husbands and settled near ARVN camps, most enlisted men saw their families no more than once a year. Also unlike the Communists, their lack of education meant they had little chance of escaping the lowest rungs of army life, surviving as well as they could on a salary of $11 a month.

Extended absences without leave and outright desertion were common. But for the most part they accepted their circumstances philosophically. Generally neglected by their officers, given little idea of what they were fighting for, the ordinary ARVN soldiers displayed a courage and endurance that won the respect of the Americans. When asked what had been his most lasting impression of Vietnam, one U.S. adviser replied: "I think it would be the almost limitless ability of the Vietnamese soldier to bear suffering and pain without complaint. I've never heard a wounded Vietnamese cry, never heard a tired one complain." For their part, ARVN troops admired the bravery and skill of the advisers, prizing individual Americans as an endless source of food, cigarettes, and other small favors. They also understood that they had a better chance of decent treatment when the Americans were around than they did from their own commanders.

As a group, the ARVN officer corps differed in almost every respect from the men they led. The well-educated sons of wealthy, urban Vietnamese families, most had received their appointment as the result of patronage. The beneficiaries of family or political connections, they used their positions to line their pockets with money siphoned from unit budgets or extorted from local farmers. The ultimate products of a traditional, class-bound society, they looked down on the peasants they commanded and on the young Americans whom they sometimes treated with an obsequious condescension all the more irritating for its partial validity. "They are too new at the game," observed one ARVN colonel archly, "but they can learn."

The advisers wondered whether the Vietnamese really wanted American advice and complained that too much of the burden had been placed on them to "get along." Most of all, the Americans were dismayed to find that many ARVN officers had no more enthusiasm than the enlisted men for the difficult task of subduing the Vietcong.

What characterized the government side of the war in the delta was a pervasive lack of aggressiveness. By and large the army kept to the safety of district towns and the security of the roads. When operations were mounted, they tended to take place in areas of little enemy activity or were so large and noisy that the guerrillas had ample opportunity to get out of the way. There were no nighttime operations, scant interest in patrols

or ambushes, and no attempt whatever to pursue Vietcong units who did blunder into government forces. Instead, local commanders relied on artillery to keep the enemy at arm's length and regularly left escape routes open for the Vietcong to flee should an engagement become too hot.

The U.S. advisers met this discouraging situation with determination and ingenuity. They urged their counterparts to abandon their fortress mentality, close down the vulnerable outposts they nicknamed Vietcong PXs, and take the war to the enemy. They devised tactical refinements such as the flare-and-strike technique to permit night operations and the highly successful Eagle Flights, in which helicopters loaded with ARVN troops circled battle areas, ready to swoop down on Vietcong units trying to escape. They helped get needed equipment for their units and applied innovative approaches to counterguerrilla warfare.

Month by month American men and machines changed the face of war in the delta. Caught off guard, the Vietcong suffered one stunning defeat after another. As the government extended its control into insurgent areas, Communist defections grew while the rate of new recruitment dropped sharply. So grave were the new problems facing their armed forces that the National Liberation Front even considered abandoning delta strongholds they had held for thirty years. Concluded Wilfred Burchett, an Australian journalist sympathetic to the Vietcong, "In terms of territory and population, Diem made a considerable comeback in 1962."

By the end of the year many Americans were enthusiastic about the prospects for driving the Communists out of the delta entirely. With American hardware and initiative there were possibilities for "all sorts of delightful operations," chortled Lieutenant Colonel Frank B. Clay at 7th Division headquarters. It seemed as though all the Vietnamese needed was a little leadership. "These people may not be the world's greatest fighters," said one adviser, "but they're good people, and they can win a war if someone shows them how."

An American adviser flies a twin-seated T–28 during an Operation Farmgate mission in 1962. Under Farmgate, U.S. pilots could fly combat missions as long as a Vietnamese trainee rode along in the back seat.

South Vietnamese soldiers disembark from a helicopter in the Mekong River Delta in August 1962 as an American crewman looks on.

On a mission in the delta, ARVN soldiers move past a hut they set afire after discovering Vietcong propaganda inside it.

An ARVN soldier uses forceful means while questioning a Vietcong suspect arrested in a delta village in early 1963.

With at least a dozen of their comrades lying dead in the wake of an ARVN attack, a group of Vietcong prisoners (left) await interrogation. Two American advisers look on from the rear.

55

2
AMERICA TAKES OVER

When "we marched into the rice paddies on that damp March afternoon," Marine Lieutenant Philip Caputo later wrote, "we carried, along with our packs and rifles, the implicit conviction that the Viet Cong would be quickly beaten." Certain that its goals were legitimate, confident that the application of American military power would swiftly drive the enemy from the field, the United States went to war in 1965 with an almost casual assumption of victory.

So pervasive was this optimism that little attempt was made to tailor American strategy to the realities of the situation in Vietnam. As a result, U.S. policy was filled with uncertainties and questionable assumptions. The dispatch of troops was meant to halt the Communist onslaught and compel negotiations, but no one in Washington made any serious attempt to determine just what level of force would be necessary to accomplish those ends. Meanwhile, the introduction of large numbers of American units pushed the indigenous military into the background, steadily diminishing ARVN's ability to shoulder the burden of their nation's defense. Further confusing matters was Johnson's sensitivity to adverse public reaction. Fearful of domestic unrest, he sought a quick end to the war. Yet, equally concerned that an overly aggressive pursuit of victory would draw in China or the Soviet Union, he imposed limitations on his military commanders that made their missions more difficult to achieve.

For its part, the military never fully accommodated itself to Washington's restrictions. Nor did U.S. commanders adjust their vision to a revolutionary struggle in which political victories were always more important than military triumphs. Instead, MACV employed regular forces in a conventional war of attrition against an unconventional enemy in an unfamiliar setting. When that strategy failed to produce adequate results, when more and more men were sent to hold the line, the early optimism of 1965 degenerated into a bitter frustration that threatened to tear the nation apart.

First Cavalry Division soldiers head into the bush on a patrol in November 1965.

Exemplifying this strategic confusion was the air campaign against North Vietnam. The initial bombing raids were designed to meet the political need for a quick, negotiated settlement of the war. The administration was confident that U.S. air power would force the North Vietnamese to cease their support of the southern insurgency and that this could be achieved without significant loss of American lives. When the initial attacks failed to cow Hanoi, however, the goal of the air assault shifted. The primary task became a military one—to halt the flow of reinforcements and supplies to the South where U.S. ground troops were engaged in battle with Communist forces. Whether air power was suitable for either task would remain a subject of debate long after the war was over.

After the fruitless five-day bombing pause in mid-May, Rolling Thunder resumed in earnest, long-range U.S. Air Force fighter-bombers striking inland targets while carrier-based navy aircraft operated along the coast. By September, American warplanes were flying almost 4,000 sorties a month against military bases, supply depots, and infiltration routes in the southern half of North Vietnam. At Johnson's insistence major targets within the Hanoi-Haiphong restricted zone initially escaped the aerial onslaught. As the ground war below the demilitarized zone (DMZ) intensified, however, the Joint Chiefs argued that air power could not prevent the flow of men and materiel south as long as these areas remained off-limits. In June 1966, the president finally approved a full-scale assault against the North's vital petroleum, oil, and lubricants (POL) storage facilities and transportation network.

While American aircraft blasted tank farms and railroad yards on the northern outskirts of Hanoi, other American pilots flew interdiction strikes along the Ho Chi Minh Trail in southern Laos. Code named Tiger Hound, this multiservice operation utilized modern reconnaissance jets and leftover attack aircraft from World War II, propeller-driven observation airplanes and high-flying B–52s. During the first five months of 1966, Tiger Hound attacks destroyed thousands of structures and trucks, dozens of bridges, and hundreds of antiaircraft positions along the major enemy infiltration route into South Vietnam.

The tempo of air raids over the North increased steadily during the summer to a peak of 12,000 sorties in September. Two months later, under continuing pressure from the military, Johnson enlarged the target list even further to include key railroad yards on the outskirts of Hanoi. By the end of 1966 the United States had flown more than 105,000 sorties over the North. The 165,000 tons of bombs delivered by American warplanes since the beginning of 1965 had destroyed nearly 350 fixed structures and thousands of railroad cars, motor vehicles, and water craft. Estimates of the economic and military damage done to North Vietnam exceeded $200 million.

Yet the air attacks cost the United States more than $1.5 billion and the loss of 489 aircraft. Nor had the bombing appreciably affected the course of the war. Much that had been destroyed was replaced by increased aid from China and the Soviet Union. What could not be replaced was rebuilt by armies of civilian workers. In January 1967, a CIA analysis concluded that Rolling Thunder had been unable to cripple the North Vietnamese economy, weaken the North's military establishment, or significantly impede the flow of supplies to the South. The U.S. command argued that the disappointing figures were the direct result of Washington's graduated and limited application of American air power. Others, like Secretary of Defense Robert McNamara, had begun to believe that no amount of bombing would break the will of the North Vietnamese. Whatever the causes, the failure of the air campaign meant that U.S. troops would play far more than a stopgap role. By the beginning of 1967 the war on the ground in South Vietnam had long since become an American fight.

When the Marines landed at Da Nang in March 1965, there were slightly more than 29,000 U.S. military personnel in Vietnam. During the next twenty-one months U.S. soldiers, sailors, air crewmen, and Marines poured into the country in ever increasing numbers. Most came courtesy of the Selective Service, which by the end of 1965 was processing up to 40,000 men a month. Primarily the sons of lower-middle-class or working-class families unable to get the still-liberal college deferments,

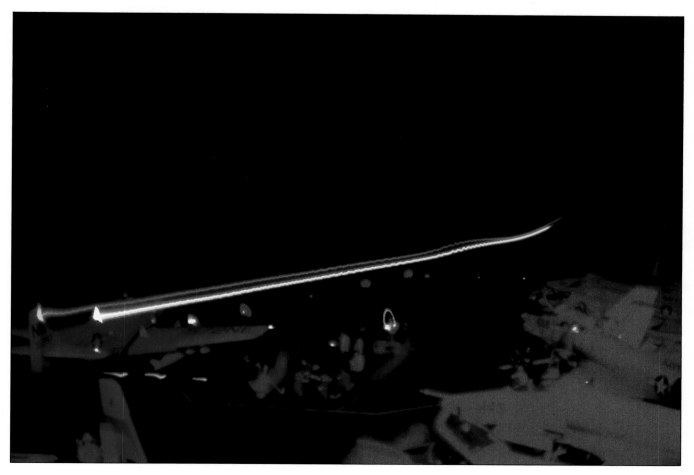

Streaks of light show the path of a navy Skyraider that moments before took off from the deck of the U.S.S. Midway *en route to a night mission over North Vietnam in summer 1965.*

these men were funneled into expanded training bases all over the country, then rapidly shipped to Vietnam.

On the heels of the 3d Marine Division, which set up shop at Da Nang in May 1965, came the army's 173d Airborne Brigade, assigned to Bien Hoa, and the 1st Brigade of the 101st Airborne Division, which landed at Cam Ranh Bay on July 29. July also witnessed the arrival at Bien Hoa of the 2d Battalion of the 1st Infantry Division. Within a month advance elements of the 1st Cavalry Division (Airmobile) were building their camp at An Khe. During the fall the remainder of the 1st Infantry Division deployed to Phuoc Vinh and Ben Cat northwest of Saigon. These months also saw the air force grow to more than 500 aircraft and 21,000 personnel at eight major air bases in South Vietnam, plus more men and machines in Thailand. Offshore, the Seventh Fleet's Cruiser-Destroyer Group patrolled the coast on gunfire support duty, while the navy's Task Force 77

launched air attacks on the North from Yankee Station, 100 miles off the coast of South Vietnam, southeast of Cam Ranh Bay.

By the beginning of 1966 U.S. troop strength in Vietnam had grown to 250,000, including nearly 160,000 soldiers and Marines comprising twenty-two army and thirteen Marine infantry and tank battalions. But the pace of deployment scarcely slackened—the 1st Marine Division went to Chu Lai in January; the 25th Infantry Division to Cu Chi in March; the 4th Infantry Division to Pleiku in July; the 196th Infantry Brigade to Tay Ninh in August; the 11th Armored Cavalry Regiment to Long Binh in September; the 9th Infantry Division, slated for duty in the Mekong Delta, in December; the 199th Infantry Brigade to Long Binh, also in December. At year's end U.S. ground combat strength had grown to fifty-nine army and twenty-four Marine infantry and tank battalions.

Battle-hardened pilots of the 12th Tactical Fighter Wing sit beneath their laundry lines and enjoy the weekly Sunday night cookout of steak and beer at Cam Ranh Bay airfield.

So rapid was the buildup of American troops that they almost immediately outstripped MACV's ability to meet their logistical needs. This huge, modern military force required a continuous flow of supplies, equipment, and manpower. But South Vietnam did not have enough ports, terminals, warehouses, or highways to handle the load. Nor was the army prepared to field combat support units without the activation of the National Guard and Army Reserve, something President Johnson had ruled out. The result was temporary chaos marked by ammunition shortages and delayed unit deployments.

To remedy the situation army engineers constructed four major deep-water ports, rebuilt South Vietnam's highway system, and greatly expanded that nation's air transport facilities. Meanwhile, the 1st Logistical Command headquartered in Saigon became one of the largest army organizations in the world. By the end of 1966 their joint efforts had turned shortages into surpluses. But there was more to logistics in Vietnam than military supplies. Convinced that the maintenance of morale was of prime importance, Westmoreland not only limited each soldier's tour of duty to 365 days, he also attempted to provide his men with "all the comforts of home." Even the troops in the field could expect regular hot meals with ice cream flown in by helicopter for dessert.

For all that, Vietnam remained an alien place for most of the young Americans who served there, a beautiful but strange land of shifting topography, climatic extremes, and enigmatic people. In the south was the delta, a watery world of flat rice fields, impenetrable mangrove swamps, and isolated forests. North of Saigon the emerald green fields dwindled to a narrow strip along the rocky coast, the area of cultivation limited by the sparsely populated mountain forests of the central highlands. Still farther north the high plateau gave way to the rugged peaks and plunging waterfalls of the Truong Son Mountains, a steep wilderness of dense rain forests rising as high as 8,000 feet above sea level.

Less varied than the land, the weather of Vietnam was dominated by the annual cycle of monsoons. During the summer, drenching torrents of rain created a perpetual humidity that rotted clothing, mired everything on the ground in mud, and made flying treacherous. In the winter months the rain was replaced by scorching heat, a mind-numbing furnace that took a man's breath away and turned the winter mud into clouds of gritty red dust.

Almost as impenetrable as the heat was the peasant population of the Vietnamese countryside. "My time in Vietnam," recalled one infantryman, "is the memory of ignorance. I didn't know the language. I knew nothing about the village community. I knew nothing about the aims of the people—whether they were for the war or against the war." Instead of grateful "natives" eager to be "liberated," U.S. troops frequently encountered indifference and suspicion. Even worse, there was often no way of distinguishing who was friend and who was enemy, no way of telling by how they acted or what they wore who was a farmer and who was a guerrilla until it was too late.

The people were different from what the GIs expected. So was the war itself. Large units were broken up and scattered across the country, major engagements with the enemy were rare and, when they did occur, usually lasted only a short time. For most "grunts," as the infantrymen called themselves, the war became an endless round of small-unit patrols. Some were designed to exploit specific intelligence of enemy concentrations, but most had no specific goal. Contact was sporadic, often limited to sniper fire but occasionally erupting into brief, savage firefights. In many areas the gravest threat came not from the enemy himself, but from the mines and booby traps he left behind. Sweltering under seventy pounds of equipment and ammunition, soldiers "humped" across the countryside enduring days of boredom punctuated by split seconds of sheer terror.

Despite the overwhelming advantage the Americans had in raw firepower, the Vietcong and North Vietnamese Army (NVA) proved elusive and deadly adversaries. Dispersed into platoon-size units that would consolidate only for carefully planned attacks, the enemy avoided contact except at their own initiative. The elaborate preparations made by U.S. units prior to an operation and the effectiveness of the Communist in-

The Seventh Fleet's U.S.S. Oklahoma City *unleashes its guns for the first time since World War II on a Vietcong ammunition dump hidden along the South China Sea coast in late 1965.*

telligence network made surprise almost impossible for the Americans to achieve. When enemy troops were cornered, they fought stubbornly, standing their ground even under the most punishing artillery and air strikes. In populated areas Vietcong guerrillas frequently fired on American troops from within villages, prompting return fire that rarely found its target but often destroyed civilian property and killed or wounded innocent villagers. In the uninhabited border regions well-trained, heavily armed regular troops of the North Vietnamese Army challenged the Americans in an escalating series of ferocious encounters that by the end of 1965 were already claiming heavy casualties on both sides.

While the White House maintained tight control over the bombing of North Vietnam, Westmoreland was given considerable freedom to develop and execute the ground war in South Vietnam. The strategy he formulated was divided into three parts. First, U.S. combat units would search out and destroy enemy Main-Force units and base areas. Next, ARVN troops would clear the area of Vietcong guerrillas left after the large-scale search-and-destroy operations had ended. Finally, local South Vietnamese units—the Regional (RFs) and Popular Forces (PFs)—would secure the area by providing a permanent defense against future attacks.

Although his plan was designed in part to protect the population of the countryside, Westmoreland's primary goal was the attrition of the enemy's Main-Force units. Once that was achieved, reasoned the general, the Communists would have no choice but to sue for peace. "We'll just go on bleeding them until Hanoi wakes up to the fact that they have bled their country to the point of national disaster for generations."

Westmoreland's strategy of attrition relied on a steadily increasing pool of U.S. manpower, on the application of American technology to the task of locating the enemy, and on the ready availability of American firepower to destroy him—artillery, naval gunfire, helicopter gunships, fixed-wing attack aircraft, and awesome B–52 bombers from air bases in Guam and Thailand. So confident was he in the impact of such weapons that even before he had significant numbers of combat troops at hand the American commander took the offensive.

Westmoreland's willingness to send his green troops against the Vietcong was also a reflection of the deteriorating position of the South Vietnamese army in the early summer of 1965. Anxious to strike back before ARVN collapsed entirely, the MACV commander urged Washington to abandon the defensive enclaves to which U.S. forces had been deployed. On June 26 Westmoreland was given permission to commit U.S. combat troops at his discretion. Within twenty-four hours the 173d Airborne Brigade began a search-and-destroy operation into War Zone D northeast of Saigon.

The first major American ground combat action of the war proved anticlimactic, the paratroopers encountering only scattered resistance during their four days in the field. But the die had been cast. Eight weeks later, when elements of the 1st and 3d Marine Divisions cornered an entire VC regiment fifteen kilometers south of Chu Lai, the Americans dealt the enemy a stunning blow.

A multipronged land, air, and sea assault, Operation Starlite, caught the VC completely by surprise. From their entrenched positions the Communists fought back furiously but could not contend with the Americans' mobility and firepower. Using helicopter-borne troops to block avenues of escape, Marine infantrymen supported by tanks and amphibious tractors trapped the enemy regiment against the sea, where it was torn to pieces by Marine air and naval gunfire. In less than a week of fighting the VC lost nearly 700 men. Their extensive tunnel and cave complexes, laboriously carved out over many years, were destroyed.

As the year wore on and U.S. troop strength grew, the intensity of combat increased. American units penetrated Vietcong base areas near Saigon, swept the central highlands around Kontum, and grappled with guerrillas in the villages along the central coast. But even as U.S. soldiers and Marines poured into South Vietnam, the Communists more than matched the American buildup. By November, total VC/NVA strength was estimated at 140,000 men. Early that month troops of the 1st Cavalry Division (Airmobile) met North Vietnamese regulars in a bloody battle that demonstrated both the advantages and limitations of the American way of war in Vietnam.

A Marine medic carries a South Vietnamese infant to safety. The child was wounded by U.S. jets in September 1965 during the opening stages of Operation Piranha on Cape Batangan.

The 1st Cavalry Division (Airmobile), or 1st Air Cav as the troopers preferred, represented a new concept in warfare: airmobility. Its roots stretching back to the old horse cavalry of the Civil War, the new "First Team" was initiated in 1963 as part of President Kennedy's insistence on a more flexible military machine. The 1st Air Cav had staged only two full-scale maneuvers with its new helicopters before it became the first full division sent to Vietnam. When Communist troops attacked the Special Forces camp at Plei Me on October 19, elements of the division's 1st Brigade helped lift the siege. In the process they discovered that two full NVA regiments were roaming the frontier area. That knowledge only whetted the appetite of the 1st Air Cav's commander, General Harry W. O. Kinnard. Eager to try out his UH–1 Hueys over the trackless mountain jungle of the western highlands, Kinnard sought permission to go after the enemy. On October 27 Westmoreland gave Kinnard the order to "find, fix, and destroy" every enemy soldier between Plei Me and the Cambodian border.

Employing the new technique of aerial reconnaissance by fire, Kinnard's helicopter pilots began sighting an increasing number of North Vietnamese soldiers in the Ia Drang Valley. After several small engagements during the first weeks of the operation, Colonel Harry G. Moore's 1st Battalion, 7th Cavalry, set down at Landing Zone (LZ) X-Ray on the morning of November 14, virtually on top of two full NVA regiments. Pinned down by rocket and grenade fire, attacked on several sides by enemy infantry, Moore called in air and artillery strikes within 150 meters of the battalion's perimeter. By nightfall reinforcements from the 2d Battalion had arrived at the LZ, but the morning of the fifteenth brought renewed assaults that were only beaten off in fierce hand-to-hand fighting. When the NVA soldiers finally retreated the next day, they left behind 834 confirmed dead plus an estimated several hundred more KIA from artillery and air strikes, including several by B–52 Stratofortresses, the first time in the war the giant bombers were used for tactical support.

The 2d Battalion moved out on foot November 17 heading for LZ Albany ten kilometers away. Discovered en route, the troopers marched straight into an ambush.

Within a few minutes NVA fire had decimated two companies, some of the terrorized green troops shooting wildly into their own ranks. Slowly the surviving Americans fell back into a coherent perimeter. Helicopter gunships raked the enemy positions, followed by air force fighter-bombers discharging loads of napalm that seared the jungle in orange sheets of jellied fire. Even with the aerial support, enemy fire remained too intense to land reinforcements or evacuate wounded. By next morning the NVA had fled. Counting the more than 400 enemy bodies littering the battleground, General Kinnard declared that the 2d Battalion had "won the day." But the price of victory had been steep. Of the original 500 men who had set out from LZ X-Ray, 150 had been killed and another 250 wounded.

After the battles at LZs X-Ray and Albany, the NVA staged one more attack against an artillery firebase, then withdrew across the border into Cambodia. During the month-long campaign the 1st Air Cavalry had moved entire battalions by air, dropped artillery batteries into the middle of the jungle sixty-seven times, and ferried 7,500 tons of supplies to the men in the field. Even more important, in the course of some 50,000 individual flights during the operation, only fifty-nine helicopters were hit by enemy fire, four shot down, and but a single aircraft lost. The concept of airmobility had been fully vindicated.

It was a sobering defeat for the Communists, who left 1,500 dead scattered on the battlefield and may have lost as many as 2,000 more to air and artillery fire. But the Communists had also gained important information from the battle of the Ia Drang Valley. They discovered that they could neutralize the worst of American firepower by fighting at close range, and they learned not to reveal their positions by firing at low-flying reconnaissance helicopters. Moreover, the extent of their losses convinced the North Vietnamese to adopt a more cautious approach that kept the initiative in their hands and made U.S. casualties their primary objective. By the end of 1965 Hanoi had adopted its own strategy of attrition, confident that eventually the bill of war would be greater than the Americans were willing to pay.

The idea that the Communists could outlast the United States was one General Westmoreland was determined to resist. Yet as the new year began the American commander had faced some serious problems. Despite the rapid deployment of U.S. troops, the president's decision not to call up the Reserves created a manpower crisis that delayed the dispatch of critically needed logistical units, sent infantry platoons into the field with as few as half their authorized complement of men, and threatened to neutralize the promise of airmobility because of an acute shortage of helicopter pilots. Westmoreland also had to contend with the inexperience of his young soldiers, who had to learn how to maneuver safely, react to ambush, and make use of the firepower at their command.

The most difficult problem for MACV, however, was the inability of the South Vietnamese army to provide security for the nation's 12,000 hamlets. Although West-

moreland's strategy called for American troops to seek out and destroy the enemy's Main-Force units in the sparsely inhabited border regions, most of his attention during the first half of the year was devoted to operations against the VC/NVA in the populated coastal lowlands and in the strategically vital region surrounding Saigon.

The task of guarding the capital fell in part to the 173d Airborne Brigade and the 25th Infantry Division. During the first three months of the year, airborne elements repeatedly penetrated VC strongholds north and west of Saigon in operations such as Marauder, Crimp, and Mallet, provoking sharp firefights but no sustained contact. For the men of the 25th Division, now stationed at Cu Chi where they threatened a prime VC supply route to Cambodia, simply clearing the area immediately around their base camp proved an arduous

The poncho-covered bodies of 1st Cavalry Division soldiers killed in the bitter battle of the Ia Drang Valley in November 1965 are gathered in a clearing for evacuation.

Marine medical corpsman Josiah Lucier is escorted by three Vietnamese children, including one badly burned by napalm, as he conducts his rounds south of Da Nang.

process. Withstanding intense engagements against stubborn Vietcong defenders, they captured large amounts of materiel but only after deliberately working their way through enemy bunker and tunnel complexes.

The American unit most active in III Corps during the first half of the year was the 1st Infantry Division. Ranging north, east, and west of Saigon, elements of the division swept the Boi Loi Woods and the region around Long Thanh in February, then worked their way through the jungles of coastal Phuoc Tuy Province in April. That month the division also sent two battalions north to Tay Ninh in Operation Birmingham, while other men of the "Big Red One" struggled through hip-deep mud in the mangrove swamps of the Rung Sat Special Zone southeast of the capital. After a fruitless sweep in May around Loc Ninh, division commander Major General William E. DePuy pushed his men into War Zone C during June, where they met the 9th VC Division in Operation El Paso II. After several sharp encounters, the Americans drove the enemy into Cambodia, forestalling a threatened offensive against Saigon.

While the 1st Infantry Division struggled to keep the enemy at arm's length from the political center of South Vietnam, the 1st Cavalry Division brought its airmobile tactics out of the mountain jungles and onto the lowlands of Binh Dinh Province 400 kilometers north. Beginning with Operation Masher/White Wing in January and continuing through the remainder of the year, the 1st Air Cav combed the Bong Son Plain and the mountain valleys to the west, a Communist stronghold since World War II. Making effective use of their own helicopters and the added firepower of B–52s, air force fighter-bombers, and the guns of the Seventh Fleet, the Cav decimated three enemy regiments, capturing numerous VC suspects and tons of war materiel.

Farther north, in Quang Ngai Province, the men of the 1st Marine Division pushed out from their Chu Lai enclave into the Vietcong-dominated villages that surrounded them. Between February and early April they battled the enemy and the monsoon rains in four separate excursions into the An Hoa basin. During Operation Utah, a joint effort with South Vietnamese forces, the Marines encountered NVA regulars for the first time. In three days of fierce battle the heavily armed

North Vietnamese regiment lost a third of its strength but inflicted more than 500 casualties, including 98 Marines killed in action. "They're not supermen," observed one survivor, "but they can fight."

It was a lesson that the rest of the Marines would learn in July when the 324B NVA Division crossed the DMZ and headed toward Quang Tri City with the apparent intention of annexing South Vietnam's northernmost provinces. Six Marine and five ARVN battalions struck back in Operation Hastings, the largest allied operation of the war to date. Establishing a forward base at Dong Ha, the Marines attacked north and west toward Cam Lo and "Helicopter Valley," where the 3d Battalion of the 4th Marines endured a massed human-wave assault by 1,000 NVA soldiers. Only after napalm strikes within fifty feet of their position were the Marines able to drive the attackers off. For the next three weeks more than 8,000 Marines and 3,000 South Vietnamese soldiers fought a savage conventional battle against as many as 12,000 enemy troops. By August 3, when Hastings came to an end, the North Vietnamese had been sent reeling back across the DMZ with more than 800 dead.

When the NVA resumed the attack several weeks later, the Marines met them again in Operation Prairie, employing helicopter assaults, massed artillery fire, naval gunfire, air support, and tanks in a series of costly assaults against enemy strongpoints. The operation, which continued into January 1967, netted more than 1,000 enemy KIA. But the defense of the northern border cost the Marines as well. Despite lavish use of supporting arms, the fighting since July had claimed 365 Marine dead with another 1,662 wounded. Forced to counter this new threat, the Marine command shifted 3d Division headquarters plus two regiments and most of a Marine helicopter group to Quang Tri in October, leaving a severely stretched 1st Marine Division with responsibility for the three southern provinces of I Corps.

The fighting in the north was a sign of things to come. So was Operation Attleboro, a massive search-and-destroy sweep through the heart of the enemy's War Zone C. The initial penetration was made in September by the newly arrived 196th Light Infantry Brigade. For several weeks contact with the enemy was sporadic, but by mid-October the 196th was beginning to uncover considerable quantities of rice and documents. When the brigade moved closer to the Cambodian border during the first days of November, it ran smack into the 9th VC Division, returning to the site of its June battles with the 1st Infantry Division.

While the outnumbered men of the 196th, plus reinforcements from the 25th Infantry Division, fought for their survival in the tangled jungle west of the Michelin rubber plantation, MACV hurled the 1st Infantry Division, the 173d Airborne Battalion, and a brigade each from the 4th and 25th Infantry Divisions into the battle. The concentrated force of more than 22,000 American troops, backed by B–52 strikes and more than 10,000 rounds of artillery, drove the twice-beaten enemy soldiers back into Cambodia. They left behind 1,100 dead and tons of supplies.

Less pleasing to MACV were the nearly 1,000 American casualties, including 155 KIA, and the temporary disablement of the 196th, whose novice troops had been severely shaken by their rough initiation to combat. But Attleboro's resounding success convinced the American command that multidivisional search-and-destroy operations against Communist base areas and supply routes would bring the enemy to battle and destroy him. Much of 1967 would be spent testing that belief.

By the time Operation Attleboro came to an end the military dimension of the Vietnamese conflict overshadowed all other aspects of U.S. involvement in that troubled country. But alongside the cries of battle were the voices of other Americans—men and women, military and civilian, private and official, in Washington and Vietnam—who attempted in the midst of war to con-

South Vietnamese prime minister Nguyen Cao Ky (left) and president Nguyen Van Thieu (right) meet with President Johnson (back turned) at the Honolulu summit in February 1966.

tinue the job of nation-building that had first brought the United States to Vietnam.

From Washington's point of view, the key to South Vietnam's survival was the creation of a popular and effective government in Saigon. The first requirement of any South Vietnamese regime, however, was stability. In February 1966, eight months after the coup that brought Nguyen Cao Ky to power, the administration made clear its commitment to the former air force general at a summit conference in Honolulu. To South Vietnamese Buddhists, however, this signal of American support for Ky meant their continued domination by the elite Catholic minority. No sooner had the premier returned from Honolulu than the Buddhists took to the streets of Hue in a series of anti-American demonstrations that quickly escalated into open rebellion. After two months of negotiation and confrontation Ky ended the crisis with a show of force that cowed the Buddhists and gave South Vietnam at last a measure of political stability.

The Honolulu conference was designed not only to solidify Ky's position but also to win his support for a sweeping agenda of social and economic reforms in South Vietnam. To fight what Johnson called "the other war," the two nations devised an ambitious Rural Development (RD) Program featuring teams of young Vietnamese trained in propaganda and social services who would go out into the villages to build popular support for the government. Unfortunately, Saigon's interest in the program turned out to be largely rhetorical. Poorly trained and ill-supported, the RD cadres accomplished little. The fundamental problem, however, was the lack of security in the villages. Preoccupied with defeating the enemy's Main-Force units and hampered by limited manpower resources, Westmoreland left pacification— the job of destroying Vietcong political and military organizations at the local level—in the hands of the ARVN, which had even less interest in rural security than the Americans. Thus, even by the suspect methods used to measure progress, the number of "pacified" villages increased only 5 percent during the first year of the new program.

Far more successful were the thousands of individual Americans working in the Vietnamese countryside: from employees of the United States Agency for International Development (USAID), who sponsored programs in land reform, local government, and public health, to workers with the Christian and Missionary Alliance, who provided food, clothing, and medicine as well as spiritual comfort to the war-torn villages where they labored; from agents with the United States Information Service (USIS), who showed films on sanitation and democracy to rural peasants, to the young men and women of the private International Voluntary Service, who operated schools, experimented with new crops, and conducted family-planning clinics. Some of the most meaningful work was undertaken by American servicemen. Both under the official auspices of MACV's Civic Action Program and on their own initiative, U.S. soldiers and Marines dug wells, built bridges, stocked pig farms, distributed food and clothing, dispensed medicine, and trained local volunteers in rudimentary health-care techniques.

The GIs sweating over their civic action projects were part of a long-standing U.S. effort to plant "rice roots democracy" in a country that had only the most limited experience with democratic government. But democracy meant more than self-sufficient, self-governing local villages. It also meant the replacement of authoritarian military government with democratic political institutions. At the Honolulu conference the United States and South Vietnam pledged themselves to both goals. Seven months later, amid threats of Vietcong violence, 81 percent of the nation's registered voters turned out to select members of a constituent assembly that would draft a new constitution and formulate procedures for a presidential election the following year. If some observers questioned the sincerity of the government or suggested that democracy would hardly solve South Vietnam's problems, it was nonetheless a notable step in a country still very much at war.

Unfortunately, by the end of 1966 the constantly growing armed conflict threatened to overwhelm everything the United States was trying to achieve for South Vietnam: democracy, development, independence. At the same time the war rained down destruction on North Vietnam, eroded the prestige of the United States around the world, and jeopardized Johnson's Great Society. Yet neither side was ready for peace except on its own terms.

North Vietnam, which refused to negotiate at all until the bombing stopped, insisted that the United States remove its troops from South Vietnam, withdraw support from the existing Saigon regime, recognize the National Liberation Front (NLF) as a legitimate partner in a coalition government, and accept the eventual unification of North and South as mandated by the Geneva agreements. But the Johnson administration would not stop the bombing until Hanoi ceased its support of the southern insurgency, and the U.S. refused to accept any South Vietnamese government in which the Vietcong played a role, implicitly denying the possibility of unification.

The failure of a late-1965 "peace offensive" that sent U.S. representatives to foreign capitals around the world with offers to negotiate had hardened Johnson's attitude toward the North Vietnamese. But mounting international and domestic criticism persuaded him to make another effort. In November 1966 the administration reluctantly accepted a ten-point peace plan put forward by the Polish diplomat Januscz Lewandowski. As part of the new initiative, code named Marigold, Washington offered to halt the air strikes over North Vietnam in return for Hanoi's promise that it would stop infiltration within a reasonable time. Once the infiltration ceased, peace talks could begin. Contact was made with Hanoi through the Poles and an opening round of talks actually scheduled in Warsaw for December 5. Then, three days before the Warsaw meeting, U.S. warplanes struck railroad yards within eight kilometers of the center of Hanoi. The North Vietnamese immediately broke off the contact and Marigold was aborted.

Whether Johnson deliberately scuttled the talks, as his critics have charged, or simply fell victim to poor coordination within the government, as the administration claimed, made little difference. Neither Washington nor Hanoi was ready to concede defeat or compromise on the central issue that divided them—the political future of South Vietnam. The futility of the Marigold initiative simply underscored the enormous gulf that lay between the two countries and the different perspectives with which they viewed the events of the previous eighteen months.

Hanoi's attempt to crush the ARVN had been thwarted and U.S. troop strength in Vietnam now totaled 385,000. The buildup had enabled American forces to take the offensive in 1966 and make the first serious forays into major Communist base areas. Thanks to their superior mobility and firepower, American troops had yet to suffer a significant defeat. With more than a year of combat experience behind them, with base areas and lines of communication secured, with logistical problems well on the way to resolution, and with most of the restrictions on the bombing campaign lifted, both Washington and MACV looked forward to 1967 with confidence.

Yet Washington's swift victory had been denied, and the gains made had not come cheaply. During the year U.S. forces had suffered more than 35,000 casualties, including 5,008 dead. By December, U.S. KIA were averaging nearly 500 a month. At the same time, the ratio of VC/NVA to American losses was dropping rapidly, while enemy infiltration was up 250 percent over 1965. Moreover, reported the Joint Chiefs of Staff, "three-fourths of the battles are at the enemy's choice of time, place, type, and duration."

Although the president had already approved an additional 45,000 men, Westmoreland was even now developing requests for a force level of 542,000 troops. It was rapidly becoming apparent at the end of 1966 that the war had just begun. And if the Johnson administration persisted because it believed the United States would win, the North Vietnamese persisted because they believed they could not lose.

A radio operator from the 1st Cavalry Division watches for any suspicious movement near a burning Vietnamese farmhouse in Binh Dinh Province in 1965.

Focus: Masher/White Wing

When Major General Harry W.O. Kinnard brought his 1st Cavalry Division (Airmobile) to An Khe in September 1965, his mission was clear: to stop the enemy from driving to the coast and cutting South Vietnam in two. Within weeks of their arrival in-country Kinnard's men rose to that challenge in a series of violent battles along the Cambodian border. The bloody Ia Drang campaign of November 1965 blunted the Communist offensive in the central highlands and validated the concept of airmobility in land warfare. Heartened by the division's success, Kinnard immediately shifted his attention to another Communist stronghold, the northeastern corner of Binh Dinh Province.

The intended area of operations ranged from rice fields and tree lines along the thickly populated coastal plain to steep, bamboo-forested slopes and rugged mountain valleys farther inland. Designated by the Saigon government a "national priority area," the region was protected by the 22d ARVN Division, which had more than it could handle trying to keep Highway 1 open and pacify villages dominated by the Communists for more than two decades.

During the French Indochina War the province had been a center of insurgent resistance. With the signing of the Geneva accords in 1954, nearly 45,000 Vietminh cadres from Binh Dinh "regrouped" to North Vietnam. But when fighting resumed in 1960, many returned to renew family ties, re-establish a political organization, and re-create the infrastructure necessary to sustain regular armed forces. By 1966 these forces consisted of the 18th and 22d NVA Regiments plus the 2d Vietcong Regiment. Together they comprised the 3d NVA Division, also known as the Sao Vang, or Yellow Star, Division.

Kinnard divided the target area into four sectors, then devised a plan of attack that made the most of the American advantages in firepower and mobility. Operating out of Bong Son, a small airstrip and Special Forces camp, the Air Cav would mount a series of fast-moving "hammer-and-anvil" operations in which some of the troopers flushed the enemy toward other friendly units waiting in blocking positions. The men on the ground would be supported by tactical air, gunships, and artillery batteries continuously moved forward by helicopter from one emplacement to another.

The American general dubbed his conception Operation Masher and selected the 1st Cav's 3d Brigade to spearhead the attack. Normally consisting of the 1st and 2d Battalions, 7th Cavalry, the brigade was now augmented by the 1st and 2d Battalions, 12th Cavalry, the 1st Squadron, 9th Cavalry, plus assorted artillery and aviation units. Directing the 5,700-man task force was 3d Brigade commander Colonel Harold G. "Hal" Moore, a tough, hard-driving officer who had recently received the Distinguished Service Cross for his actions during the Ia Drang campaign.

The first days of the operation were bedeviled by bad weather and bad luck. Moving out from An Khe toward forward staging areas on January 25, a C–123 carrying forty-two cavalrymen crashed into a fog-shrouded mountain killing everyone on board. When the 3d Brigade launched its initial assault into the Bong Son Plain three days later, rain and low ceilings restricted helicopter flights and virtually eliminated tactical air support. These problems had little effect on the 1st Battalion, which encountered only mild enemy resistance. For the 2d Battalion, however, D-day almost turned into disaster when Company C dropped right on top of an NVA battalion at a village called Phung Du.

Enemy fire ripped through their helicopters before they ever touched down, scattering the Americans across a kilometer of rice fields. When the men tried to regroup, NVA machine guns and mortar fire methodically cut them down. Attempting to come to the rescue, Company A ran into heavy resistance just south of the village, only barely making it into a nearby cemetery, where the troopers found what shelter they could behind waist-high mounds that marked the grave sites. During the afternoon helicopters repeatedly attempted to land reinforcements but could not penetrate the intense enemy fire. By the end of the day the 2d Battalion was divided, pinned down, and cut off.

Under the cover of darkness and a heavy rain, the Americans managed to consolidate their positions and tend their wounded. Shortly after daybreak the clouds began to lift, allowing A–1 Skyraiders and B–57 Canberra bombers to pummel enemy positions with napalm and high explosives. In midmorning two companies from the 2d Battalion, 12th Cavalry, arrived on the scene accompanied by a furious Colonel Moore. "The Old Man was not pleased," remembered Sergeant Major Basil Plumley. "We moved around and talked to the men. The biggest thing they needed was leadership and guidance to move them out of there." Moore provided both, ordering preparatory artillery strikes and tear-gas barrages, then directing an assault by the 2/12 against the enemy fortifications.

Once the village had been cleared, Masher began to move forward as planned. Over the next two days the 2/7 and 2/12 swept past Phung Du while the 1st Battalion explored the intricate network of hamlets and hedgerows farther north. The two groups acted like a giant vise, using their airmobility to trap enemy units between them while constantly shifting artillery batteries to maintain an umbrella of protection. The swiftly moving troopers provoked several sharp encounters—at Tan Thanh, where the 2/12 battled an enemy company entrenched in what Col. Moore called "a rat's nest of bunkers and spider holes," and at Luong Tho, where the 1/7 lost thirteen men killed and thirty-three wounded in a contest fought at such close quarters that neither artillery nor air strikes could be brought in for support.

During the first few days of February the remaining North Vietnamese units slipped through the American net and withdrew to the west, their escape aided by bad weather that hampered U.S. reconnaissance flights. As contact with the enemy decreased, the cavalrymen returned to their forward bases and the first phase of Operation Masher came to a close. Despite the early re-

verses, the results of a week's worth of fighting were impressive: an estimated 1,358 enemy dead at a cost of 119 American lives, including those killed in the C–123 crash. U.S. intelligence estimated that two battalions of the NVA 22d Regiment had been put out of action, a "loss of equipment, personnel, and prestige," said the division report, that "will be difficult to overcome."

Even as Phase I concluded men and supplies were being readied for an immediate resumption of activity. By the time Phase II got under way, however, there had been two notable developments—the addition of Colonel William A. Lynch, Jr.'s, 2d Brigade, and a change in the name of the operation from Masher to White Wing. The former reflected the division's need for more hitting power before tackling the enemy on his own ground. The latter reflected Washington's desire to avoid overly aggressive connotations in its ongoing battle for public opinion back home.

Delayed for what turned out to be three crucial days by more bad weather, the assault into the rugged mountain valley commenced on February 7 when four cavalry battalions were lifted by helicopter onto high ground, then swept down the mountain slopes to the valley floor. The Americans expected fierce resistance to their penetration of the Communist base area, and U.S. troopers did find an elaborate system of fortifications and booby traps. But their tardy arrival had given the enemy time to escape. After three days of fruitless searching, disappointed division commanders closed out Phase II and turned their attention to the southwest sector of the operational area.

The third phase of Masher/White Wing was directed toward another mountain valley, called Kim Son but also known as the Eagle's Claw because of its distinctive shape. Reversing the tactics used in Phase II, Colonel Moore put the 3d Brigade and its supporting artillery down on the bottom of the valley, then sent patrols into subsidiary canyons to flush out the Vietcong. After subduing a VC company, the 2/7 Cavalry began scouring the valley floor. The troopers discovered a Vietcong hospital, a Communist weapons factory, and most important, documents pinpointing a VC Main-Force battalion in nearby Son Long Valley.

Moore immediately dispatched Captain Myron Diduryk's Company B, which just as quickly ran into two entrenched enemy companies near the village of Hon Mot. Diduryk blasted the well-camouflaged defensive works with his own mortars, battalion artillery from Kim Son, and cluster bombs delivered by air force A–1 Sky-raiders. Meanwhile, he prepared his 3d Platoon for a classic infantry assault. As soon as the last bomb had fallen the GIs, bayonets fixed, leaped to their feet and raced forward screaming "like mad men." Unnerved at the sudden attack, terrified enemy soldiers fled into a murderous crossfire from Diduryk's well-placed 2d Platoon. The battle left fifty-seven VC dead and scores wounded, including an enemy battalion commander. During interrogation he volunteered information that revealed the location of a Vietcong regimental head-quarters a few kilometers to the south in an area nick-named the "iron triangle" after the famous Communist redoubt north of Saigon.

Ordering the 3d Brigade back to An Khe for a well-earned rest, Kinnard put Colonel Elvy B. Roberts's 1st Brigade into the Eagle's Claw and sent his 2d Brigade—the 1st and 2d Battalions, 5th Cavalry, and the 2d Bat-talion, 12th Cavalry—against the enemy stronghold. The ensuing battle raged for four days. Backed by artil-lery and air support, the cavalrymen blasted through a labyrinth of VC defenses killing 313 and losing 23 of their own. More successful than anyone had anticipated, the two-week Phase III campaign claimed in all more than 700 enemy KIA, plus a substantial quantity of arms, ammunition, and materiel.

The final phase of Masher/White Wing—a lightning foray into the Cay Giep Mountains southeast of Bong Son—began on March 1 in spectacular fashion. After air force bombers blasted holes in the layered green can-opy, engineer teams descended on rope ladders from hovering CH–47 Chinook helicopters to hack out land-ing zones for the 2d Brigade. Swarming down the thick jungle slopes the cavalrymen braced themselves for heavy fighting with the 6th Battalion of the NVA 18th Regiment. For the second time during the operation, however, the troopers discovered that the enemy they expected to meet had gone. Fleeing south, the North Vietnamese collided with units of the ARVN 22d Di-vision. The South Vietnamese killed fifty NVA soldiers

and captured thirty of the demoralized enemy troops.

Masher/White Wing was formally closed down on March 6. The operation had been an outstanding mil-itary success, proving again the effectiveness of airmo-bility and demonstrating anew the might of American firepower. During 41 days of fighting against the NVA 3d Division, the cavalrymen had slashed their way through four Communist base areas, killing 1,342 enemy soldiers, capturing 633, and detaining 1,087 VC sus-pects. Kinnard, who judged the division's performance "at least 50 percent better" than the 38-day campaign in the Ia Drang, claimed the 1st Cav had driven Com-munist military forces from the coastal plain, rendered five of the enemy's nine battalions unfit for combat, and freed 140,000 Vietnamese "from VC domination."

The violence the Americans visited upon the enemy, however, also proved devastating to the people who lived in the Bong Son district. The lavish use of fire-power—more than 140,000 rounds of artillery alone dur-ing the six-week operation—ravaged the villages in which the Communists entrenched themselves and drove more than 16,000 civilians from their homes.

Nor were refugees the only problem. Smashing the enemy's military units was one thing, breaking up his political apparatus was quite another. Unless there was continuity between the military and pacification efforts, unless the Communist infrastructure was rooted out of the villages once the enemy's base areas had been cleared, his military forces were sure to return. But the South Vietnamese authorities were not prepared to carry out the security and pacification programs necessary to take advantage of the 1st Cav's battlefield victories. As a result, enemy soldiers began filtering back into the region less than a week after the end of Masher/White Wing, prompting new operations with names like Thayer and Irving and Crazy Horse and Davy Crockett.

But the results were always the same. Over the course of the war the men of the 1st Cavalry Division would return to the area again and again as they struggled in vain to transfer control of Binh Dinh Province from the Communists to the Saigon government. In the process they would learn to their bitter dismay what American arms and ingenuity could accomplish in Vietnam, and what they could not.

With intense enemy fire having stalled the American assault on Landing Zone 4, an LZ used during the opening phase of Operation Masher/White Wing, Captain Joel Sugdinis (squatting in foreground) and his command group from Company A, 2d Battalion, 7th Cavalry, 1st Air Cavalry Division, take shelter in a ditch and call in artillery, late January 1966.

As soldiers of the 2d Battalion, 7th Cavalry, look on, a B–57 Canberra unloads its napalm on nearby North Vietnamese positions surrounding Landing Zone 4.

Under withering fire from North Vietnamese units, men from the 2d Battalion, 7th Cavalry, crawl forward through a flooded rice field near the landing zone, January 28.

Having reached the other side of the field, one of the troopers helps a wounded soldier to higher ground.

Marines take a break and share a meal of C-rations during Operation Prairie. Marine reconnaissance teams tried to track down and destroy units from the 324B NVA Division that had recently infiltrated into Quang Tri Province.

Two soldiers from the 3d Marine Division fire upon North Vietnamese troops defending Hill 484. The Marine assault on this hill in early October resulted in one of the fiercest fights of the operation, the battle for Mutter Ridge.

Ignoring his own wounds, a Marine reaches for a buddy injured during the struggle for Hill 484. NVA troops repelled the initial attack on the hill on October 4, so the Marines pulled back and called in artillery and air strikes.

Marines carry one of their wounded to an air evacuation site near Hill 484. They captured the hill on October 5, bringing to an end the struggle for Mutter Ridge.

An abandoned helmet and rifle stand as tribute to the 200 Americans killed during Operation Prairie.

Witness: Mary Reis Stout

As the war heated up in 1966 and 1967, American soldiers all across South Vietnam took greater numbers of casualties, and the role of the thousands of American medical professionals in Vietnam became even more important. One of this group was 1st Lieutenant Mary Reis, an army nurse at the 2d Surgical Hospital (MASH) at An Khe and Chu Lai from November 1966 to November 1967. In 1987, nearly twenty years after her return from the war, Mary Reis Stout was elected president of the Vietnam Veterans of America.

When I graduated from high school in Columbus, Ohio, my class had a prophecy. Their prophecy for me was that I was going to be a nurse in the Peace Corps. I've often said I ended up being a nurse in the war corps.

I volunteered to go to Vietnam. In basic training they told us there was a need for medical people to go to the field hospitals there. A lot of my friends volunteered, and I called my parents and talked to them about what was going on. My father specifically asked me not to volunteer. He wasn't particularly crazy about my being in the army to begin with.

The thing that finally got me to put in the paperwork was the fact that Carl Stout, who is my husband now, had orders to go. We met at my first duty assignment at Fort Ord, California, where he was a field artilleryman working with basic trainees. I just decided, "I'm in the army now, there's a war going on, and my services are needed. And if Carl's going to be there it's important for our future that I understand somewhat what he's going through." We ended up pretty close together in

Vietnam; he was with the 3d Brigade of the 25th Infantry Division, and we were usually within fifty miles of each other. We saw each other about every six weeks, so that was kind of a bonus for both of us.

I guess the things that I remember most are massive wounds, primarily shrapnel wounds that had to be opened. Most people don't understand that the way you treat these war wounds is to open them even more, take out all the damaged tissue, and leave them open so that they can be cleaned, so that they don't get infected. Large chunks of people's bodies, particularly muscle, were gone. There were a lot of amputations, multiple amputations, because there was so much mining. There were a lot of gunshot wounds, but in comparison it just seemed as though there were so many more of the distance kind of injuries, where you weren't face to face with the enemy when it happened.

Our major job in field hospitals was to keep these people alive; we didn't deal with the long-term psychological effect, like the medical people at the hospitals back in the States did. We were just part of the chain. We never knew what happened to anybody when they left our hospital. We never got word back that "yeah, this person made it" or "that person didn't make it." That was something that bothered me for a long time; whatever happened to those people?

Boy, I got tough really fast. We all tried to not think too much about it all, just do what needed to be done and get through each day. I really blocked out a lot when I came back, but there were a couple of cases at Chu Lai that I still remember. Both of them happened to be named Steve, but I can't remember their last names. The first Steve had a gunshot wound in the abdomen. He seemed to be doing OK, and you know, once people stabilize you kind of let your guard down about letting yourself get close to them. He just got very bad one night, with a lot of breathing problems. His doctor said, "Just keep suctioning him out and don't call me unless he gets worse."

Well, he basically didn't get any worse, but he just all of a sudden went into cardiac arrest. We couldn't bring him back. That was unusual, because if we were right there with them normally we could get them back. His death was very traumatic for me. On top of that, the hospital commander, who just happened to be there when he went into cardiac arrest, told me it was my fault because I should have done a tracheotomy on him. I had a lot of guilt about that for years. I've taken that responsibility and understand why that happened, but it took me a long time.

The other Steve had an enormous leg wound. Normally the doctors would have just amputated his leg, but he begged them not to. When they brought him in he just kept pleading with them, "Please don't take my leg." Instead, they did an arterial graft on him, but it was such a large graft that they had real concerns that it would not hold. So we had to check on him very regularly to make sure that he wasn't bleeding around the graft. Within a few hours he started leaking around the graft, and they took him back into surgery. He begged them again, "Don't take my leg." They did another graft and that held for a couple of days.

Then one evening I looked over at him from the nurses' station and saw he was having some difficulty. I pulled back the sheet and he was lying in a pool of blood. When I pulled the dressing off his wound I could see his artery pumping. His pulse was getting thready and he was perspiring and going into shock. So I just put my hand into his leg and grabbed the artery. Sterile technique is something that's ingrained in you, but when it's somebody's life the most important thing is to stop the bleeding.

They took him back into surgery, and on the way in he was saying to the doctors, "Take it off, I don't want to die."

We had him for a while after surgery, and he started talking and wondering what his life was going to be like without his leg. We were all trying to be positive, saying you can ski and you can ride horses, you're not going to have any problem. But it was tough. He asked, "How is my girlfriend going to feel about this?" That wasn't something we had to deal with very often in our patients, because they usually left so soon after surgery. You don't have the answers. You can be really positive and confident about it, but I wonder how he dealt with that later in life.

It's amazing how adrenaline keeps you going in camp from month to month. When I got back home it was very difficult. I got off the plane at Seattle, went to Fort Lewis, and got processed out—thirty-six hours from the intensive-care ward to my parents' kitchen. I wanted to get right back to work. I thought about going back to the hospital where I had trained, to volunteer in the emergency room. I really felt the need to keep that adrenaline going. But my parents said no, you need to rest, you're getting married in a month, why don't you take some time off. So I didn't go back to work.

In fact, I never really went back to nursing after Vietnam. I spent several years raising our three daughters and moving all over with Carl as a military wife. I kept my nursing registration current until 1982, always with the thought that I would go back. But after I went to college and got my degree in social welfare, a new world opened up. I spent time as a volunteer for the USO, school programs, an outreach program for military wives in Germany, even Girl Scouts with my daughters. Then suddenly, all I could think of was Vietnam.

I had thought about it before, of course, but I had become very good at deciding not to think about it too much or really deal with it. But when Carl was sent to Korea in 1981 and we were separated for the first time in our marriage, I took over a lot of the responsibility and a lot more stress. When stress increases for whatever reason, it's very common that post-traumatic stress and memories of Vietnam have an impact along with the other stress. For some reason, I thought, Maybe if I could talk to some other Vietnam veterans they'd help me understand why this is happening. Soon after that I joined the Columbus chapter of the VVA and got more involved. I became national membership director in 1983, then national secretary, then, in 1987, president.

In many ways, what I'm doing now encompasses the best aspects of what I cared about in nursing—especially the holistic approach of caring for people. Recently I met Lillian Dunlap, a retired brigadier general who was chief of the army nurse corps when I was in Vietnam. I told her I haven't done any nursing since Vietnam. She said, "You do it every day, dear. We're very proud of you." And it struck me that she was right. You picture nursing as working in a hospital, but nursing is really caring for people. That's what I'm about, and that's what VVA is about. So I guess I'm in the right place.

3
STALEMATE

General Westmoreland's strategy for defeating the Communists required a military force large enough to protect the populated areas of South Vietnam and to take the war to the enemy in the remote jungles along the border. Despite the increasing tempo of fighting during 1966, the first eighteen months of active U.S. involvement had been devoted primarily to building up that military machine.

By the beginning of 1967 Westmoreland had at his disposal substantial South Vietnamese assets, including eleven army divisions, two independent regiments, a marine brigade, ten armored cavalry groups, twenty Ranger battalions, six artillery battalions, plus a host of territorial and police units scattered about the country. In addition, the American commander could call upon the services of two Korean infantry divisions, a Korean marine brigade, and a combined Australian–New Zealand task force.

Westmoreland's plans for the new year, however, depended chiefly on the 430,000 U.S. soldiers and Marines who now called South Vietnam their temporary home. Organized into seven infantry divisions, two paratrooper brigades, two light infantry brigades, one armored cavalry regiment, and a reinforced Special Forces group, it was these men who would bear the primary responsibility for meeting the enemy's Main-Force units in battle and defeating him.

Or, rather, it would be the 20 percent of these men who comprised American combat units in Vietnam. Although television news reports suggested that U.S. troops spent their time leaping from helicopters into hot LZs or hacking their way up jungle hillsides in search of their elusive quarry, most Americans who served in Vietnam were staff and support personnel. For every mud-coated soldier humping through the rain there were a half-dozen mail clerks, typists, maintenance men, air traffic controllers, briefing officers, military policemen, transport pilots, supply sergeants, nurses, chaplains, or truck drivers. And for all the newspaper photos of mortar-blasted fire support bases carved out of the

Marines herd Vietcong suspects captured in the Mekong River Delta onto a helicopter.

jungle, most Americans who served in Vietnam spent their tours of duty at sprawling rear-echelon bases like Bien Hoa, Tan Son Nhut, Qui Nhon, Nha Trang, Phu Bai, Da Nang, or Cam Ranh Bay.

Aside from an occasional rocket attack and the threat of VC terrorism, life in the rear could be quite agreeable. Living accommodations were comfortable, if not luxurious. The menus at messes and snack bars featured steaks and ice cream, while nearby officers' and enlisted men's clubs served liquor and cold beer at rock-bottom prices. Off-duty soldiers could read a book in air-conditioned libraries, play volleyball, go water-skiing on the Saigon River, or catch their favorite television shows on the Armed Forces Television Network. GIs stationed at the larger U.S. installations could choose from two or three different first-run films a week at base movie theaters or pick up anything from potato chips to portable stereos at the local PX.

The stateside food and drink, the elaborate recreational facilities and bountiful consumer goods were a deliberate effort by MACV to maintain morale. Coupled with tight restrictions that isolated most servicemen from the surrounding Vietnamese community, however, the material abundance had a disorienting effect on many soldiers who found it difficult to reconcile their relatively plush existence with the death and destruction that surrounded them. Critics charged that the profusion of clubs, slot machines, steam baths, luxury purchases, and other "nonessentials" overtaxed the U.S. logistical system and created endless opportunities for corruption. It also exacerbated the division between rear-echelon personnel and those assigned to combat units.

For the men who actually fought the war, "home" was apt to be a good deal less comfortable. It might be a huge, dusty compound like the 1st Cav's headquarters at An Khe, which lacked many of the amenities of Saigon but still boasted its own twenty-five-acre "entertainment area" complete with bars and brothels. Or it might be the much smaller and starker confines of a fire support base. There a soldier could still count on a hot meal, a drink—sometimes even a cold one—and a change of clothes, but little more than sandbags and dirt to protect him from either the weather or enemy sapper attacks.

It was from these outlying bases and strongpoints that Westmoreland initiated Phase II of his strategy of attrition—moving out from the populated areas into the enemy's sanctuaries where the Communist Main-Force units could be located and destroyed. With Operation Attleboro as its model, the American command launched a series of multibattalion thrusts against Communist base areas and supply corridors. These huge search-and-destroy operations utilized superior American firepower and technology to reap a punishing harvest of enemy dead. But they also left behind a growing toll of American casualties while steadily drawing more and more U.S. forces farther and farther from South Vietnam's cities and villages.

During the second week of January, elements of the 1st, 25th, and 9th Infantry Divisions, the 196th Infantry Brigade, the 173d Airborne Brigade, and the 11th Armored Cavalry Regiment—in all, some 16,000 American soldiers—joined an equal number of ARVN troops in Operation Cedar Falls, an enormous search-and-destroy sweep directed against a long-time Communist stronghold northwest of Saigon known as the Iron Triangle. Preceded by B–52 strikes and 20,000 airdropped leaflets warning inhabitants to leave the area, twenty battalions crashed into the sixty-square-mile triangle on January 8 in search of the 9th VC Division. By the end of the first day the Americans had cordoned off the fortified village of Ben Suc, removed 6,000 villagers to refugee camps, bulldozed the town's dwellings, and destroyed an elaborate network of tunnels and supply caches that honeycombed the ground beneath the surface.

Over the next eighteen days American and South Vietnamese soldiers evacuated the region's four main villages as air strikes, artillery, and giant Rome plows demolished the surrounding jungle. Meanwhile, 6–10-man teams of "tunnel rats" crawled through nearly twelve miles of underground corridors unearthing tons of supplies and thousands of enemy documents. By the time the operation ended, the Vietcong had suffered the discovery and seizure of a key headquarters complex, the destruction of twenty years' worth of tunnels and fortifications, and the loss of nearly 800 men. But the elaborate operation had not been able to trap the main body

American servicemen sunbathe on the deck of the swimming pool at the U.S. Army's enormous headquarters at Long Binh, South Vietnam, in September 1969.

In January 1967, U.S. forces attacked the Vietcong stronghold northwest of Saigon called the Iron Triangle, focusing on the village of Ben Suc. Here some of Ben Suc's 3,800 inhabitants, headed for a refugee camp, sit in an evacuation helicopter with their belongings; their village will soon be razed so it can no longer be used by the Communists.

of enemy soldiers, who filtered through allied lines toward the Cambodian border.

Four weeks later Westmoreland took up the pursuit, sending twenty-two American battalions northwest of the Iron Triangle into War Zone C as part of Operation Junction City. Spearheaded by the 503d Airborne Brigade, which on February 22 conducted the first U.S. combat parachute assault since the Korean War, Junction City was a classic "cordon and sweep" maneuver designed to trap the Vietcong division with speed and numbers, then hammer it to pieces with overwhelming firepower.

The paratroopers formed the eastern side of an enormous horseshoe. To the west were the 196th Light Infantry Brigade and the 3d Brigade of the 4th Infantry Division. To the north were eight battalions of the 1st Infantry Division, carried into battle by some 250 helicopters in one of the largest air assaults in the history of army aviation. As soon as the blocking forces were in place, units of the 25th Infantry Division and the 11th Armored Cavalry swept north through the thickly wooded terrain while Rome plows and heavy bulldozers stripped away great chunks of jungle to deprive the Communists of concealment. When the advancing troops collided with enemy concentrations, the Americans called in prodigious quantities of artillery and air power, including airdropped cluster bombs (CBUs) that ripped through the tangled foliage with devastating results.

Such collisions were rare. When they did take place the Vietcong were handled severely. But the large size of the operational zone, the ruggedness of the terrain, and the noise generated by large, mechanized American units made it almost impossible to surprise the enemy, most of whom scattered west across the Cambodian border. The high point of the allied effort in III Corps during 1967, Junction City demonstrated MACV's ability to swiftly penetrate heretofore-inviolable enemy sanctuaries in force, but the massive shock power of the multidivisional operation had largely spent itself in futile

In one of the few combat jumps made in the war, paratroopers of the 173d Airborne Brigade parachute into Tay Ninh Province on March 3, 1967, during Operation Junction City.

pursuit of an elusive quarry at a cost—$25 million, 282 Americans killed, 1,576 wounded—that some thought well out of proportion to the results.

Two hundred miles north, in the western reaches of the central highlands, the U.S. 4th Infantry Division fought a different kind of border campaign during 1967. Operating out of its base camp near Pleiku City, General William R. Peers's men had the job of guarding the rugged frontier region against the 1st and 10th NVA Divisions. It proved an arduous task, an endless round of patrols through steep rain forests in temperatures that could fluctuate sixty degrees during a twenty-four-hour period. So skilled was the enemy that his presence was often never suspected until the lead elements of a column had been cut down in a hail of fire. So thick was the jungle that aircraft frequently could not locate beleaguered American units.

Between January and April, in a series of engagements known as Operation Sam Houston, the division devoted its attention to the area west of the Nam Sathay River in Kontum Province. At first the infantrymen encountered only light resistance as they systematically uncovered and destroyed enemy tunnels and fortifications. But in mid-February the North Vietnamese began to strike back. Shadowed by NVA reconnaissance teams and trail watchers, harassed by daytime snipers and nighttime mortar attacks, the GIs endured a growing number of vicious ambushes that sapped both their numbers and their morale. The North Vietnamese learned to position themselves so close to the Americans that effective supporting fire was impossible. Counterattacks typically resulted in heavy casualties from carefully prepared enemy flanking positions. And although such firefights could last well into the night, by daylight the enemy had invariably disappeared, taking his dead and wounded with him.

With the beginning of the summer monsoon in early April, the 4th Division shifted its energies south into western Pleiku Province. For this new operation, code named Francis Marion, the Americans relied with greater success on supporting firepower, including indigenous armored personnel carriers and the tanks of the 10th Cavalry in a series of violent encounters that raged across the rolling hills south of the Se San River. For three months the NVA attempted without success to drive the division away from its border sanctuaries, the fierce battles culminating on July 23 when air force fighter-bombers annihilated an entire NVA regiment as it vainly attempted to overrun an isolated American company.

For all its difficulties and dangers, however, the contest against the NVA in the western highlands could not compare in scope or savagery to the continuing battles waged by the U.S. Marines along the shattered hills of the demilitarized zone. By the end of 1966 the 3d Marine Division had established a series of combat bases strung out between Route 9 and the DMZ. From these isolated strongpoints bristling with artillery and barbed wire, the Marines fought a succession of costly battles during 1967, as heavily armed Communist regulars tested the Americans in their own bloody war of attrition.

Heavy fighting broke out on February 27 when a Marine reconnaissance patrol intercepted an entire NVA regiment near Cam Lo, precipitating a series of ambushes against a hastily dispatched relief force that left one Marine battalion commander and dozens of his men dead. The same pattern was repeated on a much larger scale in April at Khe Sanh when a squad from Company B, 9th Marines, ran into advance elements of the 325C NVA Division. As reinforcements poured into the small western outpost over the next three days, it quickly became apparent that the enemy was heavily entrenched in the hills surrounding the base. It took twelve days of continuous battle, a relentless bombardment by Marine artillery, helicopter gunships, attack aircraft, and nearly 600 American casualties to drive the North Vietnamese back across the DMZ.

The Marines immediately sought to press their hard-won advantage with Operation Hickory. Launched on May 18, this multibattalion strike marked the first time that U.S. forces had penetrated the demilitarized zone. The complex scheme of maneuver utilized the full range of Marine combat assets, including helicopter gunships, fighter-bombers, and amphibious landing craft. Backed by a cascade of supporting arms the Americans smashed through heavily fortified NVA bunker complexes all the way to the Ben Hai River, then wheeled south to sweep up the remnants of enemy units scattered by the lightning assault.

The first battle of Khe Sanh had cost the North Vietnamese an estimated 1,000 KIA, Hickory at least as many. But neither defeat had any appreciable effect on Hanoi. With the luxury of rear bases in Laos and North Vietnam secure from U.S. attack, battered enemy units simply regrouped, refitted, and returned to battle. By midsummer the NVA was threatening U.S. defenses in the eastern part of the demilitarized zone where the Marines labored to construct the first stage of a massive anti-infiltration barrier. Dubbed McNamara's Line after its chief proponent, Secretary of Defense Robert S. McNamara, this combination of mines, electronic sensors, guard towers, and physical obstacles was an attempt to accomplish by other means what the bombing of North Vietnam had failed to do. Of dubious value and inordinate expense, the grandiose project did not survive the year. Nonetheless, the barrier and its initial terminus—the combat base at Con Thien—became the focal point of NVA artillery, rocket, and ground attacks.

Attempting to relieve the steadily growing pressure on Con Thien, three Marine battalions fought a furious battle with the 90th NVA Regiment in early July. Against waves of North Vietnamese infantry backed by intense enemy artillery fire, the Americans directed a thunderous bombardment of air, artillery, and naval gunfire that claimed more than 1,300 enemy lives but did nothing to stop the steady encirclement of the besieged combat base. Throughout August and September the two sides engaged in a fearful contest of supporting arms that drove Con Thien's defenders burrowing into the ground for protection and left the tortured landscape littered with the bodies of thousands of North Vietnamese soldiers (see page 120). Only under the devastating impact of nearly 800 B–52 bombing runs did the enemy finally retreat in early October.

Driven back along the northern frontier, the Communists struck farther south, attacking an ARVN outpost in Phuoc Long Province on October 27 and the Cambodian border town of Loc Ninh two days later. Both assaults were thrown back with heavy enemy casualties. Then on November 3 a defector revealed that the NVA 1st Division, after months of elaborate prep-

While one Marine checks a fallen buddy, others charge toward North Vietnamese positions on the ravaged slopes of Hill 881 North during fierce fighting near Khe Sanh in spring 1967.

aration, was poised to attack the highlands town of Dak To. Seizing the opportunity to engage the enemy in force, the American command deployed all sixteen battalions of the 4th Infantry Division, the entire 173d Airborne Brigade, a brigade from the 1st Air Cavalry, and six ARVN battalions into the narrow valleys and onto the precipitous, jungle-canopied ridges that surrounded the remote district capital.

As allied units probed south from Dak To during the first two weeks of November they clashed repeatedly with well-armed NVA regulars. From the labyrinth of tunnels and camouflaged fortifications they had labori-

ously carved out of the steep hillsides, the Communists took a steady toll of American lives during these encounters, including a Veterans Day ambush that left 20 dead, 154 wounded, and 2 missing from a 200-man airborne task force. Four days later a North Vietnamese mortar attack on the Dak To airfield destroyed two C–130 transports and blew up an ammunition dump in an explosion that sent an enormous fireball shooting thousands of feet into the night sky.

The blazing airfield proved the high-water mark of the Communist attempt to take Dak To. By the middle of the month the weight of men and machines that

American soldiers stationed at the remote U.S. Army camp at Dak To near the Cambodian border take time out to attend Sunday Mass.

MACV had hurled into battle began to tell, pushing enemy units southwest toward their Cambodian sanctuaries. As they retreated the North Vietnamese fought tenacious rear-guard actions, forcing the Americans to literally obliterate whole hilltops with supporting fire before units on the ground could claw their way forward in vicious hand-to-hand engagements. During the course of the operation U.S. forces fired 151,000 rounds of artillery, flew 2,096 tactical air sorties, and mounted 257 B–52 bombing strikes against enemy positions. Finally, after a savage five-day battle for Hill 875 (see page 132) in which 158 Americans and at least twice as many NVA were killed, North Vietnamese resistance came to an end.

As the battered 1st NVA Division limped into Cambodia, the American command celebrated the tremendous effort that had transported 16,000 allied troops into some of the most hostile territory in South Vietnam, maintained an astonishing level of logistical and fire support, and driven one of the enemy's best divisions from the field with losses estimated as high as 1,600 killed in action.

The bulk of enemy casualties at Dak To, as they had been in every other major battle during the year, were the result of air strikes. The expansion of American ground forces during the previous two years had been more than matched by the increase of U.S. air assets in Southeast Asia. By the end of 1967 the air force had more than 60,000 personnel organized into one air command wing, nine tactical fighter wings, three strategic bombardment wings, and one air commando/special operations wing, plus communications groups, tactical control groups, and a welter of subsidiary units operating out of sixteen major air bases in South Vietnam, Thailand, and Guam. Alongside the air force were the 70–100 carrier-based U.S. Navy aircraft flying from Yankee Station some 100 miles off the northern coast of South Vietnam and the six air groups—representing approximately 500 helicopter and fixed-wing aircraft— of the 1st Marine Air Wing scattered throughout I Corps.

The aircraft used to wage the in-country war over South Vietnam included B–57 Canberra light bombers,

F–100 Supersabres for close air support, supersonic F–4 Phantoms, and prop-driven A–1 Skyraiders. Above North Vietnam and Laos the air force relied heavily on the F–105 Thunderchief, while navy pilots flew the F–8 Crusader, the A–6A Intruder—the first all-weather attack aircraft—and later the A–7 Corsair. Utilized extensively for close air support and interdiction over South Vietnam and Laos but not yet subjected to North Vietnam's main air defense system were the giant B–52 Stratofortresses based in Thailand and Guam.

American warplanes were far outnumbered, however, by the thousands of observation, reconnaissance, cargo, tanker, transport, and command aircraft that daily filled the skies over Southeast Asia, not to mention helicopters of every kind and description flying cargo, troop transport, gunship, rescue, and medevac missions around the clock. By 1967 this aerial armada was responsible for more than 53,000 air traffic "movements"—takeoffs, landings, and major flight pattern changes—in South Vietnam alone every single day.

Along with this growing aerial armada came mounting pressure on Lyndon Johnson to employ it without restraint against the enemy's heartland. The North Vietnamese weakened the hand of those in Washington who argued for caution when they took advantage of a February 1967 bombing pause to resupply their forces in South Vietnam at an unprecedented rate. Just as important, the steady increase in the number of U.S. casualties had begun to undermine public confidence in the president's handling of the war. Most troublesome to Johnson, however, were Congressional hawks led by Mississippi senator John C. Stennis whose August hearings into the conduct of the air war sharply challenged White House control over the air campaign.

The result was a continuing escalation of the bombing throughout Indochina. American pilots on Tiger Hound missions over the Laotian panhandle flew more than 12,000 sorties during the first four months of 1967. By year's end the air force recorded 1,718 B–52 raids alone. But the activity along the Ho Chi Minh Trail paled beside what was happening over North Vietnam, where total sorties increased from 79,000 in 1966 to 108,000 in 1967, the amount of bombs dropped climbing from 136,000 to 226,000 tons of high explosives.

Behind these figures lay a steady expansion in both the number and type of targets authorized by Washington. Johnson met Hanoi's increased infiltration of February with mine-laying operations in North Vietnamese rivers south of the twentieth parallel and strikes against manufacturing targets near Hanoi and Haiphong. In March, American warplanes hit the Thai Nguyen steel and chemical plant thirty-five miles north of the capital. During April they struck power plants, ammunition dumps, cement factories, and airfields within the Hanoi-Haiphong restricted zone. The most important target that month was the 32,000-kilowatt thermal power plant in downtown Hanoi, which U.S. Navy pilots knocked out with television-guided "Walleye" bombs. Eight weeks later Johnson approved attacks against petroleum storage sites near Hanoi and Haiphong. In July the president added forty new transportation and military installations to the Rolling Thunder target list, including the crucial Paul Doumer Bridge on the outskirts of Hanoi, which air force fighter-bombers hit for the first time on August 2. That same month strikes were made against previously prohibited regions within the city limits of Hanoi and along the buffer zone near the Chinese border, a series of raids culminating on August 20 when U.S. aircraft flew more than 200 sorties over North Vietnam, the greatest single day's effort since the bombing began. During the remainder of the year American pilots were let loose on virtually every military, industrial, and transportation target recommended by the Stennis committee.

By December 1967 the United States had delivered a total of 864,000 tons of bombs on the North Vietnamese—70 percent more than had been dropped in the entire Pacific theater during World War II. The bombing had inflicted an estimated $300 million in damage on North Vietnam, seriously disrupted its agricultural production, and crippled its fragile industrial base. Although civilian casualties had generally been kept low, some cities were severely damaged; others were almost entirely destroyed.

Soldiers in an AC–47 gunship fire its electrically driven Gatling guns into the twilight sky, showing why the aircraft was nicknamed "Puff the Magic Dragon."

A North Vietnamese transport truck crosses a pontoon bridge that was built to replace the one destroyed earlier outside Nam Dinh by U.S. bombers.

The actual dollar cost of the air war to the United States, however, was far greater—some $900 million in lost aircraft alone, not to mention enormous operating and munitions expenditures. Had the bombing been successful such deficit spending might have been accepted with equanimity. But the hard fact was that the air campaign against North Vietnam had failed utterly to meet its original objectives.

The United States constructed its military strategy in Southeast Asia around the assumption that air power would so devastate the North Vietnamese economy, so impede the flow of men and materiel south, and so discourage the people of North Vietnam that Hanoi would have no choice but to sue for peace. Yet, after an aerial onslaught unparalleled in history the North Vietnamese were no closer to giving up than they had been at the beginning of 1965. Despite the destruction, the economy functioned. Despite the shortages and dislocations, there was no evidence of a significant loss of morale. And despite everything that American air power could do to stop it, the infiltration of men and supplies to the southern battlefields during 1967 was nearly three times greater than it had been before the bombing began.

The reasons for these failures were many. American military planners had underestimated the limitations on air power posed by Vietnam's monsoon climate, triple-canopy jungle, and mountainous terrain. After focusing their doctrine on Europe for two decades, they had to adapt aircraft designed primarily for strategic nuclear warfare to the demands of a limited political conflict and had to retrain pilots in conventional bombing techniques. Beyond this, the air war was saddled from the beginning with shortages of equipment, ammunition, and pilots. Washington's gradualist approach gave Hanoi time to disperse its economic assets away from urban centers, while the administration's tight control of target selection resulted in unwieldy chains of command. Even worse, from the pilots' point of view, were the plethora of prohibited zones and restrictive rules of engagement that diminished both the effectiveness and the safety of many missions.

Compounding these problems were the ingenuity and resourcefulness of the North Vietnamese. By evacuating civilians from the cities, dispersing industries, scattering petroleum and other storage facilities across the countryside, and cleverly camouflaging those targets that could not be moved, they were able to minimize the damage done by the American air raids. By raising an army of civilian workers armed with picks and shovels, they were able to effect repairs with remarkable speed and keep vital roadways open. And by creating one of the most sophisticated air defense systems in the world, they were able to make the United States pay a heavy price for its air offensive.

In the end, however, North Vietnamese survival rested on the material aid and technical assistance they received from their Communist allies, especially the Soviet Union and China. Hanoi's leaders took full advantage of Sino-Soviet rivalry, skillfully playing one superpower against the other in their quest for increased aid. The success of their efforts was measured in the vast quantities of rice, small arms, ammunition, vehicles, fighter planes, surface-to-air missiles (SAMs), and tanks that their allies supplied. This cumulative contribution, estimated to be in excess of $2 billion between 1965 and 1968, more than made up for all the damage inflicted by the bombing.

To Defense Secretary Robert McNamara the figures called for a reassessment of strategy. Convinced that the North Vietnamese would not give in "no matter how much bombing we do," McNamara proposed an unconditional bombing halt in hopes of appeasing antiwar critics within the United States and prodding Hanoi toward negotiations. He also urged the president to revise American ground strategy and place a ceiling on American troop levels. Although he did not put it in so many words, by the middle of 1967 the man who had once been a major proponent of escalation no longer had any hope of victory.

For if air power had not brought the Communists to their knees, neither had General Westmoreland's strategy of attrition. The commitment of nearly half a million troops had saved South Vietnam from defeat and taken a heavy toll of enemy casualties. U.S. soldiers had fought well under adverse conditions, utilizing an enormous advantage in mobility and firepower to drive the Vietcong from even their most secure strongholds. Indeed, whenever American forces actually engaged VC or NVA units, they almost always prevailed. But the primary goal of grinding down the enemy until he hollered "uncle" was not happening. Despite official estimates of as many as 220,000 enemy soldiers killed since the deployment of U.S. combat forces, overall Communist strength in South Vietnam stood at approximately 350,000 troops, compared to some 200,000 in June 1965.

In trying to account for this state of affairs some questioned the accuracy of MACV's enemy casualty figures. There was little doubt that the confusions of battle, the difficulty of distinguishing Vietcong guerrillas from ordinary peasants, command pressure, and the ambitions of junior officers all inflated the notoriously unreliable "body count"—by at least 30 percent according to one Defense Department analysis. Far more important, however, Westmoreland's strategy ignored the fact that some 200,000 North Vietnamese reached draft age each year, a manpower pool far in excess of the number of enemy KIA, even when estimated by the most optimistic methods. Moreover, the Communists had time and terrain on their side. By fighting only when and where they chose, the Vietcong and North Vietnamese were largely able to control how many casualties they suffered. When losses became too high, they simply scattered into the jungle or crossed the border into sanctuaries immune from U.S. attack.

In short, Westmoreland's vaunted "cross-over point"—when enemy casualty rates would exceed the number of soldiers the Communists could replace through recruitment or infiltration—was never reached. Meanwhile, U.S. casualty rates steadily increased, averaging 816 killed in action per month during the first half of 1967, compared to 477 per month during 1966. Along with swelling draft calls, the mounting American death toll further eroded domestic support for the war. On the other hand, Communist morale remained intact despite formidable losses and staggering hardships, thanks to an effective system of internal discipline and a firm conviction that they were defending their country against foreign invaders.

Neither the Americans nor their own political leaders had been able to inspire the same spirit of resistance among the people of South Vietnam. Much of the blame for this lay with the Saigon government, whose corrupt agents were more intent upon lining their own pockets than improving the living standards of the South Vietnamese people. Some of the onus rested on the ARVN, which ceded de facto control of whole provinces to the Vietcong while alienating the rural population with its ineffectiveness and, often, its arrogance and brutality. But an important measure of responsibility also belonged to the U.S. military command. The massive search-and-destroy operations that occupied so much of MACV's time and resources diverted attention from the social and political roots of the insurgency. They also wreaked havoc among the civilian population of the countryside.

The job of the combat officer in Vietnam, wrote one brigade commander, was to "spend firepower as if he is a millionaire and husband his men's lives as if he is a pauper," and so he did. Armed with automatic weapons, recoilless rifles, grenades, mortars, and machine guns, able to call upon artillery, naval gunfire, helicopter gunships, and supersonic fighter-bombers carrying everything from high explosives to cluster bombs, defoliants, and napalm, American commanders let loose a storm of shot and shell against the enemy whenever he appeared. Since it was common practice for the Vietcong to fire on American troops from within villages, the reliance on firepower contributed to a soaring rate of damage and death among the civilian population of the countryside. The widespread use of "free fire zones" and "harassment and interdiction" fire as a means of controlling enemy movements only made matters worse. So did the calculated attempt to discourage villagers from aiding the VC by burning their homes and evacuating them to crude refugee camps that eventually housed more than 20 percent of South Vietnam's population.

The results, observed one official pacification report, were highly counterproductive: "It becomes relatively easy for the VC to replace losses from a population resentful and disgruntled at the destruction of their lives and property and therefore hostile to the GVN [Government of Vietnam] and its allies." Informed at a press briefing that U.S. forces had moved into one rural district behind 365 tactical air strikes, 30 B–52 sorties, and a barrage of more than a million artillery shells, an American correspondent had a similar reaction. "It ap-

American soldiers use metal detectors to examine a South Vietnamese farmer's harvest of dried rice plants for any hidden weapons or ammunition, 1966.

pears you [have] leveled virtually every village and hamlet, killed or driven more than 50,000 peasants off the land with your firepower. My question is, how do you intend to go about winning the hearts and minds of these people?" "I'm afraid you'll have to take that up with Civic Affairs, sir," replied the briefing officer, "but, jeeze, it's a real good question."

What the United States had achieved in Vietnam after nearly three years of war was stalemate, but stalemate at a much higher level of commitment.

In the air and on the ground American forces were scoring ever greater victories. But the war was not being won. It was not being won because it was being fought largely on the enemy's terms. By devoting U.S. military assets to the pursuit of enemy Main-Force units in remote war zones and base areas, the American command was losing men and machines with no commensurate increase in security for the bulk of the South Vietnamese population. Although most of the giant operations were "successful" in capturing Communist supplies and temporarily clearing enemy units from the area, once the Americans left in search of new targets the Communists returned. After 30,000 U.S. and ARVN troops spent three weeks blasting their way through the Iron Triangle in Operation Cedar Falls, 1st Division commander Major General William DePuy called the destruction of the Communist stronghold "a blow from which the VC in this area may never recover." Yet scarcely two weeks later an American officer reconnoitering the area by helicopter reported that "the Iron Triangle was again literally crawling with what appeared to be Viet Cong riding bicycles or wandering around on foot."

The border battles of 1967 exacerbated the security problem, stretched American forces to the limit, and enabled the Communists to regain the military initiative. With major U.S. units lured into large frontier engagements, prophesied North Vietnam's General Vo Nguyen Giap, strongholds along the coast such as Da Nang and Chu Lai would become "isolated islands in the open sea of the people's war." The heavy cost in casualties was one Giap was more than willing to pay as long as sufficient replacements were available and substantial losses could also be inflicted on his adversary. As one authority on North Vietnamese strategy pointed out, it was not by battles won or lost but "by the traffic in homebound American coffins that Giap measures his success."

In that regard the North Vietnamese general was most astute, for by the end of 1967 the war had produced sharp divisions among the American people. Believing that the strategy of attrition was bearing fruit, that the solution in Vietnam was "more bombs, more shells, more napalm . . . till the other side cracks and gives up," military leaders and Congressional hawks pushed the president to remove remaining restrictions on the bombing, increase American troop strength by as many as 200,000 men, and permit Westmoreland to take the war to the enemy in Laos and Cambodia. At the same time, the growing antiwar movement castigated the government for its involvement in Southeast Asia, demanding that the administration end the bombing of North Vietnam and cease propping up the Saigon regime.

Meanwhile, opinion polls charted a steady decline in public support for the war and an equally steady rise in the number of Americans who disapproved of the way the president was handling the situation in Vietnam. What the polls revealed more than anything else was a profound confusion and uncertainty about the war. "I

want to get out," explained one housewife, "but I don't want to give up."

Lyndon Johnson might well have said the very same thing. Discouraged by the lack of progress in Vietnam yet reluctant to expand the war any further, sharing some of McNamara's reservations about the likelihood of military victory yet unwilling to concede defeat, he once more sought a middle ground. To appease the hawks he enlarged the Rolling Thunder target list, but he gave Westmoreland only a quarter of the 200,000 additional men the general sought. To keep his options open he placed no ceiling on American troop levels, but he began to consider ways of transferring greater responsibility for the ground war to the South Vietnamese. If he was not prepared to go further, Johnson surely was not ready to retreat. The American commitment to Vietnam would continue.

Having made his decision to stay the course, Johnson mounted a frenzied public relations campaign during the last month of the year, dispatching government "truth teams" around the country and recalling General Westmoreland to Washington to reassure the nation with an optimistic speech before Congress. "We are not going to yield," declared the president. "We are not going to shimmy. We are going to wind up with a peace with honor which all Americans seek." Yet, even as he spoke, Communist troops in unprecedented numbers were marshaling their forces all across South Vietnam. The stunning blow they were about to deliver would take the true measure of American determination.

One of the 1,500 Marines defending Con Thien near the DMZ braces for an incoming mortar round during a four-day battle with North Vietnamese troops in late September 1967.

Witness: Sam Davis

From the murky paddies of the Mekong Delta to the skies over Hanoi, Vietnam was the scene of countless acts of bravery. For their intrepidity in the face of battle and valor in Vietnam "above and beyond the call of duty," 238 Americans received their country's highest award, the Medal of Honor. One of them was Sammy L. Davis, a twenty-one-year-old private first class in November 1967, when his 9th Infantry Division base came under attack in the Mekong Delta.

Looking back I find it difficult to believe that I or anyone else was cited for individual heroism. The situation that I faced on the night of the action was difficult and dangerous, to be sure, but difficult and dangerous are words that address all the experiences that made up Vietnam. As honored as I am to have been chosen to receive the Medal of Honor, it seems that there should be some way to honor all the rest of the men in my unit and in all the other units that served in Vietnam. Vietnam was indiscriminate in its selection of whom it called and when, and once called there was no refusing its demands. The overwhelming majority of men passed the test and met the challenge—not for politics or medals or any high sense of righteousness, since those things can't be felt by people covered with mud. Things happened because men made them happen, just because we were all in it together.

C Battery, 2d Battalion, 4th Artillery, was a terrific, hard-working unit. We did our jobs very, very well. In fact, our call sign was "Automatic Five-Niner," which was a statement in itself because we were able to put out so many more rounds than the average artillery crew. The reason was that the unit had trained together and was used to working together as a crew. I was one of the first replacements to join it, and I learned how to work with them.

On the night of November 17 we were at Forward Base Cudgel, right on the Mekong River, south of My Tho. Just before dark the major came to the camp in his helicopter and said, "The probability of you guys getting mortared tonight is very good." He didn't say anything about a ground assault. So we prepared ourselves as well as possible. Because of the water table you could dig down only about fourteen inches, then fill sandbags to put around it. We also stocked our artillery: beehive rounds filled with fléchettes, little arrows about an inch and a quarter long, very devastating; high-explosive rounds; white phosphorus; and propaganda rounds, filled with chieu hoi notes for the enemy.

At 2:00 on the button we heard the first enemy mortar slide down the tube. They were very close. Usually if a mortar attack lasts more than five minutes, it's a really long one. So when this one lasted half an hour, we knew something big was coming. And sure enough, at 2:30 we could hear the NVA starting to yell and run fast toward us. They were coming en masse from immediately across the river and from my right. We had four guns, each covering a different direction, and the majority of the NVA were coming from my direction.

We jumped up from our foxholes, dropped the tube on the 105 MM gun for direct fire, loaded up a beehive, and started firing. I was the assistant gunner of our crew, the one firing the piece. When I pulled the lanyard on the third round, the NVA fired a rocket-propelled grenade right at our muzzle blast. It hit the shield that I was hiding behind and the shield kind of exploded. I got thousands of little bitty pieces of steel in my right side and was knocked unconscious, lying half in and half out of my foxhole. The other guys just gathered up the guys they thought were alive and would make it and fell back to the next piece. That's why my guys left me. They thought I was dead.

Our guys fired beehive to keep the NVA off the gun, and when they fired the round some of the darts hit me and woke me up. I had a tremendous buzzing in my head, and it took a long time for me to get it together. After maybe a few minutes I realized what was happening and what I had to do. I picked up my M16 and fired it until it quit. Then I fired the M60 machine gun in my foxhole until it quit. Then I didn't have anything else to fire and they just kept coming. The only alternative was to get hold of the 105 and see if I could get it fired up. So that's what I did.

My head was still ringing, but I fired quite a few rounds. It was dark, and I couldn't tell what round was what, but I fired at least four more beehives and some white phosphorus rounds and even some propaganda rounds. The NVA were still on the other side of the river, about twenty-five to thirty meters away. I guess if I hadn't fired that gun we would have been overrun from that side. The grenade had hit the recoil mechanism on the howitzer, so when I fired it the gun went crazy. It just rolled over onto me and broke some vertebrae in my back. If it hadn't been for the soft mud, it probably would have killed me. Every time I fired it, it just kept jumping back and back. It ended up in a little creek eight feet away. I had to load the last round underwater, but it went off.

After I finished with the gun I saw one of our guys lying wounded across the river. I knew I was hurting bad and couldn't get to him by myself, so I took an air mattress and made it across that way. On the other side, I reached the wounded guy and found two more with him. One was shot in the back, another in the head, and the third in the foot. I threw the guy who had been shot in the head over my back, and the two other guys leaned on each shoulder. We all kind of leaned on each other and helped each other back toward the river. Some NVA ran right past us; I don't think they thought there would be anybody on their side of the river.

I took the guy who was wounded the worst across first. Our guys saw me swimming across the river so they helped me get him up on the bank. Then I went across and got the other two guys. I spent the rest of the time just tending to business, taking care of some of the guys who had been wounded. By that time the NVA had been pretty well whipped.

I had more problems when I was medevacked the next day. One of the beehive darts had penetrated my kidney and I got a kidney infection, then my whole body just kind of deteriorated. I had a 106-degree temperature for more than a week. I had lost a lot of blood anyway, and the fever dehydrated me to the point where my blood had almost turned to buttermilk. They would give me a transfusion, and within twenty-four hours my body would just suck all the moisture back out. They gave up on me and put me out in the hallway to die. Then one of the guys I swam across the river for told them to take blood out of his arm for me. He lay down in the hallway beside me. They hooked us up, and I lived.

Years later I had more health problems. I was one of the point men used by the New Jersey Agent Orange Commission in its original studies, and that's when they determined that I was exposed to dioxin from the Agent Orange that was sprayed all throughout the delta. Most of the things that are wrong with me today, except for my back problem, can be attributed to dioxin. Because of my exposure to it, my internal organs work at the rate of a seventy- or seventy-five-year-old man—which is really confusing when you're only forty. But I'm hanging in there.

I don't think that a person can be honest and say, "I only took care of myself in Vietnam." No one who served there could escape or endure the terror, the heat, or the tremendous physical demands made by the war simply by applying himself to the task. Most of what carried us through the experience came out of the sense that everyone needed everyone else, that if you helped me today I would help you tomorrow. We would both help a third the next day. I would never have made it to that riverbank if it had not been for the efforts of the other men, and if the other men came away from the riverbank because of what I did there, then it simply was my turn. We all looked out for each other.

This is a trait we brought home with us as well. The signs that have been coming out over the last few years—the building of the Wall in Washington, the parades and ceremonies in various cities, the books, the movies, with the more realistic understanding and view of events—are largely the product of our efforts, because we're the ones who understand what has to be done. We're just taking care of each other. It's what we do best.

Focus: Con Thien

Nothing better symbolized the stalemate reached by the end of 1967 than the struggle over Con Thien near the DMZ and the battle for Hill 875 in the central highlands. Both were long and hard fought, with each side taking heavy casualties. And both seemed, at least to the American troops who fought them, exercises in futility.

It was known to local missionaries as the Hill of Angels, but to the Marines who occupied it, it was a little piece of hell. Just two miles from the DMZ, Con Thien was a barren, bulldozed plateau of red dirt 160 meters high. The cramped outpost, barely big enough to hold an understrength battalion, was ringed by barbed wire, studded with artillery revetments, and crisscrossed with trenches and sandbag-covered bunkers. To the east stretched the Trace, the 600-meter-wide firebreak the Marines had cleared for the McNamara Line. Equally important, the hilltop strongpoint overlooked one of the principal enemy routes into South Vietnam as well as the vast U.S. logistics complex at Dong Ha ten miles away. If the enemy ever occupied Con Thien, observed Colonel Richard B. Smith, commander of the 9th Marines, "he would be looking down our throats."

The men of the 1st Battalion, 9th Marines, who garrisoned the outpost, suffered from blazing heat and choking dust, from snipers and threats of ground attack. But what made duty at Con Thien a special misery was the rain of artillery from NVA batteries tucked away in the northern hills of the DMZ. The Communist guns were not only well camouflaged but also sheltered in caves and other protected positions. Rolled out to fire, then rolled back again, the guns were frequently shifted to prevent U.S. spotters from fixing their locations for air force bombers. Although the Americans retaliated with artillery and air strikes of their own, they were not able to stop the hundreds of shells that each day took a steady toll of Con Thien's defenders.

The heaviest fighting took place outside the wire, however, as other Marine battalions clashed with enemy units trying to draw a noose around Con Thien. On July 2 a North Vietnamese ambush killed or wounded nearly 275 men from a single U.S. company. During the fighting, the NVA fired more than 1,000 artillery and mortar rounds at Con Thien and Gio Linh, while American air and artillery punished the North Vietnamese with more than 100 tons of napalm and high explosives. The ambush set off a week of violent encounters climaxing on July 6, when American units backed by tanks, naval gunfire, artillery, attack aircraft, and helicopter gunships fought off a ferocious nighttime Communist ground attack. The battle left behind a scene of indescribable carnage, with some 800 enemy bodies and tons of demolished equipment scattered over the smoking, blasted landscape. By the time the NVA had retreated across the DMZ in midmonth, nearly 1,300 enemy soldiers had been killed and at least one first-line North Vietnamese regiment virtually destroyed.

Yet their horrendous casualties seemed to have little effect on the North Vietnamese. In late August the enemy returned to the attack and by early September, when the 3d Battalion, 9th Marines, took over from the 1/9, ground assaults had erupted south of the base. On September 10 the 3/26 Marines engaged an entire NVA regiment four miles from Con Thien, which itself was hit three days later.

Meanwhile, the Marines were experiencing one of the heaviest shellings of the war. Over one six-day period Con Thien endured twenty-four separate bombardments, during which a total of more than 3,000 rounds of artillery, rockets, and mortars crashed into the beleaguered garrison. On September 25 alone, more than 1,200 rounds fell within the perimeter. Under that thunderous cascade of shells the Marines tried to pick out the sounds that could mean the difference between life and death—the "whump" of mortars that gave a man five to ten seconds to seek cover, the whine of artillery shells that could be heard three seconds before impact, and the terrible whisper of enemy rockets that gave no more than a second's warning. But the combined volume of fire from U.S. and enemy guns left many temporarily deaf, so that even when the shelling stopped the men had to shout to make themselves heard.

Adding to their misery was the northeast monsoon that arrived a month early in September, flooding trench lines, collapsing bunkers, and washing out land lines of communication. The rain turned the laterite soil into a muddy quagmire that absorbed some of the shrapnel from high-explosive artillery shells, but which also made it difficult to run for cover and eventually concealed so many dud rounds that Con Thien became a minefield of unexploded ordnance. At night, fog shrouded the base, creating an even greater sense of isolation and magnifying every sound into an enemy attack. When it was not raining it was drizzling, the perpetual moisture producing skin rashes so painful that a mere touch was agony and feet so sodden that skin a pale shade of green sloughed off in long strips.

They called themselves "the walking dead," the men of Con Thien—living in dank, filthy bunkers they shared with rats, eating only one or two C-rations a day to save space on resupply choppers for ammo and replacement troops, carrying wounded men through a sea of mud, and all the while listening for the constant cry of "Incoming!" In addition to the random pattern of deadly barrages that made superstition a way of life, there were also recoilless-rifle fire and rocket-propelled-grenade (RPG) sniping to contend with, full-scale attacks that sent the adrenaline surging, and small probes along the wire that stretched a man's nerves to the breaking point. Shell shock, relatively unheard of elsewhere in Vietnam, was not unusual at Con Thien; nor was a growing anger and confusion among the Marines about their predicament.

They were frustrated with having to sit and take it and bitter about being asked to die for "a shit hole place," as one of them put it, whose value did not seem to measure up to that of the men beside them who were being wounded and crippled and killed. Despite the hazards of the journey, reporters and cameramen—including the great war photographer David Duncan [who took the pictures on the following pages]—came to record what was happening at Con Thien. Some of them, too, questioned the wisdom of holding the isolated base, portraying a grim siege they likened to the French disaster at Dien Bien Phu. Westmoreland scoffed at their warnings. Happy to have the North Vietnamese stand and fight, he sent four Marine battalions circling the combat base to keep enemy units at arm's length and hammered at the NVA with "one of the greatest concentrations of firepower in the history of the Vietnam War."

It was called Operation Neutralize, a forty-nine-day campaign involving the entire spectrum of U.S. supporting arms—strike aircraft, strategic bombers, offshore naval guns, and heavy artillery—along with forward air control pilots who pinpointed targets for aerial strikes and special long-range reconnaissance patrols that infiltrated the demilitarized zone to assess bomb damage and locate additional targets. The concentrated, seven-week assault pummeled an area the size of Manhattan with nearly 20,000 rounds from land artillery and naval gunfire and more than 40,000 tons of bombs. Together, air force, navy, and Marine pilots flew 5,200 sorties during the siege, including 820 B–52 Arc Light missions. Like a terrible plow, the torrent of firepower furrowed the earth for mile upon mile, saturating NVA troop sites, demolishing more than 200 enemy gun positions, and leaving the land a desolate moonscape of water-filled craters devoid of life.

The fearful onslaught finally broke the back of the North Vietnamese offensive. Although willing to accept more than 2,000 dead and many times that number wounded, NVA units were never able to concentrate sufficient forces for an all-out attack. Toward the end of September enemy shelling began to taper off, and on October 4 MACV headquarters announced that the siege of Con Thien was over. As North Vietnamese troops staggered back across the DMZ, the 1/9 Marines relieved the battered 3d Battalion. But the combat base itself remained, a grim, depressing place of danger and misery. From that there was no escape—not at Con Thien or anywhere along South Vietnam's northern frontier in the third year of a war whose end was nowhere in sight.

At night inside the catacomb-like bunkers under Con Thien, Captain Frank Breth (center) briefs platoon lieutenants from Mike Company of the 3d Battalion, 9th Marines, whose men were among the occupants of the Hill of Angels during a two-month-long siege in September and October 1967.

A moment of relative relaxation at the landing zone in the rear of the Marine base.

Photographer David Duncan's original caption to this picture, first published in his book War Without Heroes: "One man was black—one white; the endless nights and days, the rain-flooded trench, constant enemy shelling, cigarettes, and the grim life they shared were the same."

127

Opposite and above. *Marines dive for cover as enemy gunners "walk" their artillery in on the landing zone in the rear of the base, firing each volley progressively closer to the LZ until they finally score a direct hit.*

Focus: Hill 875

By the time of the "border battles" in late 1967, of which Con Thien was the first, the war had become a bloody contest of regular armies and conventional arms. Nowhere was this more evident than at Dak To, where beginning in early November 16,000 allied troops took on the 1st NVA Division in the steep, jungle wilderness of western Kontum Province.

For two weeks American and Communist units fought a series of costly engagements until the incessant pounding of U.S. air and artillery drove the North Vietnamese from the battlefield. Pursued by elements of the 4th Infantry Division and the 173d Airborne Brigade, the Communists withdrew southwest toward their Cambodian sanctuaries. Left behind to guard their retreat was the 174th NVA Regiment. On November 18 a Special Forces mobile reaction company ran into the heavily entrenched enemy on Hill 875, ten miles from 173d field headquarters at Ben Het. The next day brigade commander General Leo H. Schweiter ordered the 2d Battalion, 503d Infantry, to take the hill. What followed was one of the most savage battles of the Vietnam War.

Covered with closely spaced trees, dense brush, and bamboo thickets, Hill 875 rose gradually from the surrounding jungle toward two ridge lines that leveled off at the top into a broad "saddle." The enemy had turned the hill into a fortress, lacing the slopes with bunkers and trenches linked by tunnels and well-constructed trails cut into the sides of the hill. The elaborate fortifications spiraling downward from the summit were camouflaged with natural vegetation that had grown up in the several months since they had been built and protected from air and artillery bombardment by up to twelve feet of overhead cover. The slit gun ports of the underground bunkers commanded excellent fields of fire, while the interconnecting tunnels enabled the enemy to shift troops rapidly from one bunker to the next without exposing them to danger. Six days earlier, men of the 2d Battalion, 503d Infantry, had been badly mauled trying to take out a pair of NVA bunkers on another nearby hill. As the GIs checked their weapons in the early morning mist, they had few illusions about what lay ahead.

At 9:43 A.M., after preparatory artillery and air strikes, Companies C and D started up the northern slope. At the base of the hill Company A began cutting a landing zone out of the thick jungle. The men of the lead companies advanced slowly over the tangled trees and splintered bamboo left by the bombing until they neared the crest of the first ridge. Suddenly, the NVA opened up with automatic weapons from a concealed bunker only five meters from the point squad. Two men fell within seconds. The rest of the squad dropped their packs and spread out behind fallen logs. As the Americans came forward the enemy added recoilless-rifle fire and grenades to the withering barrage, then B40 rockets launched from farther up the hill. When the firing eased momentarily, the paratroopers resumed their advance, tossing grenades into the bunker as they passed. But no sooner had it stopped than the shooting resumed—both from above and from the bunker where those killed by the grenades had been replaced by other NVA soldiers scrambling through hidden tunnels.

Artillery and tactical air tried to take the pressure off by pounding enemy positions above the line of advance. But the men on the ground were being hit by machine guns, mortars, and sniper fire. Then NVA attackers, helmets camouflaged, faces painted black, rifles wrapped in burlap, rushed the Americans from every direction. "Jesus, they were all over the place," remembered one GI. "The noncoms kept shouting, 'Get up the hill, get up the goddam hill.' But we couldn't." With the assault bogged down and casualties mounting, Company C commander Captain Harold J. Kaufman ordered the men to pull back. The headlong withdrawal was so precipitous that Kaufman had to fire his pistol in the air to forestall a rout. Their panic averted, the paratroopers established a perimeter within a few meters of where the battle had begun, then dug in furiously with anything that came to hand.

At the bottom of the hill, meanwhile, a squad from Company A was just collecting some power saws and other equipment dropped by helicopter when North Vietnamese soldiers tore through the clearing. A brief firefight drove the squad up the hill toward Company A's main position, the GIs dropping fragmentation grenades back down the trail in a futile attempt to slow the enemy assault. As they reached the rest of the company, mortar shells erupted around the Americans followed by waves of screaming NVA infantrymen. Defense lines disintegrated under the impact of the mass attack that also killed Captain Michael Kiley and five other members of the Company A command group. After fifteen minutes of vicious hand-to-hand combat, platoon Sergeant Jack Siggers collected what remained of the company and staggered up the hill toward Companies C and D, whose men compounded the carnage by firing on the retreating men until cries of "Friendly! Friendly!" enabled the survivors to gain the perimeter.

Together, the Americans temporarily halted the main NVA assault. The battalion was now surrounded by up to 300 North Vietnamese soldiers, who continued to attack the paratroopers with mortars, automatic weapons, and B40 rockets. One soldier had his M60 machine gun blown out of his hand. Nearby a wounded sergeant was dragged to a tree for cover by a medic who himself was shot through the head. Despite the sergeant's shouted warnings, a lieutenant tried three times to reach him, suffering a new wound with each attempt. The sergeant finally died, still pleading with the officer not to try to rescue him.

Supplies of water and ammunition dwindled steadily during the afternoon, but relief helicopters were driven off by heavy enemy fire that brought down six of the choppers. Just before dusk helicopter crews dodging snipers in trees dropped two pallets of ammunition inside the American perimeter. The beleaguered paratroopers reloaded their weapons, but few believed they would make it through the night.

What hopes they had rested largely with air support. As darkness fell F–100s, propeller-driven A–1 Skyraiders, and helicopter gunships bombarded enemy positions within fifty meters of U.S. lines. One fighter-bomber, screaming toward the enemy at 300 miles an hour, dropped a 500-pound bomb short of the target. The high-explosive canister fell on the battalion command post and aid station, killing forty-two men and wounding forty-five more in a gigantic concussion that sent human limbs, bloody bandages, and pieces of charred uniforms hurtling through the night. "Heaps of dead after that bomb," recalled a stunned defender. "You didn't know where to go, you didn't know where to hide. You slept with the corpses."

With most of the battalion's company commanders dead or wounded, junior officers and NCOs took charge of the situation, which continued to deteriorate. After the mistaken bombing, U.S. artillery rounds started to hit the men until a platoon sergeant crawling frantically from one shattered radio to another finally raised the fire direction center and adjusted the errant guns. As the ninety-degree daytime temperature fell toward fifty, the troopers cursed the warm clothing left in rucksacks scattered across the battlefield. Soldiers seeking protection from man and nature by burrowing into the earth found their task complicated by discarded ammo boxes, splintered weapons, and worse. Said one survivor, "Every time you tried to dig you put your shovel in somebody."

All during the hours of darkness AC–47 gunships flew over the hill, illuminating the eerie scene with brilliant flares. But nothing could abate the terror of that night: sporadic mortar and recoilless-rifle fire ripping across the perimeter, wounded men begging for water that did not exist, GIs hollering in frustration and rage at enemy soldiers who taunted them with threats of destruction. Meanwhile, at the bottom of the hill, reinforcements checked their weapons and filled their packs with extra ammunition as they prepared to relieve their fellow paratroopers.

On the morning of November 20 Lieutenant Colonel James H. Johnson's 4th Battalion, 503d Infantry, moved up the hill through a litter of smashed vegetation, abandoned gear, and lifeless bodies. Climbing cautiously, the battalion spent all day negotiating the 7,000 yards to the 2d Battalion. Along the way they passed so many dead Americans they began to wonder whether anyone was left alive to save. In fact, the situation at the perimeter remained precarious. As the Associated Press's Peter Arnett reported from the hill, "Some of the wounded cracked under the strain.

" 'It's a goddam shame that they haven't gotten us out of here,' gasped one paratroop sergeant with tears in his eyes early afternoon Tuesday [the twenty-first]. He had been lying on the hill for fifty hours with a painful groin wound. All around him lay scores of other wounded. You could see who had lain there the longest. Blood had clotted their bandages, they had ceased moaning, their eyes were glazed." Enemy snipers firing automatic weapons from treetops continued to drive off relief helicopters. Just before dark one medevac chopper managed to land and carry out five critically wounded men, but dozens more were left to suffer through another night. As the clatter of helicopter blades faded in the early evening darkness, the 4th Battalion's Bravo Company finally reached the men of the 2d, who cried openly at the sight of their rescuers. By 10:00 the remainder of the 4th Battalion had arrived at the U.S. perimeter.

Early the next morning, the North Vietnamese renewed their furious attack, pounding the Americans with 82MM mortars throughout the day. Peter Arnett wrote that "the foxholes got deeper as the day wore on. Foxhole after foxhole took hits. A dog handler and his German shepherd died together. Men who were joking with you and offering cigarettes would be writhing on the ground wounded and pleading for water minutes later. There was no water for them or anyone else."

That day, however, the paratroopers cut a hillside landing zone out of the bullet-scarred trees surrounding their position. Helicopters were finally able to bring in desperately needed food and water and evacuate the 2d Battalion's wounded. The dead would remain on the hill for another day. While these tasks were going on halfway up the north slope, the top of the hill was being pounded with every supporting arm II Corps could muster. For seven hours air strikes and artillery battered the summit with more than 15,000 pounds of napalm and

high explosives. At 3:00 in the afternoon, behind a last-minute wall of artillery, the 4th Battalion resumed the assault.

Armed with flame throwers, shoulder-fired antitank rockets, and 81MM mortars, the troopers had moved out through a ravine and started uphill when a mortar barrage crashed down on the head of the column, killing or wounding dozens of men. While medics tended the casualties, the battalion grimly pushed forward. Crawling up the steep slope, the soldiers found themselves under intense fire from mutually supporting bunkers. Not until they managed to pull themselves within a few meters of the concealed fortifications, however, could they locate the bunkers by the muzzle smoke of enemy rifles. Their ranks had been steadily thinned by NVA machine-gun fire and grenades during the climb. Now, when they finally found the enemy entrenchments, their weapons proved useless.

Part of the problem was that none of the men had been trained to use flame throwers. More to the point was the care the North Vietnamese had devoted to their fortifications. Mortar shells failed to penetrate the thick dirt covering that protected the bunkers, while rockets required a direct hit into narrow bunker firing holes. Even when marksmen occasionally managed to do so, the results were not always satisfactory. One group of troopers fired a dozen rockets directly into a bunker porthole, only to be met with grenades and machine-gun fire from enemy soldiers who had taken refuge in a connecting tunnel during the barrage. Some platoon commanders tried sending individuals with satchel charges or napalm and grenades against the bunkers, but the intensity of fire made it difficult to get close enough.

Making matters worse, the NVA began firing rockets of their own that bounced down the slope and exploded among the fallen logs and mounds of dirt that sheltered the paratroopers. As the advance began to falter, enemy infantrymen using prepared avenues of entry and withdrawal from the battlefield attacked the battalion's flanks and rear, isolating small units and wiping them out one by one as they had done to the 2d Battalion two days earlier. By sheer determination the Americans captured a pair of trench lines within 250 feet of the summit, but the gains could not be consolidated and the assault ground to a halt. After dark the battered troopers gathered their casualties and pulled back to the original perimeter, more than half their number killed or wounded.

Since the beginning of the battle on November 19, Major General William R. Peers, commander of the 4th Infantry Division, had promised reporters at his headquarters that Hill 875 would soon be in U.S. hands. Now, after two attempts to do so had failed, Peers vowed to end North Vietnamese resistance once and for all. All day and into the night of November 22, American aircraft blasted Hill 875 with tons of bombs, napalm, and rockets in a thunderous effort to soften up the enemy before a final assault by the airborne troopers. Simultaneously, Peers placed the fresh 1st Battalion, 12th Infantry, in a supporting position south of the hill. By 11:00 A.M. on November 23, Thanksgiving Day, everything was ready.

Led by Bravo Company, the 4th Battalion scrambled back up the hill behind a shield of 81MM mortars. Although they encountered some sniper fire as they clambered over the horrific landscape left by five days of fighting, there was little resistance. Twenty-two minutes later, shouting "Geronimo!" and "Airborne!" the troopers scaled the ravaged summit. But their cries echoed hollowly in the smoke that still swirled around the bomb craters and clung to the charred tree stumps. Sometime during the previous night the NVA had slipped away, taking most of their dead along with their weapons. All that remained of the enemy presence atop the hill were a few blackened bodies and the NVA's trench-works and bunkers. To cover their retreat, the Communists harassed the paratroopers arriving on the summit with mortar fire from a nearby ridge-top, but their fire soon ended. Said 1st Lieutenant Alfred Lindseth of Company B, 4th Battalion, "It was a happy day when we found they had left the hill."

After all the sweat and all the blood there would be no final battle. The weary GIs simply sat down in the dust and surveyed what remained of the enemy fortifications. Later that afternoon helicopters carried in a Thanksgiving dinner of hot sliced turkey, cranberry sauce, and potatoes.

The battle of Hill 875 was the climax of the Dak To campaign. During the remainder of November enemy resistance in the area disappeared as the 1st NVA Division withdrew into Cambodia. The battle had cost the North Vietnamese an estimated 325 dead and sufficiently damaged the 174th NVA Regiment to keep it out of action during the next phase of the Communist winter-spring offensive. General Westmoreland lauded the paratroopers for their part in denying the enemy the spectacular victory he sought, and the 173d received a Presidential Unit Citation for what it had accomplished on Hill 875.

But the men of the 2d and 4th Battalions, 503d Infantry, had paid a stiff price for their heroism: 158 dead and 402 wounded—nearly 15 percent of the brigade's strength. "With victories like this," wondered a U.S. correspondent watching the wounded disembarking from helicopters, "who needs defeats?" If that question was being asked more and more as 1967 came to a close, it was not a question for soldiers to answer. While journalists and politicians debated the course of the war, the men of the 173d held a service for the dead, laying out the boots of their fallen comrades in simple tribute to those who had perished in a terrible battle on a nameless hill in the middle of a jungle half a world from home.

A paratrooper rushes past his buddies toward a more secure position farther up Hill 875. Although stripped of its vegetation by napalm and bombs dropped by U.S. aircraft, the hill was covered with triple-canopy jungle at the beginning of the battle, making it difficult for the paratroopers to detect North Vietnamese bunkers.

136

4

THE TET OFFENSIVE

At 10:30 P.M. on January 2, 1968, the bark of a sentry dog at Khe Sanh Combat Base in northwestern Quang Tri Province alerted U.S. Marine lookouts to the presence of someone just outside the defensive wire. Peering through their night-vision Starlight scopes, the Marines could see six men, all dressed in American uniforms, nonchalantly walking along. Since no friendly patrols were reported in the area, a squad led by Second Lieutenant Nile B. Buffington was sent to investigate. As he approached the perimeter, Buffington called out to the men to identify themselves. There was no reply. The lieutenant repeated the challenge. At that point one of the strangers made a quick movement, as if reaching for a weapon or grenade. The Marines opened fire. Five of the intruders fell dead, while the sixth escaped into the darkness carrying what was believed to be a case of maps. Intelligence later identified three of those killed as the commander, operations officer, and communications officer of a North Vietnamese regiment.

When news of the incident reached MACV headquarters in Saigon, General Westmoreland was not surprised. In recent weeks the pace of NVA infiltration into northern I Corps had increased dramatically, particularly in the vicinity of the isolated Marine outpost at Khe Sanh. American intelligence analysts believed that one, perhaps two full North Vietnamese divisions had moved into the area, while elements of two other divisions had been sighted inside the demilitarized zone within striking distance of the base. Convinced that the enemy intended to "restage Dien Bien Phu," where Ho Chi Minh's Vietminh had decisively beaten the French fourteen years before, Westmoreland had ordered the Marines to reinforce Khe Sanh in mid-December. Now, faced with fresh evidence of the enemy's presence, the American commmander decided to meet the Communist challenge head-on.

To bolster allied manpower in the north, Westmoreland shifted more than half of his maneuver battalions to I Corps, beginning with the redeployment of the 1st Cavalry

A Vietcong rocket explodes into Da Nang Air Base in the early morning hours of January 30, 1968.

Division (Airmobile) on January 9. He also dispatched two more battalions of Marines to Khe Sanh, along with a battalion of South Vietnamese Rangers. In the meantime MACV officials began laying plans for the most concentrated application of aerial firepower in the history of warfare. Called Niagara, a name chosen "to evoke the image of cascading bombs and shells," the operation called for the use of some 3,000 strike aircraft to pound suspected enemy positions around the clock, as well as 2,000 helicopters and cargo planes to keep the base resupplied.

Back in Washington, President Johnson closely monitored the impending confrontation with growing unease. Haunted by the specter of the massive French defeat fourteen years before, the commander-in-chief began making nightly visits to the White House Situation Room, where a large photomural and sand table model of the Khe Sanh area had been installed at his request. As the prospect of a major attack grew more imminent, the president repeatedly questioned his advisers about the wisdom of holding the base and ultimately took the unprecedented step of requiring a written endorsement of General Westmoreland's decision from each member of the Joint Chiefs of Staff.

The high-level debate over the investment of Khe Sanh was still going on when, on the afternoon of January 20, a North Vietnamese officer holding a white flag suddenly materialized at the eastern end of the combat base. Identifying himself as First Lieutenant Le Than Tonc, the soldier told Marine interrogators that he wanted to defect. He then proceeded to provide a wealth of information about the enemy's intentions that confirmed what the Americans already suspected. According to Tonc, the 325C NVA Division and the 304th NVA Division, an elite home-guard unit from Hanoi, were preparing to overrun Khe Sanh, then sweep eastward across Quang Tri and Thua Thien Provinces toward Hue. The campaign was to begin that very night with attacks on the main base and two outlying hills occupied by the Marines.

Though Tonc seemed to know more "than would be expected of an officer in his position," Marine General Rathvon McC. Thompson decided that "we had nothing to lose and stood to gain a great deal," by acting on

the intelligence. As a result, when the North Vietnamese assaulted Hill 861 at half past midnight on January 21, the Marines were waiting for them. After turning back the NVA's initial charge, the men of Company K, 3d Battalion, 26th Marines, counterattacked down the hill and overran the enemy in savage hand-to-hand combat. No sooner had the fighting subsided than a heavy barrage of artillery and rocket fire slammed into the main base, blasting holes in the airstrip, destroying several helicopters, and detonating some 1,500 tons of stored ammunition. The Marines scrambled for cover, expecting a mass assault. It never came. For reasons that would become clear only later, the NVA had decided not to exploit their advantage, at least for the moment. The siege of Khe Sanh had begun.

While Westmoreland and the president focused their attention on the showdown in northern I Corps, some American military officials were becoming equally concerned about the pattern of Communist activity elsewhere in South Vietnam. In Saigon, II Field Force commander Lieutenant General Frederick C. Weyand was troubled by reports that several Main-Force Vietcong units had left their jungle base camps and moved closer to the capital. Uncertain what to make of it but assuming the worst, Weyand convinced Westmoreland in early January to pull fifteen American battalions back from border assignments to the outskirts of Saigon. U.S. and ARVN forces meanwhile uncovered a series of enemy orders calling for attacks on other population centers. On January 4, soldiers of the 4th Infantry Division captured Operation Order No. 1 calling for an assault on the provincial capital of Pleiku. On January 20, the 23d ARVN Division discovered similar plans for an attack on Ban Me Thuot, capital of Darlac Province. A week later, South Vietnamese military security agents in Qui Nhon broke into a meeting of Vietcong cadres and seized two prerecorded tapes declaring the "liberation" of the port town and calling on the local population to rise up against the GVN.

Aside from the redeployment recommended by General Weyand, however, the American command paid little heed to the accumulated evidence that had fallen into its hands. Believing the enemy incapable of mounting serious attacks on the cities, most U.S. intelligence

A B–52 Stratofortress leaves Guam heading for a mission in support of the beleaguered Marine outpost at Khe Sanh in early 1968 during the Communist Tet offensive.

specialists dismissed the captured orders as empty boasts designed to lift flagging Communist troop morale. Others concluded that the documents represented an attempt to divert attention and resources from the main battlefield to the north. As one high-ranking MACV intelligence officer later conceded, "Even if I had known exactly what was to take place, it was so preposterous that I probably would have been unable to sell it to anybody."

The plan that defied the credulity of the Americans was hatched in Hanoi in the spring of 1967, the product of a major strategic reappraisal by the North Vietnamese leadership. Under pressure from the southern Communists to accelerate the timetable for "liberation," yet unable to break the military stalemate brought on by the introduction of U.S. troops, the Politburo decided to inaugurate the third and final stage of the revolutionary struggle—the General Offensive, General Uprising—

with a wave of simultaneous attacks on virtually every population center in South Vietnam. By taking the war to the cities, the Communist leaders hoped to achieve several purposes at once. At the very least, they would shatter any illusions of American invulnerability as well as the sense of security felt by hundreds of thousands of refugees who had fled from the war in the countryside. At best, they would break the back of ARVN, instigate a popular overthrow of the GVN, and force the Americans to accept a negotiated settlement.

Responsibility for planning the campaign was placed in the hands of General Vo Nguyen Giap. Now the North Vietnamese defense minister, he had orchestrated the Vietminh victory over the French at Dien Bien Phu. Although Giap had personally opposed the idea of launching a general offensive, considering it too premature, too risky, and potentially too costly, he dutifully carried out the Politburo's will. During the fall of 1967, in an effort to lure the Americans away from the cities and screen the infiltration of fresh troops and supplies from the North, he initiated a series of major confrontations along the South Vietnamese frontier—at Con Thien along the DMZ, at Dak To in the central highlands, at Loc Ninh in the Fishhook region along the Cambodian border, and finally at Khe Sanh.

In each case the Americans responded as Giap presumed they would, diverting large numbers of troops to the remote battle zones in the hope of dealing the Communists a crushing blow. In the meantime the NLF attempted to lay the groundwork for a general uprising of the people of South Vietnam by stepping up its political activity in urban areas. To undermine the Thieu government and sow discord between the Americans and South Vietnamese, Vietcong agents established clandestine contacts with U.S. Embassy officials, spread rumors of imminent peace talks, and encouraged neutralists to form a new "popular front" in anticipation of a negotiated settlement.

In January 1968 Vietcong guerrillas began infiltrating the cities disguised as civilians or ARVN soldiers returning home for the upcoming Tet (Lunar New Year) holiday. Weapons and munitions were also smuggled in, concealed in false-bottom trucks or vegetable carts and then buried at predetermined sites. Preparations intensified during the last week of the month as unit commanders learned for the first time what their missions would be. Finally, on January 29, the eve of Tet, came the order to attack. Broadcast by Radio Hanoi, it took the form of a poetic exhortation written by Ho Chi Minh to mark the advent of the Year of the Monkey.

> This Spring far outshines
> the previous springs
>
> Of victories throughout the land
> come happy tidings
>
> Forward!
> Total Victory will be ours.

During the next twenty-four hours more than 70,000 soldiers of the People's Liberation Army—the Vietcong—backed by regular units of the North Vietnamese Army launched attacks on thirty-six of forty-four pro-

vincial capitals, five of six major cities, sixty-four district towns, and fifty hamlets across the length and breadth of South Vietnam. The coastal town of Nha Trang, headquarters of the U.S. I Field Force, was the first to be hit, shortly after midnight on January 30. Assaults on other towns within the II Corps area—Ban Me Thuot, Kontum, Hoi An, Qui Nhon, and Pleiku—followed in rapid succession. The next night the Communists expanded the scope of the offensive, penetrating in strength into Quang Tri City, Tam Ky, and Hue in I Corps, Tuy Hoa and Phan Thiet in II Corps, the Capital Military District of Saigon, and every provincial and district capital in the Mekong Delta.

Not surprisingly, the Communists directed their heaviest blow against Saigon and its densely populated environs, hurling thirty-five battalions into the battle under the command of North Vietnamese General Tran Van Do. Assigned the task of paralyzing the "nerve centers" of the allied war effort, the highly trained men and women of the Vietcong C–10 Sapper Battalion spearheaded the assault with a series of daring raids on the presidential palace, the ARVN Joint General Staff headquarters, the national radio station and, most memorably if not most successfully, the United States Embassy compound. A 19-man sapper squad occupied part of the embassy grounds for six hours that night while a small contingent of Marine guards held the consulate building, until an assault force of U.S. paratroopers relieved them and killed or captured the sappers. Some 4,000 to 5,000 Vietcong local troops struck other key targets simultaneously, including the Tan Son Nhut airfield, while small squads of armed political cadres fanned out into the city's residential districts and exhorted the Saigonese to rise up against "the dictatorial Thieu-Ky regime." Outside the capital, NVA and VC Main-Force units tried to pin down allied reaction forces by assaulting the U.S. military bases at Bien Hoa, Lai Khe, and Cu Chi.

Elsewhere the enemy's plan of attack was much the same, and so were the results. Although caught by sur-

One of the few survivors from the Communist sapper team that penetrated the U.S. Embassy compound in Saigon is led away by military police.

146

prise, South Vietnamese and American forces reacted swiftly, using their superior mobility and firepower to maximum advantage and with devastating effect. Poor timing and faulty execution also undermined the Communists' efforts, as did the unwillingness of most civilians to take up arms in support of their would-be "liberators." Only in a dozen places, such as the populous district of Cholon in Saigon, did the invaders manage to hold on for more than a few days, and even then only at staggeringly high cost. U.S. estimates of Communist casualties during the Tet campaign ranged as high as 40,000 killed, the vast majority of whom came from the ranks of Vietcong Main-Force units. The NLF political infrastructure also suffered crippling losses, as many previously unidentified local cadres exposed themselves in an attempt to foment a general uprising.

The exception to the pattern was the brutal battle of Hue. After storming the city and seizing the imperial Citadel on the night of January 31, 7,500 NVA regulars held out for more than three weeks in the face of an increasingly furious counterattack. While the fighting raged, the Communists set up their own "revolutionary government" and began rounding up alleged "collaborators," more than 2,000 of whom were summarily executed. By the time the ordeal came to an end, much of the once beautiful city had been reduced to ruins, "its streets choked with rubble and rotting bodies."

Years later, a number of high-ranking Communist officials candidly admitted their disappointment at the outcome of the Tet offensive. "During Tet of 1968," wrote General Tran Van Tra, a senior Communist commander in the South at the time, "we did not correctly evaluate the specific balance of forces between ourselves and the enemy" and set goals "that were beyond our actual strength." As a result, "we suffered large losses in materiel and men, especially at various echelons, which clearly weakened us." General Tran Do put it more succinctly: "In all honesty," he told an American interviewer in 1982, "we didn't achieve our main objective, which was to spur uprisings throughout the South."

South Vietnamese soldiers drag away a Vietcong guerrilla killed on January 31, during the enemy's surprise attack on government buildings in Saigon.

Air force security police block a Vietcong assault on Tan Son Nhut Air Base outside Saigon on January 31.

Yet if the Communists failed to achieve their ultimate objectives, they succeeded nonetheless in altering irrevocably the course of the Vietnam War. The unprecedented magnitude and intensity of the offensive stunned the South Vietnamese and sent shock waves across the United States. Though initial news reports tended to exaggerate the enemy's military successes, the sense of pervasive confusion that they conveyed was not far off the mark. Having been repeatedly assured in recent months that the allies were making "steady progress," that "the light at the end of the tunnel" had at last come into view, many Americans shared the reaction of venerable television newsman Walter Cronkite. "What the hell is going on here?" Cronkite reportedly exclaimed soon after the fighting erupted, "I thought we were winning the war!"

General Westmoreland's attempts to downplay the significance of the attacks, including his claim that they were "diversionary" from the fight over Khe Sanh, did little to lessen the widening credibility gap between official pronouncements and popular perceptions. Dramatic videotape footage of the bloody fighting in Saigon and Hue, the stark photograph of the South Vietnamese police chief, General Loan, executing a Vietcong prisoner at pointblank range, the offhand remark of an army major at Ben Tre that "it became necessary to destroy the town to save it"—all seemed to confirm the growing conviction, as the editors of the Cleveland Press put it, "that something enormous has gone wrong [that] cannot be shrugged off with the kind of flimsy explanations given so far."

Characteristically, President Johnson's initial response to the mounting chorus of criticism was to hang tough. At a White House press conference on February 2 he described the offensive as a "complete failure." "We have known for some time that this offensive was planned by the enemy," the president declared. "The ability to do what they have done has been anticipated, prepared for, and met." For all his apparent confidence, however, Johnson was deeply troubled by the unexpected turn of events. Although Westmoreland continued to assure him that the situation was "well in hand," the president still feared the possibility of a major military setback at Khe Sanh. Insisting that the combat

base must be held and that Westmoreland be given whatever reinforcements he needed, Johnson told his senior advisers to "review all options," including an extension of enlistments, a call-up of the Reserves, a troop increase in Vietnam, even a declaration of war.

To the chairman of the Joint Chiefs of Staff, General Earle Wheeler, the president's new mood of urgency offered an opportunity to resolve fundamental issues that had been deferred too long. Since 1965 Wheeler and the other Joint Chiefs had urged Johnson to mobilize the Reserves, not only to meet the demands of the escalating Vietnam War effort but to insure that the nation continued to meet its other global military commitments. But LBJ, remembering the public outcry that greeted President Kennedy's Reserve call-up during the 1961 Berlin crisis, had repeatedly vetoed the idea. Now, in the wake of Tet, it suddenly seemed that the president might at last accede to a full mobilization, provided that Wheeler played his cards right.

Rather than press the case for mobilization directly, Wheeler decided to coax Westmoreland into making a troop request that would force a decision on the Reserves. Beginning on February 3, he sent Westmoreland a series of back-channel cables conveying Johnson's continuing alarm over the threat in northern I Corps and strongly suggesting that the field commander put in a request for more troops. "The United States is not prepared to accept a defeat in South Vietnam," Wheeler asserted. "In summary, if you need more troops, ask for them." As a further enticement, Wheeler indicated that the White House was actively considering an expansion of the ground war into eastern Laos, or perhaps even into North Vietnamese staging areas across the DMZ, to relieve pressure on Khe Sanh. When Westmoreland replied that another division might be needed later in the year "if operations in Laos are authorized," Wheeler prompted him again, explaining that his message had been "interpreted" as something less than a "firm demand" for reinforcements.

This time Westmoreland took the hint. The "signals from Washington" had become so strong, the general later recalled, that "it seemed to me that for political reasons or otherwise, the president and the Joint Chiefs of Staff were anxious to send me reinforcements." Ac-

In a shocking episode that later appeared on American television, South Vietnam's General Nguyen Ngoc Loan executes a suspected Vietcong officer on a Saigon street on February 1.

cordingly, on February 12 Westmoreland submitted a formal request for additional troops, couched in language that contrasted sharply with his previous assessments of the post-Tet situation in South Vietnam. "A setback is fully possible if I am not reinforced," he wrote. "I desperately need reinforcements. Time is of the essence."

It was then that Wheeler, a skilled military bureaucrat, tried to force the president's hand. In forwarding Westmoreland's request to Johnson, he emphasized that the JCS could not endorse the deployment of additional troops to Vietnam unless more than 100,000 army and Marine Reservists were concomitantly recalled to service. As in the past, however, the president declined

to make a firm decision on the matter. Instead he ordered an "emergency" deployment of 10,500 more troops to Vietnam while consigning the question of mobilization to further study.

Undeterred by the president's refusal to settle the Reserve issue, Wheeler flew to Saigon on February 23 to confer with Westmoreland. During his two-day visit, as Westmoreland later put it, the chairman of the JCS "conned" him into believing that the Johnson administration was about to authorize a change of strategy. Pointing out that Secretary of Defense McNamara was about to be replaced by the hawkish Clark Clifford, Wheeler intimated that the president at last seemed ready to relax long-standing constraints on ground operations in Laos and Cambodia. The two generals then discussed the forces that would be required to carry out such operations as well as to replenish the strategic reserve if a major troop increase were approved. In the end they settled on a figure of 206,000 men, approximately half of whom would be sent to Vietnam by May 1. Deployment of the rest was to be contingent upon approval of a more aggressive ground strategy; otherwise they would be added to the strategic reserve.

When Wheeler returned to Washington to lobby for the gigantic troop increase, however, he said nothing about contingencies or new strategies. Instead, he portrayed Westmoreland as a beleaguered field commander in dire need of immediate reinforcement. Describing the Tet offensive as "a very near thing . . . that has by no means run its course," he told Johnson that "MACV will be hard pressed" to meet the continuing threat in northern I Corps and to restore security in the cities. "We must be prepared to accept some reverses," Wheeler concluded, unless the troop increase was approved. Left unspoken, but nonetheless clear, was that any sizable deployment would require a mobilization of the Reserves.

For President Johnson, Wheeler's somber report posed an agonizing dilemma. Acceptance of the general's recommendations meant putting the nation on a virtual war footing in an election year amid growing criticism of his management of the conflict. Yet to deny the troop request was to invite an indefinite continuation of the war and perhaps even to risk military defeat. Unable to reach a decision without a full-scale review of the options, Johnson turned the matter over to an "intensive working group" headed by his long-time friend and newly appointed secretary of defense, Clark Clifford. "Give me the lesser of evils," the president told Clifford. "Give me your recommendations."

Although Clifford initially believed his charge was to determine how, not whether, the troop request could be met, the sheer magnitude of the proposed deployment led him to raise fundamental questions that had been avoided for years. "How long would it take to succeed in Vietnam?" Clifford asked. "How many more troops would it take? Were 200,000 enough? What was the plan to win the war?" When clear answers were not immediately forthcoming, Clifford demanded that the JCS provide precise information on how the additional troops might be used and instructed officials at the Defense, State, and Treasury Departments to study the implications of the troop request and review possible alternatives.

Seizing the opportunity to express views that had long been ignored or suppressed, senior civilians at the Pentagon responded with a thoroughgoing indictment of the prevailing policy. "Our strategy of attrition has not worked," reported systems analyst Alain Enthoven, challenging the argument that a large troop increase could shorten the war. Since North Vietnam had already demonstrated its ability to match each U.S. escalation with an escalation of its own, there was no reason to believe that 206,000 more American soldiers would somehow break Hanoi's will to fight. Other Defense Department officials contended that a fresh infusion of troops would reinforce the belief of South Vietnam's "ruling elite that the U.S. will continue to fight its war while it engages in back-room politics and permits widespread corruption." It would also "entail substantial costs," including higher American casualties, new taxes, possibly even a wage-price freeze, thus risking "a domestic crisis of unprecedented proportions."

As an alternative to the search-and-destroy tactics employed in the past, the Pentagon civilians proposed that U.S. forces in South Vietnam pull back to the cities and adopt a new "population control strategy." The military bitterly opposed the idea, however, contending that such a strategy would lead to increased civilian casualties and concede the tactical initiative to the enemy. In the end, the report that Clifford submitted to the president on March 4 contained elements of both views but few specific recommendations. "Big questions remained," recalled William Bundy, assistant secretary of state for Far Eastern affairs. "There were stop signs—caution signs—all over the draft. Anybody could see that . . . no president would decide on the basis of these recommendations."

Children try to extinguish the fire that engulfed their father's machine shop on February 6 when U.S. and South Vietnamese aircraft bombed four blocks of Saigon's Cholon District.

Though the findings of the Clifford task force effectively killed any chance of a major troop increase, news of the proposed escalation soon filtered back to the press, eventually producing a front-page story in the March 10 edition of the *New York Times*. "Westmoreland Requests 206,000 More Men," the three-column headline blared, "Stirring Debate in Administration." For the Johnson administration, the leak could hardly have come at a worse time. In recent weeks public opinion had begun to shift decisively against the president, as hawks and doves alike registered their dissatisfaction with prevailing Vietnam policy. A series of opinion surveys taken in late February 1968, for example, revealed that only 26 percent of the American people approved of the president's handling of the war and that a near majority considered U.S. involvement in the conflict a "mistake." Perhaps more significant, many of the more influential members of the national news media had withdrawn their support. On February 23, the prestigious *Wall Street Journal* ran an editorial declaring that "the American people should be getting ready to accept, if they haven't already, the prospect that the whole Vietnam effort may be doomed." Four days later, CBS anchorman Walter Cronkite rendered a similarly bleak judgment, telling an estimated audience of 9 million Americans that "the only rational way out . . . is to negotiate, not as victors, but as an honorable people who had lived up to their pledge to defend democracy, and did the best they could."

The expansion of antiwar sentiment was also evident on Capitol Hill, where the challenge to Johnson's leadership had become increasingly open and direct in the wake of the Tet offensive. "A year ago one couldn't count 10 doves in the Senate," observed Senator Thurston Morton, a Kentucky Republican who had gained national notoriety when he turned against the war in late 1967. By late February 1968, however, Morton estimated there were 25 outright antiwar senators in the Senate and another 16 "leaning to the doves." Reflective of the new mood in Congress, on March 11 and 12

The Imperial Palace at Hue lies in ruins following the month-long drive by allied troops to clear North Vietnamese invaders from the city in February 1968.

the Senate Foreign Relations Committee grilled Secretary of State Dean Rusk for a total of eleven hours over the possibility of another troop increase. A week later 139 members of the House of Representatives cosponsored a resolution calling for a full review of American policy in Southeast Asia.

The most dramatic indication of the president's growing political vulnerability, however, came on March 12, when Senator Eugene McCarthy of Minnesota came within 300 votes of defeating Johnson in the New Hampshire primary election. An avowed peace candidate, McCarthy had been given little chance of mounting a serious challenge to Johnson when he announced his candidacy for the Democratic nomination the preceding December. But after Tet the senator's quixotic crusade had steadily gained momentum, in part due to the efforts of several thousand student volunteers. Since the president's name did not appear on the ballot, Johnson supporters responded by organizing a vigorous write-in campaign, implying in their advertisements that a vote for McCarthy was a vote for the enemy. Read one Johnson campaign slogan, "The Communists in Vietnam are watching the New Hampshire primary." Ironically, subsequent studies found that more self-described hawks than doves voted for McCarthy, so deep was their disenchantment with Johnson's management of the war.

The president barely had time to absorb the shock of McCarthy's stunning showing when, on March 16, Senator Robert Kennedy of New York announced that he, too, would run against Johnson on a platform of opposition to the war. A late convert to the antiwar camp, Kennedy had been an outspoken critic of the administration in the weeks after Tet but had resisted appeals to throw his hat in the ring. By hesitating until after the New Hampshire primary, he opened himself up to charges of opportunism. Nevertheless, as Johnson well knew, with his name and his powerful party connections Kennedy made a far more formidable opponent than the scholarly maverick McCarthy.

Instinctively, if imprudently, Johnson decided to fight back by taking his case to the country and demanding "a total national effort to win the war." "We must meet our commitments in the world and in Vietnam," he told a business group in Chicago on March 17. "We shall and we are going to win the war!" The next day his tone became even more strident during an address to a convention of farmers in Minneapolis. Recalling every crisis of the century from the sinking of the *Lusitania* to Pearl Harbor and the Berlin blockade, the president declared, "The time has come when we ought to stand up and be counted, when we ought to support our leaders, our government, our men, and our allies until aggression is stopped, wherever it has occurred."

When the public response to Johnson's speeches proved overwhelmingly negative, the president's advisers became deeply worried. Pointing out that "McCarthy and Kennedy are the candidates of peace and the president is the war candidate," campaign strategist James L. Rowe, Jr., strongly urged Johnson to "do something exciting and dramatic to recapture the peace issue" before the April 2 Wisconsin primary. "Hardly anyone today is interested in winning the war," Rowe asserted in a blunt memorandum. "Everyone wants to get out, and the only question is how." The message sank in. The next morning Johnson telephoned Defense Secretary Clifford: "I've got to get me a peace proposal."

On March 20 and again on March 22, Johnson conferred with his senior advisers about a possible new peace initiative. While most agreed that the president should propose to limit in some way the bombing of North Vietnam, fundamental differences of opinion over the purpose of such a gesture undermined any firm consensus. Convinced that the North Vietnamese would reject the offer, Secretary of State Rusk and national security adviser Walt Rostow hoped to placate public opinion long enough to allow for U.S. participation in the war to continue. In Clark Clifford's view, however, the task was not simply to stabilize the home front but to find a way out of the "hopeless bog" in which the United States had become mired. He therefore argued that a partial bombing halt should be implemented as the first in a series of concrete "de-escalatory steps" leading to a negotiated settlement and total American withdrawal.

Though for the moment the president made no decision about the bombing halt proposal, the deliberations persuaded him that any further expansion of the U.S. war effort was no longer an option. At the March 22 meeting he formally rejected the Wheeler-West-

moreland troop request, instead approving only a modest deployment of 13,500 support troops to augment the emergency reinforcements dispatched in March. He also informed his advisers that he had decided to recall Westmoreland from South Vietnam to assume the position of army chief of staff. Whether the move had been planned long in advance, as the general himself later claimed, or rather resulted from Westmoreland's failure to anticipate the Tet offensive, is not clear. It seemed nevertheless to signify that the Johnson administration had decided upon a change of course.

Clifford, however, was still not convinced that Johnson fully appreciated the need to take bold and decisive action toward an acceptable peace. Concluding that the president required "some stiff medicine to bring home to [him] what was happening in the country," he proposed that the president reconvene a group of elder statesmen—the so-called wise men—who had endorsed his Vietnam policy in April 1965 and again in November 1967. The group, numbering fourteen, included many of the more prominent members of the post–World War II American foreign policy establishment, including former Secretary of State Dean Acheson, George Ball, McGeorge Bundy, Arthur Goldberg, Henry Cabot Lodge, Cyrus Vance, and Generals Omar Bradley, Matthew Ridgway, and Maxwell Taylor.

Before meeting with the president, the wise men assembled on the evening of March 25 for a series of briefings from officials of the State Department, the CIA, and the JCS. Many of those present were shaken by what they learned. Asked how long it would take to win the war at the current level of commitment, Deputy Assistant Secretary of State Philip Habib replied: "Maybe five years, maybe ten." A dramatic exchange between United Nations ambassador Arthur Goldberg and General William DePuy proved equally unsettling. After DePuy asserted that the enemy had lost more than 80,000 troops since the beginning of the year, Goldberg inquired about the number of wounded. DePuy responded that standard military estimates were based on a ratio of three to one. Then Goldberg asked, "How many effectives do you think they have operating in the field?" DePuy cited the official MACV estimate of 230,000. "Well, General," Goldberg said, "I am not a great mathematician, but with 80,000 killed and with a wounded ratio of three to one, or 240,000, for a total of 320,000, who the hell are we fighting?"

The following day the group met with Johnson and rendered their verdict. "The majority feeling," said McGeorge Bundy, "is that we can no longer do the job we set out to do in the time we have left and we must begin to move to disengage." Although they disagreed over the next step to take, with some favoring a bombing halt and others a shift in ground strategy, all concurred with Cyrus Vance's view that "unless we do something quick, the country may lead us to withdrawal."

Johnson, who listened impassively as each man expressed his views, later complained bitterly about the outcome of the meeting. "The establishment bastards have bailed out," he told one of his aides. In the end, however, he knew that he had no choice but to accept their collective judgment.

Five days later, on the evening of March 31, Lyndon Johnson addressed the nation. Accepting Rusk's proposal, he announced in the televised speech that the bombing of North Vietnam would henceforth be limited to the area just north of the demilitarized zone and held out the possibility of a "complete bombing halt" if the

A weary President Johnson reworks the text of his March 31 speech in which he stunned a nationwide television audience by announcing that he would not seek re-election.

North Vietnamese responded favorably. Emphasizing Clifford's concerns, he characterized the unilateral move as "the first in what I hope will be a series of steps toward peace" and made it clear that the United States was prepared to begin talks at any time and any place. When he reached the end of his speech, Johnson paused briefly before reading words that he had appended at the last moment. "I have concluded that I should not permit the presidency to become involved in the partisan divisions that are developing this political year," he said. "Accordingly, I shall not seek, and I will not accept, the nomination of my party for another term as your president."

Johnson's concluding statement electrified the nation and the world. But perhaps it should not have. By the end of March 1968, Lyndon Johnson was a weary man. The war in Vietnam had taken a heavy toll on him. It had cost him his credibility, and it had eroded his political authority to the point where he could no longer govern effectively. All that remained to be salvaged was what mattered most to him—the respect of his "fellow Americans." By withdrawing from the presidential race, Johnson hoped to underscore the sincerity of his desire for peace. More than that, he sought to restore unity to a nation divided by a war he had chosen to fight.

On April 1, 1968, the day after President Johnson spoke to the nation, a combined U.S.-ARVN task force totaling some 30,000 troops set out along Route 9 in Quang Tri Province to relieve the Marine garrison at Khe Sanh. In a spectacular display of airmobility, soldiers of the U.S. 1st Air Cavalry Division spearheaded the drive, leapfrogging ahead of a seemingly endless column of tanks, trucks, and troops on foot. Meeting with only token resistance along the way, the first wave of cavalrymen finally linked up with the Marines outside the base on the morning of April 8. Seventy-seven days after it began, the siege of Khe Sanh was over.

A South Vietnamese Ranger crouches alongside a badly wounded civilian during a second wave of Communist attacks in Saigon in early May.

Witness: Ron Harper

In the early morning hours of January 31, 1968, the Vietcong attacked the U.S. Embassy in Saigon. As American military commanders and the news media waited in uncertainty, nineteen enemy sappers roamed the courtyard of the embassy complex and tried, unsuccessfully, to penetrate the embassy building. More than any other incident of the Tet offensive, the attack suggested to the American people, who awoke that morning to screaming headlines announcing the embassy raid, that the U.S. was far from victory. The sole American defending the front lobby was twenty-year-old Sergeant Ronald W. Harper of the Marine Security Guards.

Saigon was quiet. It was a very peaceful town. There wasn't much going on, considering the time. But the war was sort of quiet, too—until Tet.

As usual, there were two guards scheduled to work in the embassy building that night—myself and Corporal George Zachuranic—in addition to the two army MPs who were always at the gate. But that night the command said it was going to start putting extra men on posts because something might be going on. No one took it seriously because we'd had these alerts before, on and off. And they couldn't have been too serious because they put only one more person at the embassy. I don't think anyone thought that anything big was going to happen.

Zach was posted in the lobby and I was the "roving guard," so I went upstairs and talked to the third man

on that night, Sergeant Rudy Soto. At about 2:30 A.M. I went next door to the consulate compound, on the other side of an eight-foot wall from the embassy. I was talking to the two guards over there at about 2:45, when I heard a big explosion. Sappers had blown out part of the front wall of the embassy complex.

My first thought was that I had the master key to the embassy, that Zach was new and might not know which key to use to lock the door. So I left the consulate, went through the gate, and scooted to the back door of the embassy lobby. On the way I ran right past a Vietnamese guy just wandering around by the consulate in shock. He wasn't one of the local guards, because they weren't working there that night. I didn't realize until later that he was actually one of the Vietcong.

As I got to the back door I looked over at the side gate for the MPs. The Vietcong had shot heavy machine-gun fire at those guys and they were apparently down already. All I could see was a cloud of dust, flying dirt, and no people. I ran into the lobby and Zach was on the phone, apparently calling for help. So I ran out to the front door, got the old Vietnamese guard, and pulled the big teak doors shut.

I pushed the old man into an office and ran to lock the rear doors, too. I still didn't know what was going on. All I knew was that there was machine-gun fire, crap was flying all over the place, and there were flashes outside. As I was running to the armory, right near the desk where Zach was standing, an antitank rocket came through the side windows at the front door and hit the wall near us, knocking me on my rear end and blowing Zach's eardrums out and hitting him with shrapnel. It exploded in the wall right over my head, ripping apart the seal of the United States.

When I got up, there were dust and smoke all over the place. Zach was moaning and groaning and couldn't hear me. I dragged him into the armory and bandaged his head to stop the bleeding, but he was in shock and kept making noise. I said, "Zach, be quiet!" because I knew someone was outside. But I didn't know if we were being attacked by one person or ten people.

I grabbed a Beretta machine gun along with my .38 pistol and went back to the armory area, because the desk was right in the line of fire. I didn't know where the MPs were. I didn't know where Rudy was. I waited for help. I guess I thought I was going to die.

The phone started ringing almost immediately. Allan Wendt, a civilian on duty upstairs, called down to find out if we were OK. When I told him Zach was hurt, he came down in the elevator and brought him upstairs. I told him to lock the elevator on his floor so if anyone broke into the lobby they couldn't get upstairs.

The phone kept ringing. Every time it rang I had to crawl out to the desk and answer it, so I hated that damn thing ringing because it was tipping off someone outside that I was there. Of the people I talked to, no one would believe me that the Vietcong weren't in the embassy. Some major on Westmoreland's staff called and said, "My God, are you sure the VC aren't in the building? Are you positive? Check that bottom floor. Make sure there's no one else in there." So I had to run down and check the rear doors.

When I ran back I found the old Vietnamese guard. I'd forgotten all about him. I took him back to the armory and gave him a smoke grenade—not a gun, because I didn't exactly trust him. He didn't speak English, so I motioned to him to throw it if the Vietcong came through the front doors. He waited with me all night.

There was enemy fire inside and outside the lobby all night. The bullets ricocheted off the granite walls and occasionally it got heavy. The lobby was always lit so anyone outside could see me when I moved around, but I couldn't see them. I could even hear them chattering outside. But still no one came in.

It was little things that night, stupid little things that happened that probably saved everyone. I found out later that Rudy was on the roof. He fired down and probably killed one of them and slowed them down. The embassy was supposed to be completely dark, but there were a few lights left on upstairs. So after Rudy fired, the Vietcong started shooting into those offices, thinking more people were up there guarding the place than there actually were. They could have walked in and taken us, but they thought we were a lot more heavily manned and armed. These things slowed them down long enough for us to get help.

I felt better when it got light at about 5:30 or 6:00. I could see outside, but there wasn't anything happen-

ing. Finally at about 8:00 a platoon from the 101st Airborne came down into the lobby from the roof and some others broke through the front gate in a jeep. But there was no one left to shoot—all of the enemy had been killed by this time. At first there were a few television cameras on me, but they all shifted to General Westmoreland when he arrived. After about six hours, it was all over.

I didn't get to bed for another forty-eight hours. No one got a lot of sleep. There was still fighting in the city, and we were under martial law for several weeks. We were looking for another attack the following night, and we lived on our toes for quite a while. We were getting rocket attacks into the city every morning, big six- or eight-foot-long rockets a foot around. All of a sudden we were in a war, and we hadn't been in a war before. I think the whole country felt the same way. There was no one who wasn't vulnerable anymore.

(For his actions during the attack on the embassy, Sgt. Harper was later awarded the Bronze Star. He was honorably discharged from the Marines in 1969.)

Focus: The Battle for Hue

Like most of the larger cities of South Vietnam, Hue had been spared from extensive damage in the first few years of the war. Refugees fled there from the surrounding countryside of Thua Thien Province, and South Vietnamese and American military authorities had established headquarters there, but there was relative calm in the city. Although Hue in recent years had been the scene of protest by both Buddhists and students against the Saigon government, the former seat of the Nguyen emperors was the South Vietnamese social and religious center and a virtual oasis from war. Some called the beautiful city "a lotus in a sea of fire."

The calm had been shattered in the early morning hours of January 31, 1968, the second day of Tet, when Communist 122MM rockets screamed through the low fog and exploded in the center of the ancient Citadel, a fortress on the north bank of the Perfume River surrounded by a moat and zigzag stone walls. Almost simultaneously soldiers of the 800th and 802d Battalions of the 6th NVA Regiment stormed through the lightly defended western gates of the Citadel and made for the headquarters of the ARVN 1st Division in the northeast corner of the fortress. Attacks on Da Nang and cities in II Corps the night before had put some of them on guard, and Brigadier General Ngo Quang Truong, commander of the ARVN 1st Division in Hue, had placed men on alert that night. Thus, when the 800th Battalion arrived at the Tay Loc airfield in the middle of the Citadel, they were met by the elite ARVN Black Panther Company and forced to turn south into the residential sections of the Citadel. The 802d initially penetrated the ARVN compound but was also driven back by the Black Panthers.

Elsewhere in the city, though, defense was scattered, and waves of enemy troops continued to fan out into the streets. As daylight broke and the chilly fog lifted, the gold-starred, red-and-blue flag of the NLF flew over the old emperor's palace. Hue was in Communist hands. The only significant pockets of resistance were the ARVN and MACV compounds, where the besieged occupants could only wait for reinforcements as they watched the NVA and VC dig in.

For General Westmoreland and the American and South Vietnamese command, the loss of Hue would have meant disaster. "Taking it," the American general wrote later, "would have a profound psychological impact on the Vietnamese in both the North and South, and in the process the North Vietnamese might seize the two north provinces as bargaining points in any negotiations." For all its strategic significance, however, the initial efforts to retake Hue were unsuccessful. The Marine command at Phu Bai, eight miles to the south, believed that the attacking force was small and dispatched a single company to Hue. Along the way the unit, Company A, 1st Battalion, 1st Marines, met up with four American tanks and headed up Highway 1. A sudden barrage of intense fire from one of the two NVA battalions blocking the approaches to the city pinned down the Marines, and the call went out for reinforcements. A second company arrived and the combined American force broke through to MACV headquarters, but only after taking forty casualties, including ten dead. The fight for Hue would demand more manpower: over the next three days three more companies, three command groups, and a tank platoon—about 1,000 Marines in all—arrived to join in the fight. After a failed American attempt to cross the river, it was decided that the Marines would concentrate on the south side of the river, while ARVN forces worked to dislodge the NVA and VC from the Citadel.

The South Vietnamese had a more difficult task. General Truong had been able to pull back his troops to consolidate defense of the ARVN compound, but enemy control over the two square miles inside the Citadel was strong. NVA troops and supplies continued to flow into the old fortress through the well-defended west gates; over the next week ten battalions totaling more than a division would be committed to the battle for Hue. The twenty-foot-thick, thirty-foot-high walls, built to defend the old emperors from ancient enemies, now provided the modern-day attackers a virtually impregnable fortress.

In the first week of February, American and South Vietnamese troops locked themselves in violent seesaw combat with the North Vietnamese and Vietcong. Marines attacked house by house, street by street, in a gloomy and almost constant cold drizzle, taking sniper fire at many turns. The younger troops had fought only in the countryside and were unaccustomed to street fighting. To some older Marines, the scene harked back to a city battle in the previous war; "Seoul was tough," said one commander, "but this—well, it's something else."

For several days Marines surrounded and stormed buildings, supported by fire from tanks, recoilless rifles, and machine guns. Howitzers fired huge shells at enemy positions, while fighter-bombers dropped 500- and 750-pound bombs and navy ships off the coast hurled shells several miles from five-, six-, and eight-inch guns. Beautiful pagodas, modest stucco houses, and sprawling French villas all crumbled under the rain of firepower as Americans, enemy troops, and civilians scurried to safety or became casualties.

Despite the best efforts of the Americans to clear the south bank of the Perfume, the well-entrenched and well-supplied enemy held on. The NVA contested each step the Marines took and often carried the day. By the end of the first week it was estimated that the Americans had not yet taken half of the south bank of the Perfume while incurring 250 casualties. In the damp weather the stench from the dead soldiers and civilians became unbearable, and the almost constant cloudiness lent a funereal dankness to the city.

By February 10 the area on the south bank of the Perfume River was finally declared secure, and most of the fighting there abated, though there were still occasional mortar explosions and sniper attacks on Marine patrols. Exhausted and chilled, the Americans looked through the fog and smoke at their next objective: the Citadel.

On the north side of the Perfume, the 1st ARVN Division had not been able to match the apparent success of its American allies. The South Vietnamese had been able to regain some territory around their base, but the NVA still held 60 percent of the Citadel, including the southern sector of the fortress. The North Vietnamese established their command post in the middle of this territory, in the Imperial Palace.

In the heart of the city, the Communists tightened their grip: NLF cadres quickly established a revolutionary government, headed by a Hue University professor and the principal of a local girls' high school. A former police chief became the new mayor. In the streets, soldiers and sympathizers hoisted banners denouncing the South Vietnamese and Americans and exhorting the people to join them.

The Communists also employed more heavy-handed methods to try to control the population. Using lists compiled by local agents, small bands moved in search of those who had been deemed "cruel tyrants and reactionary elements"—government officials, foreigners, and anyone who was considered sympathetic to the Saigon government. Hundreds of these detainees were marched, hands tied behind their backs, to what their captors claimed were political reorientation sessions. Some were shot on the spot when they resisted. Most were taken away and never heard from again.

It was later estimated that approximately 3,000 people were systematically executed by the Communists during their occupation of Hue. Many were found months after the battle for Hue in shallow, mass graves; others were never recovered and were presumed dead. Later American and South Vietnamese authorities would point to the massacre of these civilians as evidence of the ruthlessness of the North Vietnamese and Vietcong and a ghastly hint of the massacre that would ensue if they won the war.

While the Communists rounded up their enemies, the Americans on the south bank of the Perfume prepared to cross the river to the walls of the Citadel. On the evening of February 11, the men, tanks, and Ontos armored vehicles of the 1st Battalion, 5th Marines, crossed the Perfume. In their first assault on the south wall the next day, the battalion lost fifteen men killed and forty wounded; the fighting at the ramparts promised to be even bloodier than the clashes on the south bank of the Perfume.

The Saigon government told the Americans that they could use whatever weapons were necessary to dislodge the occupiers. Only the sacred Imperial Palace was to be spared. Once again the barrage commenced. Countless buildings were pockmarked or reduced to rubble as the Americans moved from house to house. Confused civilians wandered the streets, trying to get back to their homes, only to be shooed away by Marines in the thick of a firefight. Hundreds of homes were destroyed around them, but the Communist soldiers continued to fire from their entrenched positions.

Corpses littered the streets. "A woman knelt in death by a wall in the corner of her garden," wrote one correspondent. "A child lay on stairs crushed by a fallen roof. Many of the bodies had turned black and begun to decompose, and rats gnawed at the exposed flesh."

Many of the dead were Americans: In the first week it was estimated that the Marines took one casualty for every meter of ground gained. The scores of wounded were carried out on top of tanks or on the backs of fellow Marines. Those who had been spared physical injury began to show the strain, bursting into tears or simply staring blankly into the distance, victims of a form of shell shock.

On February 16, an NVA radio transmission from inside the Citadel was intercepted, disclosing that the enemy commander had been killed and that his successor had asked permission to withdraw. The request was denied by NVA superiors, but it was evidence that enemy morale was dissipating. The end was near for the occupiers.

Heartened by the new intelligence, the Americans and South Vietnamese intensified their efforts. As the Marines continued to work the Citadel, the 1st Air Cav soldiers fought their way to its northwest corner, and the 101st Airborne moved in to close the North Vietnamese supply lines in the west wall. The price had been high: The two army units had lost as many men in five days as the Marines had in the past three weeks.

The end of the three-week battle proved to be anticlimactic. NVA resistance inside the Citadel crumbled, and Vietnamese marines and the ARVN 1st Division pushed the remaining enemy up against the south fortress wall where they were scattered or destroyed. In the early morning hours of February 24 the 2d Battalion, 3d Regiment, of the ARVN 1st Division arrived at the main flagpole at the Imperial Palace, where they tore down the NLF banner and replaced it with the South Vietnamese flag. The next day ARVN Rangers stormed the Imperial Palace, only to find it empty. The enemy had fled in the night.

The battle for Hue was over, but it was unclear who had emerged the real victor. For their part, the American and South Vietnamese commands pointed to the favorable casualty figures as an indicator of their success. Enemy losses were estimated at more than 5,000 killed and 89 captured. American losses totaled 216 killed and 1,364 seriously wounded, and ARVN figures were 384 KIA and 1,830 wounded.

But while the Americans and South Vietnamese regained the city, the jarring fact was that the Communists had been able to seize and hold it for three weeks; in fact, North Vietnamese commanders claimed later, the original plan had been to hold it for just seven days. In its length and severity the occupation contributed to the devastating psychological impact of Tet upon the Americans and South Vietnamese, setting in motion events that ultimately proved more advantageous to the Communists than a military victory.

Whatever standards of victory were applied, the certain losers were the people of Hue. The war that seemed far away had erupted in their midst and destroyed half the homes in the city, leaving 116,000 homeless from a total population of 140,000. Another 5,800 people had been killed in the crossfire or executed by the Communists. The war had finally come to the cities all over South Vietnam. But in Hue there was a unique agony, as the nation's most beautiful city seemed to die a painful, lingering death. What had been "a lotus in a sea of fire" had been engulfed in a storm of death.

During the battle for Hue in February 1968, two Marines take shelter against incoming shells.

Behind a bombed-out schoolhouse, Marines take a moment out from the fighting in Hue.

Moments after throwing a grenade, this Marine was killed when another grenade exploded in his hand.

A Vietcong suspect cowers before his American captors in the embattled city.

Wounded Marines are rushed to a field hospital.

A medic carries to safety a Vietnamese
child wounded in crossfire.

173

175

Focus: The Siege of Khe Sanh

It remains one of the most memorable engagements of the Vietnam War, a contest of nerves as well as arms that pitted 6,000 U.S. Marines against an estimated 20,000–40,000 NVA regulars. Yet twenty years later, no one outside a small circle of North Vietnamese leaders is certain what it meant. Was the seventy-seven-day siege of Khe Sanh a failed attempt on the part of General Giap to re-enact his dramatic victory over the French at Dien Bien Phu, as many American officials believed at the time? Or was it instead, as many military historians have since concluded, part of a clever "feint" that succeeded in luring American forces away from the cities on the eve of the cataclysmic 1968 Tet offensive?

In late 1967, when North Vietnamese troops began infiltrating into northern I Corps in regiment strength, American military officials knew that the Communists were preparing to launch a major new offensive campaign. They were also well aware that the remote Marine outpost at Khe Sanh offered an especially inviting target. Situated on a small plateau in the sparsely populated northwest corner of Quang Tri Province, the combat base lay within easy striking distance of NVA base areas across the Laotian border and inside the DMZ. Moreover, it was surrounded by dense forests and fog-shrouded valleys that made it difficult to detect the presence of even large numbers of troops. And it could be reinforced and resupplied only by air, since the principal overland road into the base, Route 9, had been cut off by the North Vietnamese in August 1967.

So vulnerable was Khe Sanh, in fact, that the Marines initially balked at the idea of defending the site. Former JCS chairman General Maxwell Taylor, President Johnson's chief military adviser, believed that the base was simply too isolated to be adequately defended. Noting the parallels between Khe Sanh and Dien Bien Phu, pointing out further the problems of resupplying the base, and emphasizing that any defensive position can be taken if the enemy is willing to pay the price, Taylor urged the president to consider ordering a withdrawal.

Such concerns, however, did not deter General William Westmoreland from pressing ahead with plans to defend Khe Sanh "at all costs." Convinced that the enemy intended to overrun the base as the first step in an all-out drive to seize Quang Tri and Thua Thien Provinces, he reinforced the outpost with three additional battalions of Marines and deployed more than half of all U.S. maneuver battalions to northern I Corps.

To ease the fears of his jittery commander-in-chief, Westmoreland dismissed as groundless any comparison between Khe Sanh and Dien Bien Phu. Though both outposts were isolated, he pointed out, Dien Bien Phu had been located in a valley while Khe Sanh rested on a plateau. The French had held no high ground, while the U.S. Marines commanded most of the important hills surrounding their base. Most important of all, the French had had few aircraft and only moderate artillery support, while American firepower "differed by orders of magnitude over that at Dien Bien Phu."

Nor were these the only considerations behind Westmoreland's resolve to hold the line at Khe Sanh. After years of chasing an elusive enemy through the jungles, mountains, and rice fields of South Vietnam, he longed to fight a set-piece battle where the full weight of the Americans' vastly superior firepower could be brought to bear. In a war of attrition in which enemy "body counts" represented the chief yardstick of battlefield success, a major confrontation in the barren reaches of northern I Corps afforded an opportunity to score a victory of unprecedented proportions.

To meet the threat of a massed enemy assault, Westmoreland assembled an awesome armada of more than 2,000 strike aircraft for what he personally dubbed Operation Niagara. Beginning on January 22, U.S. aircraft flew an average of 300 sorties per day over the base, dropping a total of 35,000 tons of bombs on suspected enemy positions. Giant B–52 Stratofortresses based in Guam, Thailand, and Okinawa emptied their payloads every three hours, twenty-four hours a day. Additional fire support was provided by the behemoth 175MM artillery guns at the Rockpile and Camp Carroll, seventeen miles east of Khe Sanh, as well as some two dozen 105MM and 155MM howitzers inside the base.

To ensure that the Marines remained adequately supplied, 3,000 transport planes and helicopters were committed to the defense of Khe Sanh. Although hampered by poor weather, exposed to heavy antiaircraft fire as they approached the base, and even more vulnerable to enemy artillery guns and rockets when they landed, C–130 and smaller C–123 cargo planes made more than 450 flights into Khe Sanh during the course of the siege. Only 4 were destroyed by enemy fire. When "zero-zero" weather set in, helicopters took the place of the fixed-wing transports. In other instances, supplies and ammunition were delivered by parachute.

Yet, for all the measures and countermeasures that Westmoreland took to protect Khe Sanh, the 6,000 Marines stationed there knew that they alone would bear the brunt of a full-scale enemy assault. Every day they had to endure the shocks of 50, or 200, or 500 incoming rounds, a form of random terror that one Marine compared to "sitting in an electric chair and waiting for someone to pull the switch." Every day they reinforced their positions—digging their holes a little deeper, filling a few more sandbags to add to their bunkers. And every day they stared into the opaque gray mists surrounding their base and wondered, Are they coming tonight?

Tension ran especially high following the outbreak of the country-wide Tet offensive on the nights of January 30 and 31. Even though the NVA had failed to exploit the dire ammunition shortage caused by their opening rocket attack ten days before, it seemed likely that the enemy would take advantage of the Tet attacks and hit Khe Sanh hard. Convinced that that had been General Giap's intention all along, Westmoreland later claimed that a massive B–52 raid on a North Vietnamese headquarters complex inside Laos on January 30 had fore-

stalled an assault on the Marine base. In any case, aside from an NVA ground assault on one of the outlying hills on the night of February 5, Khe Sanh remained quiet in the immediate aftermath of Tet.

The next moment of crisis came on the night of February 7, when the North Vietnamese attacked a camp at Lang Vei manned by U.S. Special Forces and locally recruited Civilian Irregular Defense Group (CIDG) soldiers seven miles southwest of Khe Sanh. Striking from three directions behind Soviet-made PT76 tanks, a battalion-size force of NVA sappers and infantrymen, some armed with flame throwers, smashed through the perimeter and quickly overran the fortified compound. By morning 200 of the 500 CIDG troops at Lang Vei were dead or missing, along with 10 of the 24 Americans, while the camp itself had been reduced to bleak, smoldering ruins.

The fall of Lang Vei had a profound psychological impact on the Marines at Khe Sanh, stirring their most deep-seated fear. Despite recent reports that the enemy was moving armored vehicles into the area, no one knew—perhaps because no one wanted to believe—that the NVA had tanks. Now, observed journalist Michael Herr, who was present at the time, "how could you look out of your perimeter at night without hearing the treads coming?"

The ebb and flow of anxiety and adrenaline took a toll on the Marines, many of whom developed that blank look in the eyes known as the "10,000-yard stare." To relieve the stress and fatigue, they did what soldiers often do: They played cards and exchanged news from home, sang songs and listened to music. They accumulated omens of good fortune and displayed them prominently—a lucky playing card stuck in a helmet band, a soldier's cross or even a peace symbol chained around the neck.

On Hill 881 South, the 200 men of I Company, 3d Battalion, 26th Marines, began each day with a ceremonial flag raising. As the company bugler belted out a choppy version of "To the Colors," the sound of the day's first incoming shells could be heard in the distance. Knowing that they had exactly twenty-one seconds before the rounds hit, the Marines stayed at attention until the last possible instant, then dove for cover as artillery fire erupted all around. Moments later, another banner ascended their makeshift flagpole, a pair of red panties called "Maggie's Drawers"—the traditional symbol of a miss on the training camp firing range.

The base commander, Marine Corps Colonel David E. Lownds, had other ways of keeping his men occupied. Throughout the siege he continued to send patrols outside the perimeter to look for signs of the enemy's presence, a practice that some Marines openly questioned. "They would go out on patrol, to do what I don't know, and they were promptly slaughtered," recalled medical corpsman Richard Heath. But Lownds's superiors thought otherwise. Resentful of their defensive posture, which they considered contrary to the heritage and spirit of the Corps, they wanted the men at Khe Sanh to maintain the initiative. For the record, in fact, the Marine command repeatedly cited the patrols as evidence that the combat base was not officially under siege.

By mid-February, as the Tet offensive ran out of steam, fighting in and around Khe Sanh also abated. Although the NVA's long-range 130MM and 152MM artillery guns continued to pound the base with regularity, there were no major ground attacks on outlying U.S. positions. At the end of the month, however, a Marine patrol discovered a maze of enemy trench lines, some more than a mile long, leading toward the combat base. General Westmoreland immediately dispatched a seismographic team to determine whether the enemy was attempting to tunnel under Khe Sanh as they had at Dien Bien Phu and dynamite the Marines from below. He also called in the B–52s, which soon began dropping their bombs just outside the perimeter.

The NVA nevertheless kept on digging, until some of the trenches extended to within 100 yards of the American positions. Others began to branch out into "Ts," signaling the final stage of preparation before assault ramps were put into place. With March 13, the anniversary of the first attacks on Dien Bien Phu, fast approaching, it suddenly began to look as if history was about to repeat itself. Once again the defenders of Khe Sanh prepared themselves for the big attack. And once again nothing happened. Not on March 13. Not on any of the days that followed. Though the shelling continued, toward the end of March patrols were finding that many of the enemy trenches had long since been abandoned. The siege of Khe Sanh was officially declared ended on April 8, when a relief column made up of men from the 1st Air Cavalry Division reached the Marine outpost.

Why the North Vietnamese decided to withdraw from Khe Sanh remains one the many unsolved riddles of the war. In the view of some military analysts, since it became clear by early March that the NVA could not overrun the base, General Giap probably concluded that any additional expenditure of men and materiel would be pointless. Others, including General Westmoreland, contend that the abandonment of Khe Sanh was directly related to the collapse of North Vietnamese efforts to hold Hue and gain control of Quang Tri and Thua Thien Provinces. Still others have concluded that the Communists never intended to overrun the combat base but instead sought only to divert the allies' attention from the cities. Once that had been accomplished, they no longer had any reason to maintain the siege.

Two months after the siege ended the Marines at Khe Sanh received orders to dismantle their base. Beginning on June 17, they blew up the bunkers that had served as their homes and carted away what remained of their ammunition and supplies. When journalists began to inquire why the "western anchor" of the allies' northern defense line had suddenly become expendable, they were told that the NVA had changed their tactics, that they had carved new infiltration routes, and that a fixed base in the corner of Quang Tri Province was no longer necessary. "We don't want any more Khe Sanhs," said one Marine junior officer. "To defeat an enemy, you've got to keep moving."

Food and weapons drop by parachute to Marines at the besieged Khe Sanh base in northwestern South Vietnam, March 1968. With an estimated 15,000 NVA regulars surrounding the base, Khe Sanh could be resupplied only by air.

While some Marines relax during a break in enemy shelling, others go about the Sisyphean task of improving their bunker defenses by filling sandbags and adding to their revetment walls.

Inured to the chaos outside, two soldiers (left) chat inside their large, well-fortified bunker. Meanwhile, others curl up in their trench (above) and await the impact of incoming enemy artillery. The Marines at the Khe Sanh base faced around-the-clock shelling. In one day alone in late February, the base received more than 1,300 rounds of enemy fire.

As an enemy round explodes in the back-ground, a U.S. Marine crawls over crates of ammunition to check for any burning debris that might ignite them.

The survivors of a thirty-man patrol ambushed by North Vietnamese soldiers drag their wounded back to the base.

An American tank leads the way down Route 9 toward Khe Sanh, part of the joint U.S. and South Vietnamese task force sent to relieve the Marines as part of Operation Pegasus in early April 1968.

A U.S. Army helicopter delivers ammunition to Pegasus units fighting their way westward. On April 7, the 1st Cavalry Division's 2d Battalion, 7th Cavalry, joined up with the Marines, officially bringing an end to the seventy-seven-day siege.

Witness: Walter Cronkite

In February 1968 Walter Cronkite of CBS News, then one of America's most popular and respected journalists, traveled to Vietnam for a firsthand look at the war. Cronkite reported to the American people on February 27 that, "It seems now more certain than ever that the bloody experience of Vietnam is to end in a stalemate." The only viable way out of the war, he concluded, "will be to negotiate, not as victors, but as honorable people who lived up to their pledge to defend democracy and did the best they could." Cronkite's report was the first editorial stand on the conflict by a network anchor and was viewed as a watershed in the turn of American public opinion against the war. Twenty years after the Tet offensive, Cronkite recalled the circumstances of his influential Vietnam visit and report.

President Lyndon Johnson may not have been much more surprised about our editorial conclusions on the Tet offensive than I was.

When I went to Vietnam soon after the dimensions of the offensive became obvious, my mind was wide open. I did not know what I would find or what I would conclude from those findings. Throughout the long war I had tried to report as impartially as good journalism demanded. I had done what I could to be certain that the reports of our extraordinarily talented and courageous correspondents in Vietnam were as accurate, fair, and balanced as first-person, risk-of-life, on-the-battle-scene reports can be.

My private feelings, which I believe I disguised with some success, probably reflected the opinion of a majority. I approved of President Kennedy's dispatch of military advisers to try to help preserve a corner of Southeast Asia from the Communists. I became alarmed when the advisers began taking an active role in the fighting and their numbers grew. My alarm escalated along with those numbers and as I began to understand, through my visits there, that they were in fact part of a "numbers game"; that, incredibly, America was not being told the truth about its commitment in Vietnam; that while the public was told that Congressionally approved figures defined the limits of our participation, the military was filling the pipeline with the men and materiel for a much larger involvement.

On the air, however, I tried to maintain objectivity in keeping with the CBS credo and my own conviction that those delivering the news should not comment or editorialize upon it. I always felt, and still feel, that it is too much to ask an audience to believe what I know to be true—that a good journalist can at one point deliver as objective a report as it is possible to prepare, and at the next deliver an impassioned commentary on the same event. A member of the audience, lacking background knowledge of how journalists work, could not be blamed for believing that the broadcaster's personal views must affect all of his reporting.

When the North Vietnamese and Vietcong launched their Tet offensive and within days had swept into the very outskirts of Saigon and through many areas that our military had long claimed as pacified, I began to believe there perhaps should be an extraordinary exception to that philosophy. With the offensive that had upset so many claims and predictions of our military and political leaders, I suffered a nauseous wave of doubt, uncertainty, and confusion. I felt certain that this was the feeling of a majority of my fellow Americans. We all seemed to be searching and hoping for some guidance. What could we believe? What was the truth? Were we, as our leaders claimed, winning and nearing the end of the Vietnam nightmare? Or did the Tet offensive indicate that we were still years away from victory, years that would be spent bridging rivers of blood?

I wanted to get the answers to those questions, if I

could, on the ground in Vietnam where the authoritative sources were and where I could check with my own eyes the statements versus the facts.

The question I asked myself was: Would we at CBS News be performing a public service if I broadcast my findings? Would the opinion of one reporter who had tried to maintain strict impartiality up to now be helpful in guiding at least a portion of our listeners through the maze of confusion in which we stumbled?

I discussed the matter with our CBS News president, Richard Salant. Dick and I raised the most important question with each other: By abandoning my studied neutrality on the Vietnam issue, would I compromise my future objectivity in the eyes of our viewers, and would this fallout be so severe as to jeopardize the standing of the "CBS Evening News" and even the entire reputation of CBS News itself? We decided in the end that this was too parochial a consideration in regard to an issue as large as any that had faced our nation—in fact, one that threatened to split the nation. It was agreed that I should go to Vietnam, do my best to get the answers, and broadcast my conclusions.

When I arrived, the battle for the once beautiful old city of Hue was still raging, and I huddled with civilians and American Marines seeking shelter from artillery and mortar shells as the ancient structures tumbled about us.

In Saigon I drove not far from the center of the city to the roadblocks beyond which the crunch of mortars and the staccato pop of automatic rifles, the crash of stone and the tinkling of glass, testified to the incursion of the enemy.

Out of the pages of memory of Warsaw and Paris and Brussels and Seoul, I saw refugees from the city's outskirts crowd toward the city's heart, pushing their bicycles laden with their impossible pyramids of precious belongings.

At night, from the roof of the Caravelle Hotel, correspondents' headquarters, I watched the helicopter gunships circling the city unload their hail of death on suspected enemy hot spots scarcely blocks away. And at the bar below I heard angry, frustrated American civilians and officers who had been in charge of pacification of the villages and who a few days before had claimed we were winning the hearts and minds of the people report with bitter cynicism that their villages apparently had welcomed the returning Vietcong.

At the daily press briefing (skeptical correspondents called it the "Five O'Clock Follies"), the spokesmen scarcely acknowledged that the optimistic reports of diminishing enemy strength of previous days had been either grossly wrong or grossly understated. Their glass was eternally half-full, and I seem to recall that one of them even dared to suggest that "we now have the enemy where we want him—out in the open."

At military headquarters top officers told me that now only a few score thousand more young Americans and a few score more millions of dollars in replacement equipment were all we needed to secure the victory that had long eluded them. For them the light still shone brightly at the end of the tunnel.

To me the evidence was overwhelmingly to the contrary.

The reporting and the broadcasts themselves are, I gather, history. We had anticipated some public reaction. We would have been unique broadcasters if we had not. The reaction was generally favorable, and, although I have no doubt that we lost some viewers, there was no discernible drop in our audience.

What we had not expected, and only learned much later, was that the president himself would react as he did [that March 31]. No one has claimed, and I certainly do not believe, that our broadcast changed his mind about anything. I do believe it may have been the backbreaking piece of straw that was heaped on the heavy load he already was carrying—doubt about the reports he had been getting on alleged military success in Vietnam, concern that the military was now asking for another considerable increase in troop strength to finish the job, and increasing public outcry as the nation headed into a presidential election.

Despite a considerable rewriting, or at least refinement, of history in the light of later evidence and the claim today, supported in some degree by statements of North Vietnamese military leaders, that North Vietnam actually suffered a battlefield defeat in the Tet offensive, I have found no reason to revise my belief expressed at the time that Tet proved how far we were from victory and cast doubt that it ever was attainable.

5

THE HOME FRONT

"President Johnson's decision to sacrifice himself on the altar of peace and national unity is an act of statesmanship which entitles him to the American people's deepest respect and sympathy." So wrote the editors of the *Los Angeles Times*, voicing a view shared by many in the immediate aftermath of Johnson's historic speech of March 31, 1968. Praise of the president's actions was even more widespread after Hanoi announced on April 3 that it would accept the American offer to begin preliminary peace talks. Infused with fresh hope that the Vietnam War might at last be brought to an end, a mood of near exhiliration temporarily gripped the American people. In New York throngs of well-wishers cheered the president during a visit for the investiture of Archbishop Terence Cardinal Cooke, while on Wall Street the stock market recorded its greatest single-day gain to that date.

For Lyndon Johnson there must have been more than a touch of irony in that transitory moment of renewed popularity. Barely three years had passed since he stood at the apex of power and prestige, after scoring the most lopsided electoral victory in the history of the presidency. With the Democratic party in firm control of both houses of Congress and the economy booming, his dream of creating the Great Society on the foundations of John Kennedy's New Frontier had seemed well within reach. During his State of the Union address on January 4, 1965, the House chamber had thundered with applause as Johnson laid out his agenda for the future: to extend federal aid to education and medical aid to the elderly, to eradicate poverty and refurbish the cities, and to cut excise taxes and insure equal rights for all. "This, then, is the State of the Union," the president had concluded, "free, growing, restless, and full of hope."

Only one major problem confronted Johnson as he set out to transform his social vision into reality: the war in that "damn little piss ant country," as he privately referred to Vietnam. Despite the commitment of more than 22,000 American military advisers, the

The funeral of Private Robert Damian Wuertz of Massillon, Ohio, killed in Vietnam.

might of some 12,000 American bombing missions, and the influx of thousands of tons of American war materiel, the struggle against the Communists in Southeast Asia was going badly. Even more disquieting from Johnson's point of view, it was becoming a political liability. Public opinion polls taken at the end of 1964 revealed that fully 50 percent of the public was dissatisfied with the administration's handling of the war, though the same surveys also indicated sharp disagreement over what course the president should follow. During the election campaign Johnson himself had seemed undecided, promising not to widen the war or "send American boys to do what Asian boys ought to do for themselves," while at the same time vowing never "to yield to Communist aggression."

By early 1965, however, it had become clear that the time for such ambivalence had passed. With the threat of a decisive Communist victory in South Vietnam growing more imminent with each passing day, Johnson would have to make "harder choices," special assistant McGeorge Bundy advised him. He would have to choose between "escalation and withdrawal," between using "our military power to force a change in Communist policy" and applying "all our resources along a track of negotiation, aimed at salvaging what little can be preserved." Fearful that he would be vilified by the Republican right if he "lost" South Vietnam to the Communists and confident that the nation would tolerate the war as long as its costs remained relatively modest, Johnson opted to raise the American stakes in Southeast Asia by stepping up the bombing of North Vietnam and sending U.S. combat troops to the South. In so doing, he set in motion forces that would divide the nation, shatter his plans for the Great Society, and ultimately deprive him of the presidency itself.

From the outset there had been dissenting voices. The eminent journalist Walter Lippmann, who repeatedly warned that there could be "no military solution" to the Vietnam conflict, was one. Senators Wayne Morse of

In an early antiwar demonstration, 20,000 students from across the country gather on the Mall in Washington, D.C., on April 17, 1965.

194

Oregon and Ernest Gruening of Alaska, the only members of Congress to vote against the 1964 Gulf of Tonkin Resolution, were others. With the escalation of the war in the spring of 1965, however, public opposition to the deepening American involvement in Vietnam rapidly expanded and intensified.

University students were among the first to register their protest. Beginning in late March at the University of Michigan, activists at more than 100 colleges and universities boycotted classes and staged a series of "teach-ins" to discuss the war and its implications. Others, seeking to express their dissent more directly, left their campuses to participate in the mass antiwar rallies that took place in New York on April 15 and in Washington, D.C., two days later. In Berkeley, California, the newly formed Vietnam Day Committee organized similar demonstrations during the spring and later attempted to block troop trains heading into the Oakland army terminal, the point of departure for many Vietnam-bound GIs.

Swelling the ranks of the student protesters were many clergymen, educators, and civil rights leaders, as well as members of such liberal, middle-class organizations as the Committee for a Sane Nuclear Policy (SANE) and the American Friends Service Committee. A product of the earlier "ban the bomb" movement, SANE mounted the largest single antiwar protest of the year when it attracted 30,000 marchers to Washington, D.C., on November 27. Led by pediatrician Dr. Benjamin Spock, socialist Norman Thomas, and Coretta Scott King, the wife of Dr. Martin Luther King, Jr., the demonstrators carried placards demanding an end to U.S. bombing in Vietnam and a supervised cease-fire.

In 1966 the antiwar movement continued to gain momentum, as more and more ordinary citizens began to question the American commitment to South Vietnam. In late January, a group of 100 Veterans and Reservists to End the War in Vietnam picketed the White House to protest the resumption of U.S. air strikes over North Vietnam after a thirty-seven-day bombing pause. Several days later, 5,000 American scientists, 17 of them former Nobel Prize winners, petitioned the president to review U.S. chemical and biological warfare in Southeast Asia.

Serious doubts about the war also began to surface in Congress, prompting the Senate Armed Services Committee to initiate in early February 1966 an "investigation" of the administration's Vietnam policy. Under the chairmanship of Senator J. William Fulbright, the distinguished Arkansas Democrat, the committee set out to find answers to basic questions surrounding military strategy, troop deployments, bombing policy, and peace negotiations. A long-time friend and legislative ally of Johnson, Fulbright had been instrumental in steering through Congress the August 1964 Southeast Asia (Tonkin Gulf) Resolution, empowering the president "to take all necessary steps, including the use of armed force," to defend the freedom of South Vietnam. Like many of his colleagues, however, Fulbright had become increasingly irritated by Johnson's highhanded use of that authority to escalate the war without consulting the legislative branch. Although Secretary of Defense McNamara and JCS chairman General Wheeler refused to testify before the committee, Fulbright pressed on with the inquiry, calling on a parade of high-ranking government officials to defend the administration's position.

In the end, the month-long hearings failed to produce any concrete results, since few congressmen were prepared to challenge the president directly or to cut off funds for the war. Nevertheless, by providing an open forum for a debate over American policy objectives in Vietnam, the nationally televised proceedings made dissent more respectable, thus paving the way for a flurry of nearly fifty "peace candidates" in the November 1966 Congressional elections. Though all were defeated some drew significant support, including Robert Scheer, the editor of the radical journal *Ramparts,* who received 45 percent of the Democratic primary vote in California's Seventh District. Moreover, as journalist Andrew Kopkind observed in the *New Republic,* opponents of the war could find a "measure of hope" in the election of a "miniblock" of dovish Republicans, including Senators Mark Hatfield of Oregon, Charles Percy of Illinois, and Edward Brooke of Massachusetts.

In the meantime, mass demonstrations against the war continued to proliferate, culminating in the largest antiwar rally in U.S. history—a march by 300,000

A demonstrator inserts pink carnations into the rifle barrels of military policemen during the heated confrontation outside the Pentagon on October 21, 1967.

Americans in New York City on April 15, 1967. Six months later, on October 21, a much smaller but equally determined group of protesters gathered in front of the Lincoln Memorial in Washington, D.C., to hear speakers condemn the war amid signs demanding that President Johnson "Bring Home the GIs Now!" As the last speeches came to an end, an estimated 30,000 demonstrators linked arms, crossed the Arlington Memorial Bridge, and marched on the Pentagon. Met by a line of military police as the protesters approached the main entrance to what they called "the center of the American war machine," several hundred of them attempted to break through and race up the steps. The troops responded with tear gas and truncheons, inflicting dozens of injuries as they drove the surging crowd back. After a second charge met with the same result, the demon-

strators fell back and held a nightlong candlelight vigil. By the time the protest came to an end the following afternoon, 700 people had been arrested and twice that number reported as casualties.

Although the motives of the protesters varied, from the ideological radicalism of the student "New Left" to the religious pacifism of the Quakers, the principal target of much early antiwar dissent was the same. As monthly draft calls shot up to meet the demands of the expanding U.S. war effort—from 13,700 in April 1965 to nearly 30,000 in August 1967—protest against administration policy increasingly took the form of protest against the Selective Service System (SSS). In addition to counseling potential inductees to resist conscription, antiwar activists picketed local draft boards, staged "sit-ins" at military induction centers, and publicly burned their own draft cards. Congress swiftly retaliated by stiffening the penalties for such acts and extending the range of punishable offenses. But even the vigorous enforcement of the new laws could not curtail the steady growth of the antidraft movement.

For all the publicity they generated, however, those who actively resisted the draft remained a small, if vocal, minority. Faced with the prospect of conscription, most draft-age males either accepted their lot or found other ways to avoid military service. Many took advantage of the long-standing system of exemptions and deferments instituted by the SSS to "channel" the nation's youth in "socially desirable" ways. Local draft boards were empowered, for example, to grant exemptions on the grounds of "family hardship" or "critical occupational skills" and to issue deferments to ministers, farmers, and college students "making satisfactory progress toward a degree." Other young men took their cases to court, drawing on the expertise of a growing number of draft-law specialists to establish their credentials as conscientious objectors or to challenge the procedures employed by their local boards. Still others contrived to fail their preinduction physical exams by artificially elevating their blood pressure, aggravating old sports injuries, or simulating more serious disorders.

Though the military did its best to discriminate between legitimate and illegitimate cases, in the end more than one-quarter of all prospective conscripts were disqualified from military service for medical reasons. Each year another third obtained exemptions or deferments, while 5 percent avoided serving in Vietnam by enlisting in the National Guard or the Reserves. Since the classification system by design allowed the better educated and better off not to serve, those actually inducted into the military tended to come from working-class families earning less than $10,000 a year. Inductees typically lived in cities or small towns rather than suburbs and had no education beyond high school. According to one 1968 study, a high-school dropout from a low-income

A draft-age youth from Hanford, California, appears before his draft board to learn that he will receive a deferment because he is married.

Civil rights leader Dr. Martin Luther King, Jr., an outspoken critic of the war in Vietnam, addresses a caucus of liberal Democrats in California in January 1968, three months before his assassination.

family faced a 70 percent chance of serving in Vietnam, whereas the corresponding odds for a college graduate were only 42 percent. Once in Vietnam, moreover, draftees were far more likely to be assigned to combat roles than those who enlisted voluntarily, and consequently they suffered a significantly higher casualty rate.

The social imbalances of the Vietnam army became even more glaring following the introduction of Project 100,000 in 1966. Heralded as a Great Society program designed to "rehabilitate the subterranean poor," especially young blacks, the project quickly evolved into a vehicle for funneling underprivileged and unemployed youths from the streets of America to the battlefields of Indochina. By lowering the minimum intellectual and physical standards for induction, recruiters eventually brought more than 350,000 men into the military under

the program. Of that total, 41 percent were black, and 40 percent served in the infantry. A Pentagon study later determined that the "attrition-by-death" rate of Project 100,000 soldiers was nearly twice as high as that of Vietnam-era veterans as a whole.

The racial inequities of the draft explain in part why antiwar sentiment consistently ran higher among black Americans than among whites. Already engaged in a domestic struggle to end legal discrimination in the South and de facto segregation in the North, the leaders of the civil rights movement had refrained from challenging U.S. foreign policy goals throughout the late 1950s and early 1960s. But as the Vietnam War began to take a heavy toll on black youth, as well as on the antipoverty programs of Johnson's Great Society, many blacks came to regard the conflict as an obstacle to fur-

ther social progress. The more radical activists, like "black power" advocate Stokely Carmichael of SNCC (the Student Nonviolent Coordinating Committee) and Huey Newton of the Black Panther party, were in the forefront of the opposition by early 1966.

By early 1967 even the moderate leaders of the civil rights movement had turned against the war. "A time comes when silence is betrayed," proclaimed the Reverend Martin Luther King, Jr., in a sermon at Riverside Church on April 4, 1967. "That time has come for us in relation to Vietnam." Reminding his audience that only a few years before the Johnson administration had declared a "war on poverty" at home, he traced the course of his own disillusionment with the undeclared war in Vietnam. "I watched the program broken and eviscerated as if it were some idle plaything of a society gone mad on war," King asserted, "and I knew that I could never again raise my voice against the violence of the oppressed in the ghettos without having first spoken clearly to the greatest purveyor of violence in the world today—my own government."

King's claim that the rising costs of the war had compromised the dream of the Great Society was not without foundation. Despite President Johnson's belief that the nation was "rich enough and strong enough" to fight a two-front war—against poverty at home and communism abroad—by early 1967 the American economy was beginning to show signs of strain. Faced with the threat of runaway inflation, which had been triggered by the sharp and unanticipated increase in military expenditures over the previous eighteen months, Johnson was forced to choose between raising taxes and cutting domestic spending. Politically unpalatable as both alternatives were, in August 1967 the president put before Congress a request for a 10 percent income-tax surcharge. By that point, however, dissatisfaction with Johnson's social reform agenda had become so widespread that Congressional conservatives were in a position to demand a quid pro quo. If the president wanted a tax hike, they insisted, he would first have to make deep cuts in social spending. Although Johnson ultimately agreed, by then even the combination of increased federal revenues and decreased expenditures could not cool down the overheated U.S. economy.

Opposition to the administration's domestic policies had, in fact, mounted steadily since 1965. Troubled by the recurrent outbreak of urban riots, the growth of black radicalism, and the perceived excesses of some federal antipoverty programs, many white Americans had become convinced that the government was moving too far, too fast in its efforts to remedy long-standing social problems. The so-called white backlash was especially pronounced among blue-collar workers, many of whom came to see themselves as victims of a system that had someone else's interests at heart. Forced to endure the dislocations of a rapidly changing society—crime, inflation, rising taxes, and disintegrating neighborhoods—they fought back by resisting desegregation of their schools and communities and by withdrawing their support from liberal politicians whose social programs rarely addressed their own needs.

More complicated were the attitudes of working-class whites toward the war in Vietnam. On the one hand, blue-collar workers were among the more visible and vocal supporters of the war effort, as evidenced by the 70,000 longshoremen, carpenters, seamen, and mechanics who marched down Fifth Avenue in New York City in May 1967. Carrying banners reading "Down with the Reds," "God Bless Us Patriots," and "Support Our Boys," they denounced the antiwar protesters and called upon the government to "escalate, not capitulate." On the other hand, they were well aware that their own sons were bearing a disproportionate burden of the fighting and dying in Southeast Asia. Though they deeply resented those who avoided the draft and they regarded much antiwar protest as treasonous, as time went on and casualties multiplied many working-class parents came to share the dissenters' view that the war was a mistake. Unlike the organized peace movement, however, their opposition was not so much ideological or moral as pragmatic, based on the conviction that the price they were paying was simply too high. As one Long Island construction worker put it after watching the funeral procession of a local boy killed in Vietnam: "The whole damn country of South Vietnam is not worth the life of one American boy, no matter what the hell our politicians tell us. I'm damn sick and tired of watching these funerals go by."

The pattern of gradual disillusionment with the war was also evident in the popular press. Like most Americans, the journalists who covered the war initially backed the U.S. commitment to Vietnam, believing that it was in the nation's interest to "contain" the spread of communism in Southeast Asia. As UPI correspondent Neil Sheehan later recalled, when he first arrived in Saigon in 1962 he was convinced that the U.S. was helping the South Vietnamese "to build a viable and independent nation-state and defeat a Communist insurgency that would subject them to a dour tyranny."

According to the correspondents themselves, the American government was largely responsible for undermining faith in the war effort. In their zeal to put the best face on all political and military developments, U.S. officials in Washington and Saigon repeatedly provided information that was at odds with the reporters' own observations or with intelligence gleaned from other sources. Early on, for example, correspondents were told that American forces were only "advising" the South Vietnamese, even though the reporters saw them fighting and dying. Similarly, battles in which ARVN forces were routed by the Vietcong were described as victories in official briefings. "No responsible U.S. official in Saigon ever told a newsman a really big falsehood," recalled John Mecklin, chief of the U.S. Information Service. "Instead there were endless little falsehoods."

As a result, a "credibility gap" soon emerged between the U.S. government and the Saigon press corps. That gap would widen over time. The skepticism of the correspondents manifested itself in increasingly critical accounts of the war effort that often directly contradicted what the Johnson administration was saying back in Washington. In many instances, however, their negative accounts were either buried on the back pages or revised by editors who preferred to rely on official Pentagon assessments, frequently expressed in the hard, quantitative language of enemy body counts, kill ratios, weapons captured, and hamlets pacified. "We were largely at the mercy of the administration then," said

Prowar activists stage a demonstration on the streets of New York City in early April 1967.

the late Peter Lisagor, then Washington bureau chief of the *Chicago Daily News*. "There was a tendency to believe them more because they were supposed to have the facts, and we were inclined to accept an official's word on something as cosmic as war."

Eventually, however, the flood of pessimistic dispatches from the war zone became too overwhelming to ignore. Though few correspondents went so far as to challenge the legitimacy of the U.S. presence in Vietnam, by the summer of 1967 many had come to the conclusion that the war was not being fought effectively, that the pacification program was failing, and that South Vietnam was still far from becoming a viable nation-state. "Everyone thought I was against the war," recalled Charles Mohr, who resigned his post as *Time*'s Saigon correspondent after his managing editor ordered him to rewrite a story claiming that the war was being lost. "I just thought it wasn't working. I didn't come to think of it as immoral until the very end."

Troubled by the growing perception that the war was a "stalemate," the Johnson administration launched an all-out public relations campaign in the fall of 1967 "to get the message out" that "we are winning." Under the direction of national security adviser Walt W. Rostow, who was also chief of the White House Psychological Strategy Committee, government officials inundated the major news media with an endless stream of charts, graphs, statistics, and previously classified documents showing "steady progress" on every front in the struggle against the Vietnamese Communists. Vice President Hubert H. Humphrey, Secretary of Defense Robert McNamara, and Secretary of State Dean Rusk offered equally optimistic appraisals in televised appearances on weekly news shows as well as in private chats with favored reporters. The campaign reached its high point in mid-November, when the president summoned General William Westmoreland, Ambassador Ellsworth Bunker, and pacification chief Robert W. Komer from Saigon to confirm the administration's assessment. "I am absolutely certain that whereas in 1965 the enemy was winning, today he is certainly losing," Westmoreland asserted in an address before the National Press Club on November 21. "We have reached an important point when the end begins to come into view."

As Johnson had hoped, the administration's "success offensive" brought to a halt the steady erosion of popular support for the war. Opinion polls conducted toward the end of the year showed a 7 percent increase in approval of the president's handling of the war since the preceding August. Even more striking was the shift in the public's perception of U.S. "progress" in Vietnam. Between July and December 1967 the percentage of people who thought the U.S. was "losing ground" or "standing still" plummeted, while those who thought that the Americans were "making progress" rose from 34 percent to more than 50 percent.

Then came Tet 1968. With the outbreak of the Communists' cataclysmic, country-wide offensive in late January 1968, public confidence in the American war effort suffered a grievous, and ultimately fatal, blow. Confronted with evidence of the enemy's capacity to mount coordinated, surprise attacks on a massive scale, many Americans found it difficult to believe the administration's claims that the U.S. was "winning" the war. Nor could they place much faith in General Westmoreland's sanguine prediction that "the end" had "come into view." By mid-February, two weeks after the offensive began, popular disapproval of the president's Vietnam policy had reached an all-time high of 50 percent; by the end of the month the figure was 58 percent. More telling still, only one out of three Americans now thought that the United States was "making progress" in Vietnam, and nearly one in four believed that the allies were "losing ground."

The judgments rendered by the nation's leading news organizations reinforced the verdict reflected by the polls. "After three years of gradual escalation, President Johnson's strategy of gradual escalation has run into a dead end," wrote the editors of *Newsweek,* expressing a view held by many Americans in the wake of the Tet offensive. Not only had the U.S. military buildup in Vietnam failed to quell the Communist insurgency, but the government of South Vietnam remained a "political morass," riddled with corruption and unable to earn the allegiance of its own people. What was required was "the courage to face the truth"—that "the war cannot be won by military means without tearing apart the whole fabric of national life and international relations."

Although President Johnson initially resisted the press' assessment, in the end he had no choice but to accept it. Having lost the trust of his "fellow Americans," as he always called them, he knew that he could no longer govern effectively. Not only had a majority of the public repudiated his Vietnam policies, but by mid-March 1968 Johnson could not even count on the continuing support of his own political party. Senator Eugene McCarthy's startling showing in the New Hampshire primary and Senator Robert Kennedy's subsequent entrance into the presidential race made it clear that Johnson faced a bitter fight for the Democratic nomination. By announcing on March 31 his intention to relinquish the presidency, Johnson hoped at once to salvage a measure of his own personal authority and to restore a semblance of unity to a nation increasingly divided against itself.

Yet such was not to be. On April 4, 1968, the day after the North Vietnamese rekindled hopes for peace by accepting Johnson's offer to begin negotiations, Dr. Martin Luther King, Jr., was killed by an assassin's bullet in Memphis, Tennessee. For thirteen years the charismatic leader of the black civil rights movement, winner of the Nobel Peace Prize, eloquent speaker and moral teacher, King had long stood as a symbol of nonviolent social reform. Now, with tragic irony, his murder by white ex-convict James Earl Ray became the occasion for the most widespread racial violence in the nation's history. Within minutes after learning of King's death, crowds of angry blacks began roaming the streets of many major cities, breaking windows, looting stores, and setting fire to white-owned businesses. Black colleges seethed with rage while urban high schools across the country closed down in the face of violent racial confrontations. In Baltimore, Detroit, and 4 southern cities, overwhelmed local officials were forced to request the assistance of the National Guard, while in Chicago regular army troops had to be called in after entire blocks of the West Side ghetto went up in flames. All told, 169 cities reported incidents of racial violence in the wake of the King assassination, resulting in some $130

Residents in Washington, D.C., stand by as a local store goes up in flames during one of the riots that erupted nationwide after the death of Martin Luther King, Jr.

million in property damage, nearly 24,000 arrests, and forty-three deaths, thirty-six of them blacks.

King's death was not the only reason for violence that spring. Three weeks later, on April 23, a coalition of radical white and black students at Columbia University in New York City seized a number of administration buildings, signaling the advent of a new phase in the politics of student protest. At issue were the university's decision to construct a new gymnasium in Morningside Park, a city-owned plot of land in the adjacent Harlem neighborhood, and its affiliation with the Institute for Defense Analysis (IDA), a multimillion-dollar consortium founded in 1955 to test weapons and military strategy. Led by members of the local chapter of the Students for a Democratic Society (SDS) and in loose alliance with the Students' Afro-American Society (SAS), the protesters demanded that the administration abandon its allegedly racist "land-grab" policies and end its "complicity" in the Vietnam War. When university officials failed to comply, the students moved in and occupied Low Library, the main administration offices at Hamilton Hall, and several other campus buildings. After a week of inconclusive negotiations, punctuated by a series of violent clashes between allies and opponents of the occupiers, on April 29 President Grayson Kirk called in the New York City police to clear the buildings. Crashing through a set of makeshift barricades, the police stormed Low Library, bludgeoned the students with fists and nightsticks, and then dragged them downstairs to waiting paddy wagons. A second occupation several weeks later produced even bloodier results, as students and police engaged in what amounted to hand-to-hand combat throughout the campus.

By the time it ended in late May 1968, the rebellion at Columbia had resulted in nearly 900 arrests, 180 injuries (34 to police), and the suspension of 73 students. It had also spawned similar demonstrations at hundreds of other campuses, including forty major confrontations, and provoked a torrent of criticism against the new pol-

David Shapiro, one of the student radicals who occupied administrative buildings at Columbia University in late April 1968, sits behind the desk of President Grayson Kirk.

itics of "direct action." While President Johnson condemned the Columbia militants as "young totalitarians," the editors of *Fortune* warned its readers that the new generation of student activists sought to instigate a revolution—"not a protest . . . but an honest-to-God revolution." Mark Rudd, the leader of the Columbia SDS "action faction," could only agree. "Liberal solutions . . . are not allowed anymore," he declared. "We are out for social and political revolution, nothing less."

Yet if militant blacks and student radicals had abandoned their faith in peaceful political change, the vast majority of Americans were still committed to working within the system. For those seeking to bring the Vietnam War to an end, President Johnson's unexpected withdrawal from the presidential race had opened a new range of possibilities. Suddenly it seemed that what had not been gained through protest in the streets might be achieved through the ballot, particularly after Senator McCarthy followed his astonishing performance in New Hampshire with a decisive victory in the April 2 Wisconsin primary.

But the other Democratic antiwar candidate, Robert F. Kennedy, was to steal the thunder from McCarthy's single-issue candidacy. Although his tardy entrance into the race had produced charges of opportunism, not even his enemies within the party could deny that he was a political force to be reckoned with. In part because of his name, in part because of his gift for stirring oratory, and in part because of his capacity to reach the disaffected and the dispossessed, Kennedy had an appeal that extended far beyond that of any other national political figure. His campaign entourage included members of the Eastern establishment who had served under his brother, as well as former members of the SDS. He enjoyed strong support among urban blacks and also, remarkably, among working-class whites. And he promised not only to end the war in Vietnam, but to heal the wounds that the war had inflicted on the American nation.

Recognizing that he would have to "win through the people," Kennedy launched his campaign with an exhausting whirlwind tour of sixteen states in twenty-one days. Everywhere he went the people responded, wrote one reporter, with "an intensity and scope that was awesome and frightening"—clutching at his coat sleeves as he moved through ghetto neighborhoods, chanting his name as he delivered his impassioned indictments of the Johnson administration's policies. The results at the polls were equally dramatic: victory in Indiana on May 7; victory in Nebraska on May 14. Then, after losing the Oregon primary to Senator McCarthy by six percentage points on May 28, Kennedy moved on to California. With its large bloc of delegates and "winner take all" rules, the June 4 California primary loomed as the crucial test of who would challenge the Johnson-Humphrey forces at the Democratic convention in August.

Kennedy won. In his victory statement at the Ambassador Hotel in Los Angeles, the New York senator told cheering campaign workers that their success had proved that "the violence, the disenchantments with our society, the divisions . . . between blacks and whites, between the poor and the affluent, or between age groups or on the war in Vietnam" could be overcome. Then, as he left the dais to hold a press conference in another part of the building, Sirhan Bishara Sirhan, a Palestinian Arab angered over Kennedy's support for Israel, suddenly raised a revolver and fired at the senator's head. The following day Robert Kennedy was dead.

His candidacy had for a time brought together many of the disparate elements of a perilously fragmented nation. An assassin's bullet had destroyed the hope for national reconciliation shared by Kennedy's followers. One of them, speech writer Jack Newfield, formerly a member of SDS, put it this way: "We had already glimpsed the most compassionate leaders our nation could produce, and they had all been assassinated. And from this time forward, things would get worse: Our best political leaders were part of memory now, not hope." Although it is impossible to know what might have happened had Kennedy lived, it is certain that the nation's divisions deepened after his death. Later that summer, the Democratic Convention in Chicago was to dramatize just how divided America had already become.

A hotel busboy crouches beside presidential candidate Robert Kennedy, who moments before had been fatally shot by a lone gunman at Los Angeles' Ambassador Hotel on June 4, 1968.

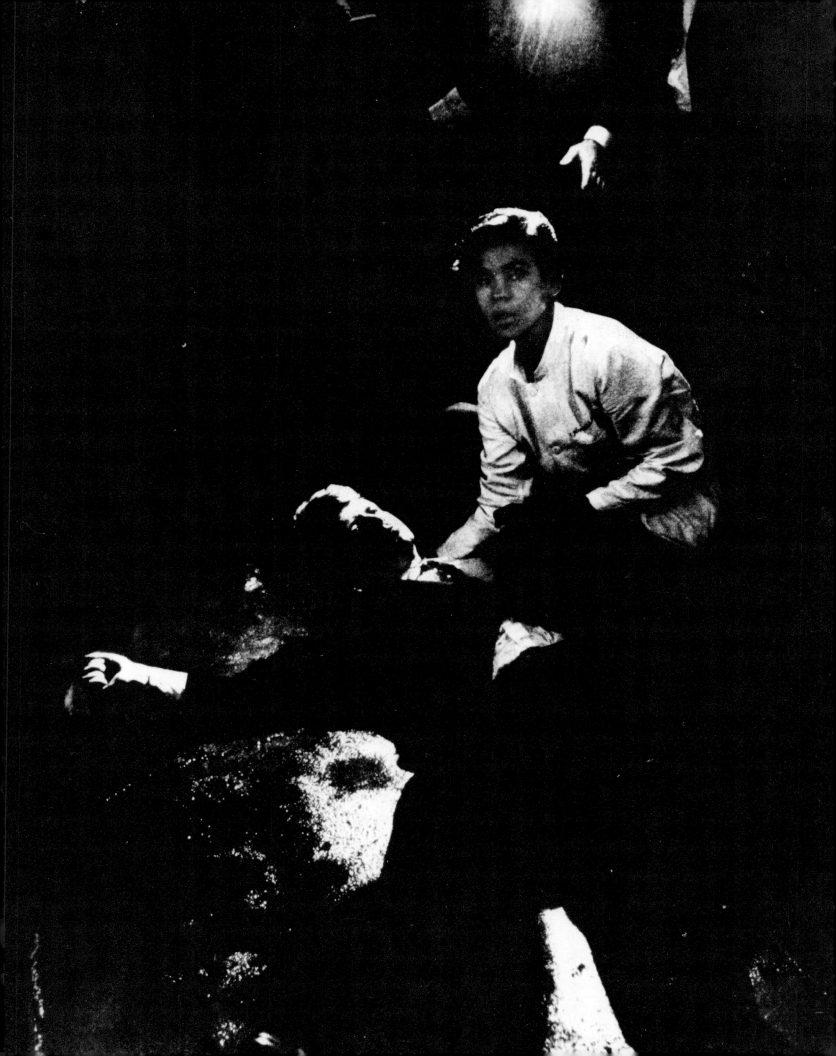

Witness: Jim Quay

Rather than answer the call to arms, thousands of American men refused to go to war. Some fled the country to avoid the draft or even went to prison for violating Selective Service laws. More than 170,000 won the classification of conscientious objector (CO) after showing their moral opposition to service. One of the COs was James Quay of Pennsylvania.

I don't recall exactly when the war in Vietnam attracted my full attention. I remember a few snapshots from the early years: a Buddhist monk protesting the South Vietnamese government, seated in the lotus position and burning like a torch; the overthrow and assassination of President Ngo Dinh Diem three weeks before President Kennedy was assassinated; the alleged attack on U.S. destroyers in the Gulf of Tonkin in August 1964. But all of these events were far removed from my life in eastern Pennsylvania. I was supposed to register at my local Selective Service board when I turned eighteen—September 26, 1964—but I forgot. Didn't go for three weeks. It was no big deal. I never considered not registering, and they didn't think my being late meant anything. That wouldn't be true later.

My family were middle-of-the-road Republicans. I favored Nixon over Kennedy in the 1960 election and found good things to say about Barry Goldwater four years later. In my junior year in high school, I applied to become a candidate to the U.S. Military Academy and took and passed all the necessary tests. I changed my mind before the selection was made, because the only degree offered at West Point was a bachelor's in science and I didn't want to limit my options. I already had an inkling that West Point might be confining in other ways, but I don't remember having any moral objection to entering the military. As it was, I never had to decide: My congressman named me only first alternate.

What turned a candidate to West Point in 1963 into a conscientious objector by 1967? My growing awareness during those years of the enormous destruction being visited upon the people of North and South Vietnam by the American military. I knew there was plenty of suffering caused by "the other side," but because of the massive technological resources America alone possessed, the U.S. had the capacity to inflict horrific damage far beyond anything available to its enemies in Vietnam. Regardless of whether Vietnam was two countries or one or whether Ho Chi Minh was a Communist aggressor or a popular Nationalist, I came to feel that the destruction America was causing was incompatible with any proper American objective in Vietnam. During the Tet offensive, an American artillery officer said of the village of Ben Tre, "It became necessary to destroy the town in order to save it." That phrase crystallized what I felt about the war. If we were killing Vietnamese and destroying Vietnam in the name of freedom, who and what would be left to be free?

Everything I read and heard about the war continually violated my deepest patriotism, my pride in what this country stood for in the world, until as an American I couldn't stand to be part of my country's war anymore. In the spring of 1967 I told my parents that I was planning to become a conscientious objector. I remember that my parents were concerned but not opposed; I think they were mostly baffled. In a journal that I kept at the time, I noted in particular my father's silence. I was rejecting the course of action he had taken in World War II. He could not help me. He could show me how a man does what his government asks of him; he could not show me how to oppose that government. But my father did me a very great kindness: He knew a member of the local draft board from a service organization he belonged to. From that day in 1967 until the board made its decision a year later, my father made it a point not to mention my case to his friend. Though I was making a choice he would not have made, he felt I had the right to make my own decision and to face its consequences. As a result, he gave me a very great gift: the gift of learning who I was and what I valued on my own and for myself.

My very first demonstration could not have been more American. In May 1967, an official from the South Vietnamese embassy came to speak at a hall at Lafayette College, where I was a junior. A dozen people I knew stood in front with signs that read "Stop the Bombing." I was not one of them. For this, they were surrounded by hundreds of fraternity boys and subjected to hours of water-and-ink bombs and verbal abuse. The campus police were strangely absent. A rally was organized to support the right of free speech; my first antiwar demonstration was really for the First Amendment.

I wrote to congressmen and received polite replies that we should support the president. I joined the Committee Against the Crime of Silence and put my name on record at the United Nations as an opponent of my government's war in Vietnam. I wrote editorials for my college newspaper and took part in antiwar demonstrations. Looking back now, you see pictures of large demonstrations, mighty throngs of people choking the streets of major cities and chanting slogans. But in the beginning, it was different. I and a dozen other students and faculty members would go down to the town square of Easton, Pennsylvania, population 30,000, and stand for one hour in silent witness, protesting the war. The people who passed us were not always friendly; we were reminding them of unpleasant events far away, and many mistook our opposition to the war as opposition to the country. I handed out leaflets at the Second Methodist Church and then attended the worship service. I heard myself denounced from the pulpit as a "tool of the Moscow line" by the minister. It was the beginning of my education into the nature and power of authority.

You see, in the beginning, I thought it would be easy. Americans were being misled by their government. All we had to do was give them more information, tell them what really was going on in Vietnam, and Americans would rise up and demand that their government stop the war. I came to see that for many citizens the issue was not truth or falsehood but obedience or resistance to authority. In arguments repeated in homes all over the country, my objections to the war were met with the reply, "The president knows more than we do. This is a democracy. We have to support the president."

Fortunately for me and for all antiwar protesters, this country has a long tradition of resistance to authority. The tradition of conscientious objection is even older, arriving with the first Quakers in 1635. James Madison, one of the architects of the U.S. Constitution, proposed making objection to war a constitutional right. Conscientious objection is as American as cherry pie. You see how fortunate I was. I could oppose American policy in Vietnam secure in the knowledge that I was upholding the finest American ideals. It was not I who was betraying America, it was Lyndon Johnson and his government.

My claim to conscientious-objector status was not based on traditional religious beliefs. In fact, I was interviewed earlier by my college's alumni magazine as an example of an agnostic. Until 1965, you could be released from military service only if you could demonstrate that your opposition to participation in war was by reason of "religious training or belief." But in 1965 the Supreme Court had ruled that a person could not be denied CO status simply because he did not belong to an orthodox religious sect. It was enough, the high court ruled, if the belief that prompted your decision occupied the same place in your life that the belief in a traditional deity occupied in the life of a believer.

I knew I objected to the war in Vietnam. What I had to discover was the ultimate source of that objection and describe it for myself and for the five ordinary Americans who comprised draft board no. 90 in Allentown, Pennsylvania, in the space provided on Special Form 150. The first question on that form was, "Do you believe in a Supreme Being?" There were two boxes: YES/NO. I checked YES. Second item: "Describe the nature of your belief which is the basis of your claim and state whether or not your belief in a Supreme Being involves duties which to you are superior to those arising from any human relation." Here is part of what I wrote:

Because I believe that from man all awareness and order come, because I believe that each man is a divine being striving to become more divine, and because I believe that divinity manifests itself only through the love and justice of human relationships, I believe that human relationships are the highest relationships. Therefore there are no duties which to me are superior to those arising from human relations.

I made a point to get letters of support not only from people who agreed with my position but from those who disagreed as well, including the dean and the president of my college, who surely didn't appreciate the trouble I was causing them but who could confirm that I was sincere. I was lucky, of course. Lucky to have heard of conscientious objection, no doubt thanks to the influence of Quakers and small peace churches in the section of Pennsylvania where I grew up. Lucky to have witnessed Martin Luther King, Jr., lead black people in civil disobedience to gain basic American rights. Lucky to live at a time when lower-middle-class kids like me were able to go to college in unprecedented numbers, and once there, lucky to read authors like Henry David Thoreau and Albert Camus and to have the time to reflect on what it might mean to be a conscientious objector to war.

I filed for conscientious-objector status on the first day of spring 1968. I did not know what I would do if the draft board refused my claim. I did know I would not enter the military. I felt I was prepared to go to prison rather than flee to Canada, but, fortunately, I never had to find out. On June 14, Flag Day, my draft board informed me that I had been classified 1–O, a conscientious objector.

Three days later I began working for the New York City Department of Social Services, where a conscientious objector I knew was performing his alternative service, and I was given a case load of families in central Harlem. My draft board informed me that they did not expect to receive a call for draftees until the fall, which meant I could sit it out and possibly not be called. Instead, I volunteered for two years' alternative service. When I was called for a physical examination in September, I informed my draft board I would not appear, which meant I would be passed automatically. All around me young men were going to war or to prison,

and I did not want to avoid service. I remember telling people at the time that twenty years into the future, if my children asked what I had done during the Vietnam War, I did not want to tell them that I had gotten out on a technicality. It is now twenty years later, and my son knows that his father is one of 170,000 who were granted CO status during the Vietnam War and one of 96,000 who completed the two years of alternative service.

The war in Vietnam and the draft of men who fought that war forced me and hundreds of thousands of other young men to ask themselves what values they were willing to suffer and die for, at an age when we were just learning to think for ourselves about such questions. One way or another, those of us who had to make a choice revealed what authority we were willing to obey, be it the authority of family, public opinion, country, or conscience. For many, the consequences of their choices have been harsh and lasting. I am one of the lucky ones; I have no regrets. And though two decades ago I took a stand different from those who volunteered or consented to fight the war, we now stand together on the common ground of grief as people who understand all too well that life is morally serious, that the choices we make matter.

Focus: Chicago

In the words of the presidential candidate nominated at the 1968 Democratic Convention, "Chicago was a catastrophe. My wife and I went home heartbroken, battered and beaten. I told her I felt just like we had been in a shipwreck." While its participants knew the convention would be a struggle, none could predict just how disastrous it would be for the Democratic party and, indeed, for the nation.

Robert Kennedy's death had all but assured that the nomination would go to Vice President Humphrey, but his accession to the party's leadership would not be unopposed. In the weeks that followed the assassination, Senator McCarthy's campaign gained fresh momentum, propelling him to victory in the June 18 New York primary and bringing a substantial influx of much-needed money. A small boomlet of support also began to gather around Senator George McGovern of South Dakota, after family members and aides of Robert Kennedy gave him their endorsement. There was even talk in some party circles of a possible convention draft for Senator Edward Kennedy of Massachusetts, Bobby's younger brother.

Nor were the politicians the only ones planning to exert their influence on the proceedings of the convention. Under the leadership of the National Mobilization Committee to End the War, a number of antiwar groups were hoping to rally as many as half a million protesters in Chicago while the delegates met. Members of the outlandish Youth International Party, or Yippies, also planned to be in attendance and hold their own mock convention, culminating in the nomination of "Pigasus," a live pig, as their party standard bearer. Far more serious were the intentions and objectives of the Reverend Ralph Abernathy, the man who had succeeded Dr. Martin Luther King, Jr., as head of the Southern Christian Leadership Conference. Determined to remind the Democratic party of the broken promise of the Great Society, Abernathy had decided to bring a group of poverty-stricken Americans to the doors of the convention hall as part of his recently launched Poor People's Campaign.

Fearing the worst, Mayor Richard Daley of Chicago prepared for the onslaught by placing the entire metropolitan police force of 12,000 on week-long, twelve-hour shifts. More than 5,000 Illinois National Guardsmen were also deployed to the city, while an additional 7,500 regular army troops were placed on twenty-four-hour alert. The convention site itself was especially well fortified, its main entrance barricaded with barbed wire and chain-link fence and its approaches guarded by some 2,000 police.

As it turned out, Daley's well-publicized security measures, together with his refusal to grant marching permits, dissuaded large numbers of would-be demonstrators from going to Chicago. The 10,000 youthful protesters who did eventually arrive, however, were among the more committed apostles of the antiwar movement. Though most had no intention of provoking violence, some clearly expected a confrontation. "To remain passive in the face of escalating police brutality is foolish and degrading," one young activist told a reporter. "We're going to march and they're going to stop us," said another. "How can you avoid violence?"

And violence there was. On Sunday, August 25, the eve of the convention, and again the next night, riot police moved in with nightsticks and tear gas to disperse demonstrators who had encamped in Lincoln Park in defiance of an 11:00 P.M. curfew. The protesters then moved on to Grant Park, where they began laying plans to march on the amphitheater. As darkness fell on Wednesday evening, August 28, a crowd of 5,000 or more gathered in the park across from the Conrad Hilton Hotel on Michigan Avenue, the city's central thoroughfare. There they remained until some caught sight of Rev. Abernathy and his supporters from the Poor People's Campaign, the only group that had been granted a legal permit to march. Beckoned by shouts of "Join us!" several thousand antiwar protesters surged forward, crossed a small bridge to Michigan Avenue, and fell in behind Abernathy's motley train.

Inside the convention hall, meanwhile, a bitter battle over the Vietnam plank of the Democratic party platform was coming to a head. Although by that point Senator McCarthy had all but conceded the nomination to Humphrey, a large bloc of antiwar delegates from New York, California, Wisconsin, and several other states were determined to put their stamp on the party's official policy. Based on a minority report hammered out at the platform committee hearings the previous week, the dissidents' position called for "an unconditional end to all bombing of North Vietnam," the mutual withdrawal of all U.S. and North Vietnamese forces from South Vietnam, and a "political reconciliation" between the Saigon government and the Vietcong leading to a coalition government. By contrast, the majority plank recommended a gradual reduction of the U.S. troop presence "as the South Vietnamese are able to take over larger responsibilities" and a cessation of bombing only "when the action would not endanger U.S. lives." As speaker after speaker rose to defend his respective position, the debate turned increasingly acrimonious. Even before the final tally was read—1,567 in favor of the majority plank, 1,041 for the minority—the New York delegation began singing "We Shall Overcome," while spectators in the gallery chanted "Stop the War! Stop the War!"

As a result of the fight over the Vietnam plank, the nomination balloting was delayed until late in the evening. It was nearly 11:00 P.M., in fact, when Mayor Joseph Alioto of San Francisco stood before the convention to nominate Hubert Humphrey as the Democratic presidential candidate. Barely had Alioto begun to speak when CBS anchorman Walter Cronkite received news of a bloody clash between police and demonstrators outside the convention hall. "There has been a display of naked violence in the streets of Chicago," Cronkite declared, as he interrupted the convention proceedings to show a tape of events that had actually taken place more than two hours before. Ordered to halt and disperse the demonstrators who had set out from Grant Park, a phalanx of helmeted riot police had intercepted the marchers at the corner of Michigan Avenue and Balbo shortly before 8:00. When the protesters refused to move, the police first made a series of peaceful arrests, then charged into the crowd with their nightsticks flailing. While some of the demonstrators fought back, many fell limp and began screaming "The whole world is watching! The whole world is watching!"

As scenes of the violence appeared on television sets throughout the convention hall, the nominating process was soon overwhelmed by a series of angry denunciations of Mayor Daley and the Chicago police. The crescendo of criticism reached its peak when Senator Abraham Ribicoff of Connecticut rose to deplore the "Gestapo tactics in the streets of Chicago," a choice of words that brought a stream of obscenities from the mayor himself. "How hard it is to accept the truth," Ribicoff replied, staring down at Daley from the podium. "How hard it is."

The formal balloting that followed proved anticlimactic, as Humphrey outdistanced his only serious challenger, Senator McCarthy, by more than 1,000 votes. For Humphrey, the nomination was a bitter prize indeed. The tumultuous Chicago convention had left the party he proposed to lead deeply, perhaps hopelessly divided, with only eight weeks to go before the general election. To defeat his formidable Republican challenger, Richard Nixon, who held a fifteen-percentage-point lead in the polls, he would have to use that time to bring the Democrats back together. In the process, he would also have to convince the electorate that he could restore unity to America by bringing peace to Vietnam.

Inside the convention hall, members of the New York delegation to the 1968 Democratic National Convention demonstrate their backing of the minority plank on the Vietnam War.

After several violent confrontations with police, demonstrators gather at Chicago's Grant Park on August 28, 1968, to prepare to march on the Democratic Convention.

217

Above. *A pair of hippies kiss in Lincoln Park.*

Left. *Police grab an antiwar demonstrator from the Logan monument in Grant Park, August 26.*

Violence in Grant Park on August 28. The demonstrator at center has just retrieved a tear-gas canister and thrown it back at the police.

Police beat back the antiwar protesters at Grant Park.

6

NIXON'S WAR

He began his 1968 campaign for the presidency with a promise "to end the war and win the peace," intimating that he had a "secret plan." Shedding the "loser" image that had plagued him since he lost the 1960 presidential race to John Kennedy, he stormed through the primaries and won the Republican nomination with ease. Now, in the early fall of 1968, Richard Milhous Nixon at last seemed poised to capture the prize that had so narrowly eluded him eight years before.

The tumultuous Chicago convention had left the Democratic party in a shambles. The liberals had all but abandoned Vice President Humphrey, and a sizable segment of the white working class had defected to the camp of populist third-party candidate George Wallace, the once and future Alabama governor who vowed to restore "law and order" to a nation in turmoil. As Humphrey set out on the campaign trail, hecklers greeted him with catcalls of "Fascist," "Warmonger," and "Dump the Hump," while state and local party leaders, wrote veteran political journalist Theodore White, "fled him as if he were the bearer of contagion."

Deprived of the funding and organizational support he needed to mount a successful campaign, Humphrey soon concluded that he had no choice but to distance himself from the president's discredited Vietnam policy. On September 30 he unveiled a new three-point peace initiative calling for a U.S. bombing halt, a turnover of the fighting to the South Vietnamese, and the withdrawal of all "foreign forces" from South Vietnam under UN supervision. Though the proposal differed only slightly from the administration's official position, it convinced many disaffected Democrats that the vice president was not simply "Johnson's boy." In the days that followed, money poured into the campaign treasury, volunteers joined up in droves, and the labor unions redoubled their efforts to bring the rank and file back to the fold. By the middle of October Nixon's lead in the polls had fallen from fifteen points to twelve; a week later it was down to eight.

Left. *Richard Nixon flashes his trademark victory sign at the 1968 Republican National Convention.*

Although Humphrey's sudden resurgence gave Nixon cause for concern, it did not induce him to panic. As in the past, the Republican challenger refused to be

wants to go," South Vietnamese president Nguyen Van Thieu flatly refused to join in any negotiations that included the Vietcong. As a result, when Johnson ap-

After the post-Tet 1969 offensive, a nun returns to her home in Dong Lach, a small village of Catholic refugees from North Vietnam thirty kilometers northeast of Saigon. The town's cluster of sheet-metal shacks, occupied by the Communists, were virtually destroyed by napalm and high-explosive bombs dropped by U.S. and South Vietnamese aircraft. At left is the body of an NVA soldier, quick-limed to dry it out and reduce putrefaction.

In the end, Nixon reluctantly shelved the Kissinger plan, at least for the time being. "I'm not sure we're ready for this," he told his aides. Whether he had actually become convinced that Vietnamization would work or simply feared the public's reaction to any bold military move remains unclear. At the time of his decision, Nixon's approval rating in the polls stood at an extraordinary 71 percent, largely as a result of his September announcement of a second troop withdrawal as well as a reduction in draft calls. Yet despite considerable public support, he had not been able to stop the spread of antiwar sentiment among the more vocal and influential elements of the population—labor leaders, educators, press commentators, clergy, and even corporate executives.

The extent to which antiwar protest had become respectable was demonstrated dramatically on October 15, when hundreds of thousands of middle-class Americans heeded the call of the organized peace movement to observe a national "Moratorium Day." Across the nation church bells tolled in remembrance of the American war dead, the names of those killed were read at candlelight services, and peaceful marchers sang the antiwar chant "Give Peace a Chance." Outside the United States, moratorium demonstrations were held in London, Paris, Copenhagen, Tokyo, and Sydney, while in Vietnam some American servicemen joined in the observance by wearing black arm bands on patrol.

Though he feigned indifference, the president was deeply angered and alarmed by the mass protests. Not only did such demonstrations encourage North Vietnamese intractability, but, perhaps more important in his view, they also threatened to undermine his own credibility. As a result, when antiwar leaders announced plans to hold a second moratorium on November 15, Nixon went on the counterattack. In a shrewdly crafted address to the nation on November 3, he staunchly defended the American commitment to Saigon, warning that an abrupt pullout would lead to a "bloodbath" in Vietnam and a loss of faith abroad in American leadership. He then proceeded to lay out his Vietnamization

Training the ARVN. U.S. Marines supervise South Vietnamese soldiers as they take aim with their M16 rifles.

238

On November 13, 1969, protesters parade
in single file through Washington, D.C.,
on the first night of a three-day antiwar
moratorium. Each of 40,000 marchers carried a candle and a sign bearing the name
of an American killed or a village destroyed by war in Vietnam.

plan in some detail, saying that it promised to reduce American casualties and bring the war to an end regardless of what the North Vietnamese did. Finally, against the advice of his entire cabinet, the president attacked the antiwar protesters as "irresponsible" and accused them of sabotaging his quest for an honorable peace. Appealing to what he called "the great silent majority," he asked for "united" support and concluded with a melodramatic admonition: "North Vietnam cannot defeat or humiliate the United States. Only Americans can do that."

Much to Nixon's delight, the response to his "silent majority" speech was overwhelmingly positive, once again boosting his standing in the polls and bringing a bipartisan vote of confidence from Congress. "We've got those liberal bastards on the run now," the president told his aides, "and we're going to keep them on the run." Entrusted with the job of keeping up the pursuit, Vice President Spiro Agnew broadened and intensified the administration's attacks on its domestic "enemies." Having already dismissed the antiwar protesters as "an effete corps of impudent snobs who characterize themselves as intellectuals," he now took on the "liberal establishment press," which he described as "a small and unelected elite" that "do not—I repeat not—represent the view of America."

Yet if the president and his men succeeded for the moment in putting their critics on the defensive, they soon learned that they could not silence them. The November 15 moratorium drew even more participants than the October demonstrations, as more than a quarter-million protesters converged on Washington, D.C., alone. Carrying placards bearing the names of U.S. war dead and describing themselves as the "Silent Majority for Peace," they served notice to the Nixon administration that there would be no lasting peace in America until there was peace in Vietnam.

Thus, as the year drew to a close, Nixon found himself engaged in a stalemate at every turn. The Paris peace talks remained deadlocked, the military balance in South Vietnam virtually unchanged, and the American public polarized over the proper course to pursue. Making matters worse, the American president was rapidly running out of options.

Nevertheless, by early 1970, as Nixon entered his second year in office, it looked as though Vietnamization might actually work. Supplied with huge quantities of the latest American weaponry and expanded to a force level of more than 1 million men, ARVN had already become one of the largest, best-equipped armies in the world. Many of its units had shown, moreover, that they could fight aggressively and effectively when well led, and in some cases they had even improved their performance after supporting U.S. forces were withdrawn.

Equally encouraging, allied efforts to extend government control over the countryside were at last beginning to bear fruit. In accordance with the "one war" strategy adopted by General Abrams in 1969, American and South Vietnamese forces had shifted their emphasis from large-scale search-and-destroy missions to smaller "clearing" operations designed to protect the rural population. Under the new pacification-oriented plan, elected village councils were entrusted with responsibility for local security, territorial defense forces were given formal training and equipped with M16s, and a variety of "civic action" programs were reintroduced to promote economic development. In conjunction with these self-help measures, the CIA's controversial Phoenix Program succeeded in inflicting severe damage to the Vietcong. According to U.S. Embassy figures, in 1969 alone nearly 20,000 VC cadres were "neutralized" through arrest or assassination under the auspices of Phoenix, sharply reducing the enemy's ability to tax and recruit.

Yet for all the new gains that had been made, many of the same old problems persisted. Despite its increased size and modern look, ARVN still suffered from a shortage of competent officers and NCOs, an abundance of corruption at almost every level, and a seemingly unshakable reliance on American advice and firepower. Despite improved security and increased democracy in the villages, signs of genuine enthusiasm for the Thieu government were still scarce. And despite the inroads of Phoenix, the Vietcong infrastructure remained intact, its relative inactivity in large part reflecting Hanoi's decision to wait until the Americans left for good.

In the opinion of many senior U.S. officials, what the South Vietnamese needed, above all, was more time. General Abrams, for one, strongly believed that the American pullout was proceeding too quickly, and he therefore urged the president to defer plans for another major troop withdrawal. But Nixon, under unrelenting domestic pressure to "bring the boys home," overruled his commander. Hoping to "drop a bombshell on the gathering spring storm of antiwar protest," as he put it, in late April Nixon announced that 150,000 more troops would be redeployed from Vietnam by the end of 1970. At the same time, however, he acceded to the military's long-standing request that allied ground forces be allowed to attack North Vietnamese sanctuaries inside Cambodia.

Nixon's decision to authorize a cross-border invasion seems to have been motivated by a variety of considerations. To begin with, he accepted the judgment of Abrams and other high-ranking military officials that such a move would relieve pressure on U.S. forces guarding Saigon and buy valuable time for Vietnamization.

In addition, he had not yet abandoned his conviction that he could bludgeon the North Vietnamese into a compromise settlement through a dramatic show of force. An unexpected thrust into theoretically neutral Cambodia would prove once again that he was willing to take more extreme measures than had President Johnson, compelling Hanoi to decide "whether they want to take us on all over again." Finally, the recent overthrow of Cambodia's neutralist leader, Prince Norodom Sihanouk, by the pro-American Lon Nol provided a previously lacking rationale for widening the war. By mid-April Cambodia was in a state of near anarchy. North Vietnamese and Khmer Rouge forces were pushing the Cambodian army back into the interior, and Lon Nol, with American encouragement, was openly calling for outside help. "We need a bold move . . . to show that we stand with Lon Nol," Nixon informed Kissinger on April 26. Even though he might fall anyway, "we must

As the war progressed, nonstandard dress became standard for the increasingly ambivalent fighting force. Here, men of the 1st Cavalry Division (Airmobile) pause in Cambodia's Fishhook region during the invasion of enemy rear bases there in May 1970.

Death at Kent State. A young woman screams in anguish as she kneels over the body of Jeffrey Glen Miller, felled in fire by National Guardsmen on May 4, 1970.

do something symbolic" for the only Cambodian leader in the last twenty-five years "with the guts to take a pro-Western and pro-American stand."

The president revealed his decision on the evening of April 30, 1970, in a televised speech that was, in Kissinger's words, "vintage Nixon." Rather than soft-selling his action simply as a matter of "good tactics," as the military had recommended, he attempted to justify the Cambodian "incursion" in hyperbolic, even global terms. The North Vietnamese, he contended, were preparing "to launch massive attacks on our forces and those of the South Vietnamese" from their sanctuaries in Cambodia. Hanoi was testing the "will and character" of the United States in an effort to expose

"the world's most powerful nation" as a "pitiful, helpless giant." Failure to respond to the enemy's "direct challenge" would only encourage "the forces of totalitarianism and anarchy [to] threaten free nations and free institutions throughout the world." Spurning "all political considerations," Nixon declared, he had decided to follow his conscience rather than be "a two-term president at the cost of seeing America . . . accept the first defeat in its sound 190-years' history."

Even as Nixon spoke, South Vietnamese forces were already operating inside the Parrot's Beak, a narrow protrusion of Cambodian territory northwest of Saigon, having first crossed the border on April 29. Two days later, on the morning of May 1, a combined U.S.-

ARVN force of 15,000 men plunged into the Fishhook region farther north. Moving behind a shield of heavy artillery fire and air strikes, columns of tanks and armored personnel carriers of the 11th Armored Cavalry Regiment led the way, followed by troop-laden helicopters of the 1st Cavalry Division (Airmobile). Though the invading troops expected to meet with heavy resistance, it soon became apparent that the North Vietnamese had fled in advance, leaving behind vast storehouses of weapons, ammunition, and other war materiel. The allied command had also hoped to discover COSVN (Central Office for South Vietnam), the alleged headquarters for all Communist forces operating in the South. Instead they found only "a scattering of empty huts" that bore little resemblance to the miniature Pentagon they had imagined. The Americans nevertheless pronounced the operation a success, since the destruction of the enemy's base camps relieved any immediate threat to the heavily populated Saigon–Bien Hoa corridor.

If the military benefits of the Cambodian invasion fell short of Nixon's hopes, the domestic reaction to it exceeded his worst expectations. As prominent media commentators lashed out at the president, university campuses across the country erupted in protest, in some instances with tragic results. On May 4, thirteen Kent State students were shot, four of them fatally, by Ohio National Guardsmen sent in to maintain "law and order." Several days later, two more students were killed at Jackson State College in Mississippi during an angry confrontation with local police. By the end of the first week in May, hundreds of thousands of students and faculty had gone on strike to protest the shootings, prompting more than 400 colleges and universities to shut down entirely.

The expansion of the war into Cambodia also provoked an angry response from Congress. In the first direct challenge to presidential authority since the beginning of the war, the Senate voted overwhelmingly in June to rescind the Gulf of Tonkin Resolution of 1964. Senators John Sherman Cooper of Kentucky and Frank Church of Idaho drafted a resolution setting a June 30 deadline for the termination of all U.S. military operations in Cambodia, while Senators George McGovern

of South Dakota and Mark Hatfield of Oregon cosponsored an even more restrictive proposal requiring a total U.S. pullout from Vietnam by the end of 1971.

Characteristically, Nixon immediately launched a counterattack. The time had come to stop "screwing around" with his Congressional opponents, he told his staff. "Don't worry about divisiveness. Having drawn the sword, don't take it out—stick it in hard. Hit 'em in the gut." Warning that if "Congress undertakes to restrict me, Congress will have to assume the consequences," he blamed his adversaries for undermining U.S. credibility and prolonging the war. He also ordered the formation of a special covert team to monitor his domestic critics and verify suspected links between radical groups in the U.S. and foreign governments. The project represented one of the most serious abuses of presidential authority in U.S. history and would later come under investigation during the 1973 Watergate hearings.

In the end neither the Cooper-Church amendment nor the more extreme McGovern-Hatfield proposal won the approval of Congress, in part because most legislators were still unwilling to accept responsibility for the war and in part because Nixon stole the opposition's thunder by removing all U.S. troops from Cambodia before June 30. Yet if the president had survived the latest crisis with his authority intact, his options for future action were more restricted than ever. The Cambodian venture may have bought time for Vietnamization, but it had neither seriously diminished Hanoi's capacity to make war nor broken the deadlock in negotiations. It had also provoked the most violent outburst of antiwar protest since the war began, intensifying pressure to speed up the pace of the American withdrawal and imposing clear limits on the future use of U.S. combat troops. A year and a half after Richard Nixon assumed the presidency, the war that he had pledged to end was still going on, and the peace that he promised to win was still not in sight.

Focus: The Cambodian Incursion

From the outset of the Vietnam War the Communists enjoyed one enormous advantage over their American adversaries: the network of secure bases and staging areas just beyond the boundaries of South Vietnam. American intelligence eventually located fourteen major enemy bases inside Cambodia, some only thirty-five miles from Saigon. MACV repeatedly sought permission to launch operations against these sanctuaries; President Johnson, who wanted to contain the ground war and feared the political repercussions of violating the territory of "neutral" states, just as regularly refused. Johnson's prohibitions frustrated American troops who believed that if they were allowed to pursue the North Vietnamese across the frontier, they could hurt the enemy where he lived. Fifteen months after he came to office, Richard Nixon gave them the chance.

On May 1, 1970, following a predawn air and artillery bombardment, tanks and armored personnel carriers (APCs) of the 11th Armored Cavalry Regiment churned across the border into the Fishhook, a narrow swath of land jutting into Binh Long Province. Overhead, wave after wave of CH–47 Chinook helicopters carried troopers from the 1st Air Cavalry Division into landing zones blasted out of the jungle by gigantic 15,000-pound bombs. "This Cambodian operation is pure blitzkrieg," one senior U.S. officer told a reporter, "like something from a World War II Panzer division's book of tactics."

While 1st Cav troopers consolidated their positions and fanned out in search of the enemy, the 11th Cavalry brushed through scattered RPG fire along the frontier, then rolled north across flat, open terrain. Late in the afternoon the tanks collided with an entrenched North Vietnamese battalion. The ensuing fight "looked like the Fourth of July," recalled 11th Cav commander Brigadier General Donn Starry. For sixty minutes the Americans blasted enemy bunkers from the ground with tank-mounted cannon fire and pounded them from the sky with tactical air strikes. When the stubborn defenders were finally driven from their fortifications, fifty-two NVA dead lay sprawled across the smoking battlefield.

By and large, however, the Americans encountered only scattered resistance. Well aware of the armored might being readied across the border, most enemy units had chosen discretion over valor and withdrawn to the west ahead of the American advance.

Most, but not all. On May 4 the 11th Cavalry was ordered to proceed to the town of Snuol, a strategically located supply depot still occupied by a large enemy force. The 100-tank column raced north along Highway 7 at speeds of up to sixty-five miles per hour, throwing armored-vehicle-launched bridges (AVLBs) across three rivers and reaching the outskirts of Snuol by the afternoon of the fifth. Immediately the tanks formed up and stormed the town's airstrip, using canisters filled with thousands of steel pellets to silence enemy positions. Once the airstrip was secured, the tanks advanced toward the central marketplace where they were met by concentrated rocket and automatic-weapons fire.

For the rest of the day and through the night air force fighter-bombers screamed through the sky plastering the town with napalm and high explosives. Periodically the tanks returned to the task, firing volley after volley of cannon fire into the crumbling, burning buildings, while helicopter gunships rocketed pockets of enemy resistance and mortars crashed into the rubble. When the 11th Cavalry entered the city on the morning of May 6 there was nothing left but ruins. The NVA had fled during the night. The only bodies were those of four civilians. "We didn't want to blow this town away," said one senior officer, "but we had no choice." American troops coined a new word after the battle—to "snuol," meaning to obliterate.

Yet the fighting of the first few days only cleared the way for what turned out to be the real work of the operation. Hoping to bag enemy troops the Americans found themselves instead the heir to the enemy's treasure, for the fleeing NVA had left behind a staggering quantity of equipment and supplies. Infantrymen from the 1st Cavalry Division organized the search around fire support bases established throughout the Fishhook. Working in tandem with teams of light observation helicopters and Cobra gunships, the troopers immediately began locating enormous hoards of enemy arms and ammunition.

One of the most remarkable finds was "The City," a two-square-mile complex buried deep in the jungle south of Snuol complete with street signs, barracks, mess halls, classrooms, firing range, lumberyard, recreation hall, swimming pool, and pig farm. Inside the 400 huts, storage sheds, and bunkers linked by three-foot-deep trenches and miles of tunnels the troopers found 60,000 pounds of rice, 16,000 pounds of corn, 58,000 pounds of plastic explosives, 1.5 million rounds of ammunition, 300 trucks, more than 200 crew-served weapons, and enough small arms for fifty-five battalions. Two days later and forty kilometers northeast, 1st Cav soldiers discovered another NVA installation the troopers dubbed Rock Island East after the Rock Island Arsenal in Illinois. The Cambodian version, the largest cache of enemy materiel ever captured during the war, contained in all some 329 tons of munitions.

The spectacular booty uncovered in the Fishhook overshadowed what was happening 100 kilometers to the south, where an elite ARVN task force scoured the Parrot's Beak, the principal enemy staging area for the 1968 Tet offensive. Driving into Cambodia two days before U.S. forces kicked off their part of the operation, the South Vietnamese had to blast their way through enemy rear-guard units before seizing the provincial capital of Svay Rieng. But here, too, the bulk of North Vietnamese troops had disappeared. Nonetheless, reinforcements poured across the border, eventually bringing ARVN strength in Cambodia to 18,000 men. Some devoted their attention to enemy base areas and supply caches. Others launched wide-ranging mobile forays deep inside Cambodian territory.

By the second week of the operation the U.S. had 30,000 troops of its own in Cambodia, including elements of the 4th and 25th Infantry Divisions. What American commanders did not have was the same freedom enjoyed by their South Vietnamese counterparts. Responding to a storm of domestic protest, President Nixon announced that the incursion would penetrate no deeper than thirty-four kilometers and conclude by June 30. Although U.S. gunships, fighter-bombers, and B–52s continued to pummel suspected enemy positions and special land-clearing units slashed through the dense forest with giant Rome plows, American ground troops had to content themselves with the backbreaking work of emptying the enemy sanctuaries. Engineers built roads to haul out as much as possible, and smaller caches were simply put to the torch. But supplies continued to be discovered faster than they could be destroyed.

In mid-May the Communists launched scattered assaults on American firebases in what appeared to be the prelude to a concerted counterattack. But the arrival of the monsoon rains in early June brought fighting on both sides to a halt. On June 28, two days before the president's deadline, the last American tanks rumbled back across the border while U.S. air and artillery hammered what was left of the enemy sanctuaries with a farewell bombardment.

When they first learned they would be going into Cambodia, many GIs had reacted with pleasure. As one helicopter pilot put it, "We had lost many men in combat assaults near the Cambodia border while the gooks would go back into Cambodia, sit there, and laugh at us, so we were all together for going in."

In American terms they largely got what they wanted. The incursion dealt the enemy a significant setback, killing an estimated 4,776 men, destroying nearly 12,000 bunkers, capturing enough rice to feed every Communist unit in South Vietnam for four months, enough ammunition for ten months, and enough individual weapons to equip seventy-four battalions. The resulting decline in enemy activity sharply reduced U.S. casualties during the remainder of the year. That enemy Main-Force units had largely escaped intact, that much of the supplies would be replaced within a few months, and that the boundaries of the war had been irreversibly widened were facts the South Vietnamese and Cambodians would ultimately have to face. U.S. ground troops had delivered their last major blow of the war.

South Vietnamese marines rush past a transport helicopter near Neak Luong during the Cambodian incursion, May 1970. South Vietnamese units initiated the invasion on April 29 with an assault into the Parrot's Beak section of Cambodia jutting into South Vietnam.

While his buddy keeps watch, a soldier from the 11th Armored Cavalry checks an enemy bunker in the Parrot's Beak, May 2.

A trooper from the 1st Cavalry Division examines one of the hundreds of SKS rifles found in this Communist bunker in Cambodia's Fishhook, another area reaching into its eastern neighbor. American combat troops spent most of their two months in Cambodia removing captured supplies and destroying abandoned enemy sanctuaries.

Men of the 3d Battalion, 23d Infantry, 25th Infantry Division, take up positions outside the village of Ph Tasuos just south of the Fishhook, five kilometers inside Cambodia, in early May.

Above. *Soldiers from the 25th Infantry Division drag away a buddy killed by sniper fire coming from Ph Tasuos.*

Right. *As other men of the 25th Infantry move to a safer position, a Cobra gunship strikes the village.*

A tank from the 3d Squadron, 11th Armored Cavalry, rumbles through the Fishhook heading toward South Vietnam. On June 28, the last American armored vehicles made their way out of Cambodia.

Witness: Al Santoli

In the wake of the Tet offensive, American and South Vietnamese units struggled to regain and control areas that had been contested or even lost in the attack. Particularly important was the populated countryside between Saigon and the Cambodian border, where North Vietnamese and Vietcong units attacked U.S. and ARVN forces, then slipped to the sanctuary of Cambodia. One of the members of a combined U.S./ARVN reconnaissance team in this area was Al Santoli, a sergeant with the 25th Infantry Division from March 1968 to March 1969.

In my time in Vietnam, I came to understand that there were actually two wars going on simultaneously, each as important as the other. The first was the conventional war against regular North Vietnamese units; the second was for the support of the population, winning the "hearts and minds" of the people, who for the most part simply wanted both sides of the war to stop disrupting their lives. It was in this second aspect of the conflict that I had my most valuable experience in Vietnam, one that gave me a unique view of the war and of human nature—my role in a CRIP platoon.

As an eighteen-year-old infantryman with the 25th Division, I had fought along the Cambodian border west of Saigon. In fierce encounters during the 1968 post-Tet counteroffensive, I was wounded three different times.

Then from October 1968 to February 1969 I served in a Combined Reconnaissance and Intelligence Platoon (CRIP) with twenty Americans and twenty South Viet-

namese and lived along the North Vietnamese invasion route to the capital, independent of American forces. Our headquarters was a small fortified village in the Kiem Hanh District, near the city of Tay Ninh and a short hike from North Vietnamese Army sanctuaries in Cambodia. We were told that the area's tunnels housed the Vietcong's elusive COSVN headquarters, from where their leaders coordinated the war in the South.

Our small group was a cross section of America: Mike Andrews, our leader, was a West Point graduate from North Carolina; Steve Zontek was from California orange country; "Tree" Maples was a small-town philosopher from Michigan; "Frenchy" was a Louisiana Cajun; and I was a street kid from Cleveland. All of us were learning to think one step ahead of the VC. Intelligence reports and assignments came to us from MACV, Vietnamese Province Command, the U.S. 25th Division, and our own sources. We were able to chart our own destiny, and we were very lucky.

American infantry units operated under a tactical umbrella of artillery support. But our CRIP platoon, far removed from American fire support bases, had to rely on the loyalty of the black-pajama-clad villagers, who were as fearful and suspicious of us as we were of them. Although the twenty GIs in our platoon had only limited knowledge of the Vietnamese language and culture, we had no choice but to learn to coexist with villagers in an area notorious for Vietcong activity.

Our objective was to monitor NVA troop movement out of Cambodia. If we could locate them in the forests of Tay Ninh and pinpoint their bases for air strikes, countless South Vietnamese and American lives would be saved. Communist strategy during and after the Tet offensive was to turn populated areas into battlefields. They wanted American firepower to "destroy villages in order to save them" and to create unintentional civilian casualties. Such destruction would cause bitter feelings toward American and South Vietnamese soldiers among a traditionally xenophobic population and produce news photos and television images that horrified the international community.

During Tet the Main-Force Vietcong guerrillas had been decimated, but surviving VC cadres still served important roles as spies, tax collectors, saboteurs, and guides for the North Vietnamese forces. In the villages along the Cambodian border they dealt swift and brutal "justice" to peasants who showed loyalty to the Saigon government or refused to contribute support.

It was hard for a regular infantry soldier to understand the pressure the people lived under. Their silence and lack of cooperation earned them the label "VC" or "VC sympathizer." After a few months of living among them, we came to understand that thirty years of continuous war and their precarious location near Communist base areas had taught them that silence was their only hope for survival. In discussions with many of these farmers I learned that they had no interest in politics, taxes, or armies. They wished only to continue their ancestral heritage and work their land in peace. I think they came to understand that we were risking our lives for them to have the peace they desperately hoped for. We awkwardly tried to understand their ways, ate their food, and attended local ceremonies. An unusual bond developed between us. We became friends. And in a contested area, friendship can have a heavy price.

COSVN did not take kindly to our success and was always seeking to destroy us. We learned that whenever we left a campsite, VC agents would come in to search through garbage and to plant booby traps, expecting us to return. We began surprising them by leaving behind an ambush team of three to six of our people who turned the tables on the saboteurs. But they kept after us; years later, in Europe, a former COSVN security chief, now a refugee, showed me on a map where the VC had sent out teams to hunt for us.

We rarely camped near any particular location for more than one or two nights. Once we got a little complacent or tired, though, and stayed almost a week near one village. Every morning a little girl would ride by us on her bicycle, giving us a warm grin. One morning an explosion rocked our camp. We ran to the road and found a huge mine crater and a crumpled bicycle blown fifty meters away. The little girl was gone. Her parents were walking circles around the crater, weeping and searching. We tried to find the child, but all that remained of her was a handful of pieces of flesh. The mother used chopsticks to place them tenderly in a plastic bag. The bomb had been meant for us.

We learned to move silently through thick underbrush, using the cover of trees to our advantage. We could not risk traveling on trails or exposing ourselves in open clearings. And we learned to look for signs like footprints or broken foliage that would often lead to NVA base camps or supply caches.

One day we received fire from what seemed to be a North Vietnamese outpost. We probed the area and found what turned out to be a regimental headquarters. Because of the small size of our patrol and teamwork we were able to maneuver quickly as we drew fire. Luck was on our side. Though we had underestimated the size of the enemy camp, they too were taken by surprise. Four or five armored personnel carriers attached to our team came to our rescue with .50-caliber machine guns providing a fierce base of fire, which gave the illusion that we were a much larger force. We were able to withdraw quickly with only one casualty.

By living with the people and sharing their fears I realized that no matter how valiantly American soldiers performed in combat, the key to winning the population's support was respect for their traditions. Through our Vietnamese platoon members we had prolonged discussions with villagers who expressed their hopes for a better life and their desire just to be left alone. Discreetly, they confided their distrust and fear of the Vietcong and North Vietnamese soldiers who took both their rice and their sons. At the same time it was obvious that there was a very effective VC shadow presence that made them reluctant to cooperate with the South Vietnamese government.

Through my relationship with these proud people I learned that regardless of our many differences, we had a lot in common. To me they weren't just "gooks." And to many of them, the soldiers in the CRIP were no longer "long nose" barbarians, as Americans were often disrespectfully called. With the passive support of the villagers we were able to beat the VC and North Vietnamese on their own turf, and we helped deny them the ability to launch surprise attacks on outposts or towns. At the same time we gained respect and understanding for the people we were protecting.

7

THE LONG GOOD-BYE

There was no longer any talk of victory in the aftermath of the Cambodian incursion. The primary U.S. objectives in Vietnam had become the rapid withdrawal of American forces and the transfer of military responsibility to the South Vietnamese. Because the Nixon administration insisted that this must be accomplished with a minimum of U.S. casualties, American combat operations would be permitted only for the purposes of defense or to "stimulate a negotiated settlement" with the Communists.

At the beginning of 1970 the United States had an estimated 450,000 troops stationed in South Vietnam. By the end of 1971 only 184,000 remained. One by one American units assembled their men for stand-down ceremonies replete with speeches and ritual flag lowerings, withdrew from outlying bases into coastal enclaves or populated areas, and prepared to return home. The 9th Infantry Division and 3d Marine Division, which had left Vietnam in the last months of 1969, were soon followed home by the 1st Infantry Division, which left in April 1970, and in October by the 199th Infantry Brigade. During December the bulk of the 4th and 25th Infantry Divisions headed home. April 1971 witnessed the departure of the 1st Marine Division, 1st Cavalry Division, and 11th Armored Cavalry Regiment, followed in August by the 1st Brigade of the 5th Infantry Division. One month later the 173d Airborne Brigade quit Vietnam after six long years of service, followed in November by two brigades of the 23d Infantry Division. By the middle of 1971, the ARVN had taken over nearly two hundred and fifty American bases and other installations.

As more and more American soldiers left Vietnam, those who remained found their role increasingly limited to protective security and static defense. Since General Creighton Abrams succeeded William Westmoreland as MACV chief in June 1968, U.S. forces had steadily abandoned multibattalion forays into remote frontier regions. Some units continued to mount sweep operations and mobile reconnaissance efforts. By the end of 1970,

During Operation Lam Son 719, a UH–1 "slick" lifts a helicopter downed by Communist fire.

though, most of the Americans' time was devoted to shielding the lowland population from attack through constant patrolling and the destruction of Communist supply caches, without which the enemy could not sustain offensive operations. The shift away from the earlier large search-and-destroy operations and General Abrams's insistence that the enemy be fought on his own terms made the war more than ever a contest in which platoons, even squads, became major actors in the military drama.

The change placed enormous responsibility on the shoulders of inexperienced junior officers and NCOs, whose jobs were made more difficult by serious manpower shortages that regularly sent companies and platoons into the field at half-strength or less. Moreover, those troops who were available exhibited little of the discipline or enthusiasm of the men who served before them. If some commanders were still able to inspire troops to effective, aggressive action, many others were less interested in hunting the enemy or capturing a tactical objective than in seeing to it that their men returned home safely.

In any case, the enemy was making himself very difficult to find. The staggering losses suffered by the Communists during the Tet offensive of 1968 and the yearlong American counterattack that followed forced Hanoi to break up most of its Main-Force and local units and curtail conventional attacks in favor of guerrilla activities that maintained military pressure without risking large additional casualties. Meanwhile, the Politburo rebuilt its forces in preparation for the day when the Americans left South Vietnam.

The Cambodian incursion and the overthrow of the Sihanouk government by pro-American General Lon Nol in the spring of 1970 made the Communist task much more difficult. Not only did these events set back Hanoi's schedule, they also forced the redeployment of four divisions from Vietnam and the border sanctuaries to protect vital North Vietnamese lines of supply in the

In November 1971, American soldiers board the "freedom bird" that will carry them back to the United States from Bien Hoa airfield outside Saigon. By then, U.S. troop strength had been reduced from its 1969 high of more than 500,000 to 180,000.

eastern half of Cambodia. Those enemy units that remained in South Vietnam continued to harass allied installations with mortar and rocket attacks and occasionally marshaled sufficient forces to mount ground assaults against U.S. fire support bases. By and large, however, the Communists avoided battle. "Things were so quiet during the final four months of 1970," recalled one army intelligence officer, "we were almost tripping over each other in an effort to find something to do."

The relative calm was shattered at the end of January 1971 when an American task force composed of artillery, airborne, engineer, armored cavalry, infantry, and aviation units—10,000 troops, 2,000 fixed-wing aircraft, and 600 helicopters—launched Operation Dewey Canyon II to clear Route 9 and reopen Khe Sanh Combat Base in preparation for a major ARVN penetration of Laos, Operation Lam Son 719. Once the South Vietnamese crossed the border on February 8, American pilots played a crucial air support and logistics role in the subsequent fighting. Battling ferocious antiaircraft fire, U.S. Army aviators flew some 100,000 helicopter sorties during a seven-week operation that ultimately cost the Americans more than 1,400 casualties, including 253 killed and missing, plus the loss of more than 100 aircraft.

During the remainder of the year American aircraft continued to pound the Ho Chi Minh Trail and provide support to government forces in Laos and Cambodia, while a renewed air campaign against North Vietnam struck military targets in the demilitarized zone and the Hanoi-Haiphong area. On the ground in South Vietnam, however, there was little action. U.S. troops near Saigon fought occasional sharp encounters against enemy bunker complexes, and the 23d Infantry (Americal) Division's 11th Infantry Brigade spent weeks in futile pursuit of the Vietcong province headquarters in Quang Ngai. When 101st Airborne troopers completed the construction of three firebases in coastal Thua Thien Province and wrapped up Operation Jefferson Glenn on October 8, they brought to an end the last major American ground combat operation of the war.

Most of the American troops remaining in Vietnam during 1971 spent their time guarding military bases, urban areas, and highways or sweeping back and forth across the so-called rocket belts that encircled major cities and critical installations. It could be a dangerous assignment, for the Vietcong laced their launching sites with booby traps. Indeed, these brutal devices were taking a far heavier toll of GIs than was enemy fire. Meanwhile, the Communists avoided direct contact except where lax security left strategically placed U.S. installations vulnerable to attack.

Such was the case at Fire Support Base Mary Ann, a 23d Infantry Division outpost in the western highlands of Quang Tin Province manned by a battalion of the 196th Infantry Brigade. In the early morning hours of March 28 a company of NVA sappers cut through the unguarded perimeter and swarmed over Mary Ann behind a barrage of 82MM mortar rounds. In no more than half an hour they were gone, having killed or wounded half of the firebase's 250 defenders, including most of the officers, at a cost of only 10 of their own dead. The disaster prompted a full-scale investigation that culminated in disciplinary action against six officers, among them the division and assistant division commanders, but did little to arrest the steady deterioration that bedeviled American forces as they waited to disengage from a war they no longer wanted to fight.

The sharp decline in the number of encounters with the enemy from mid-1970 on meant a similar decline in the number of U.S. casualties. Yet, the period of withdrawal was in some ways far more damaging to American military forces in Vietnam than the years of heaviest combat.

The defensive posture mandated by Washington left most soldiers with little sense of mission other than personal survival. This situation might have been controlled had the army's officer corps maintained the high standards of professionalism with which it entered the war. Unfortunately, by 1970 the cumulative impact of college deferments, declining ROTC enrollments, careerism within the military, and the Johnson administration's decision not to call up the Reserves had degraded the overall quality and competence of the junior officers sent to Vietnam. Coupled with an uncertain schedule of unit withdrawals and the news of mounting antiwar protests back home, these conditions provoked

Bodies of villagers gunned down by soldiers of the U.S. 23d Infantry Division (Americal) lie across a road in the village of My Lai 4 on March 16, 1968. The so-called My Lai massacre was the most publicized atrocity committed by either side during the war.

within the disengagement army an epidemic of "short-timer's fever" that corroded morale and seriously threatened discipline both on and off the battlefield.

The contagion manifested itself in growing tension between draftees and "lifers," the career officers and NCOs still intent on fighting the war in earnest. It could be seen in the "search-and-evade" maneuvers that supplanted the aggressive tactics of earlier years. It was visible in the fake patrols that some platoons substituted for the real thing when they thought their assigned patrol sector was too hot for comfort, as well as in acts of disobedience, insubordination, and outright mutiny under fire. More disturbing even than such combat refusals, however, was the mounting incidence of attacks by enlisted men on unpopular officers and noncoms. The number of these so-called fraggings more than doubled between 1969 and 1970, spurred on by bounties as high as $10,000 offered by disgruntled troops for the assassination of "overaggressive" commanders.

A significant portion of fragging incidents took place

in the rear, where racial tensions suppressed during combat added fuel to the fires of resentment. Black soldiers served as infantrymen and suffered battle casualties at rates well out of proportion to their numbers in Vietnam. In the rear, black soldiers were far more likely than whites to be assigned to low-skilled specialties. The discrimination suggested by these figures was more the result of socioeconomic factors than institutional racism, but there was no denying the hostility that black soldiers frequently encountered from some white officers and enlisted men. Energized by the civil rights revolution within the United States, many black soldiers demanded changes, adopting a militant stance that increasingly echoed black-power advocates back home. The military instituted a number of measures to reduce friction but could not forestall ugly eruptions of racial violence.

Racial prejudice also contributed to a rising tide of violence by U.S. troops against those whom they had come so far to help. Barriers of language and custom had long obstructed relations between American soldiers and

the Vietnamese. During the early years of the war mutual antipathies had been largely held in check. But the slow redeployment of U.S. troops provoked noisy anti-American demonstrations and a dramatic increase in American criminal offenses against Vietnamese civilians.

These ranged from shooting water buffaloes for sport to running cyclists off the road, from throwing C-ration cans at Vietnamese children to using peasants for target practice. As large numbers of U.S. troops withdrew into heavily populated rear areas, public drunkenness, disorderly conduct, and theft became more common. In the countryside, a deadly combination of too much frustration and too little discipline led to a substantial increase in formal allegations of war crimes, including manslaughter, rape, murder, and mutilation. The massacre by men of the U.S. Americal Division of more than 450 Vietnamese villagers at My Lai in June 1968 (but not discovered by the American public until more than a year later) was unprecedented in the numbers involved and the extent of command breakdown. But atrocities were committed by American troops and in greater numbers as the war went on.

While some U.S. servicemen reacted to the difficulties of the withdrawal years with aggressive behavior against one another or the Vietnamese, others simply tried to escape, a few through desertion, a great many more through drugs. Marijuana was the most frequently used substance, but heroin, opium, cocaine, and amphetamines were all readily available at rock-bottom prices. As was the case with racial unrest, drug use skyrocketed after 1968. One Defense Department survey in 1971 found that almost 50 percent of American troops in Vietnam were either occasional or habitual users of marijuana. Despite 20,000 arrests by the military during 1969 and 1970, the number of marijuana and heroin users within the armed forces continued to increase, as did a host of drug-related crimes from petty theft to murder. And though most drug use took place in rear areas, tales of combat troops smoking pot before going out on patrol were too numerous to discount entirely.

A soldier of the U.S. 5th Mechanized Division sits atop his armored personnel carrier at Lang Vei, the westernmost American position along the DMZ, April 4, 1971.

So serious was the crisis of discipline that afflicted the disengagement army that some feared catastrophe. "By every conceivable indicator," commented one retired Marine officer and military analyst in June 1971, "our army that now remains in Vietnam is in a state approaching collapse, with individual units avoiding or having refused combat, murdering their officers and noncommissioned officers, drug-ridden, and dispirited where not near mutinous." Although that sweeping indictment was overdrawn, there was no doubt in the minds of most professional military men that the health and effectiveness of the U.S. Army required that the war be turned over to the Vietnamese as swiftly as possible.

In September 1963, at the height of the crisis that brought down the regime of Ngo Dinh Diem, President John Kennedy observed that there were limits to what the Americans could do to help the South Vietnamese. "In the final analysis," warned the president, "it is their war. They are the ones that have to win it or lose it." Almost forgotten by the Johnson administration during the years of American military buildup, Kennedy's admonition reverberated through Washington in the wake of the 1968 Tet offensive. Unwilling to commit the substantial new forces the military wanted, Johnson called upon the South Vietnamese army to assume a greater burden of the fighting. One year later, after Richard Nixon's initial attempts at negotiation and military pressure failed to wring a settlement from Hanoi, the new president made Vietnamization the cornerstone of his efforts to extricate the U.S. from Vietnam.

The job was entrusted to General Abrams, who helped his South Vietnamese counterparts build up their forces and expand their training programs. To improve combat leadership MACV designed programs for commissioning experienced NCOs. To provide the necessary firepower and mobility, the U.S. command funneled the latest American equipment into South Vietnamese hands. And to ensure they knew how to use the new hardware, Abrams sent the ARVN on combined operations with American units.

By 1971 these efforts had resulted in a South Vietnamese army of more than 1 million soldiers, each one armed with an M16 rifle. The ARVN also boasted 12,000 M60 machine guns, 40,000 M79 grenade launchers, 2,000 heavy mortars and howitzers, plus an armada of new ships, airplanes, helicopters, tanks, and armored personnel carriers. Expanded military schools bolstered the officer corps, while enlisted men welcomed increased pay, enlarged benefits, and improved housing for themselves and their families. Similar strides were taken in other branches of the South Vietnamese armed forces: the navy, which increased from a strength of 19,000 to 43,000 sailors operating nearly 1,700 coastal craft; the Vietnamese air force, which more than tripled during these years; and the territorial militias, which increased by 200,000.

The new men and new weapons, however, could not themselves correct such fundamental problems as uninspired troops, staggering rates of desertion, lack of trained personnel to maintain the sophisticated equipment supplied by the U.S., severe shortages of experienced junior officers, corruption and incompetence among the senior officer corps, heavy dependence on the U.S. logistics system, and a continuing overreliance on American artillery and air support. These weaknesses had been to some extent obscured by the successful combined operation into Cambodia and the relatively low level of fighting the remainder of 1970. But when Vietnamization was put to the test with a pre-emptive strike into the Laotian panhandle at the beginning of 1971, the results were disastrous.

In conception, the Laotian incursion was similar to the foray into Cambodia nine months earlier. The purpose of the operation, code named Lam Son 719, was to capture NVA equipment and supplies, cut infiltration routes, and in general create as much havoc for the enemy as possible while U.S. aviation and artillery assets still remained for support. Beyond these specific objectives, Lam Son was an opportunity to demonstrate that Vietnamization was working, to show the Communists that the South Vietnamese armed forces had come of age. Although U.S. aircraft and pilots would be employed, no American ground troops or advisers would accompany the ARVN beyond the border.

The 16,000-man South Vietnamese task force crossed into Laos on February 8 against minimal resistance.

Lam Son 719. Inside Laos, wounded South Vietnamese soldiers abandon their armored personnel carrier, which hit a mine.

The main ammunition dump at Khe Sanh erupts after being blown up by NVA sappers on March 23, 1971. The former Marine base became a focus of activity as South Vietnamese soldiers driven from Laos at the end of Lam Son 719 sought the protection of the Americans stationed there.

While troops from the ARVN Airborne Division, 1st Infantry Division, and a Ranger group established bases to the north and south of Route 9, the 1st Armored Brigade advanced along the highway hampered only by rain and mud. At the end of the third day the main South Vietnamese thrust was only twenty miles from Tchepone, a main hub of the Ho Chi Minh Trail. Beginning on February 12, however, the outlying firebases began to come under heavy attack from tank-supported NVA infantry. American gunships and supply helicopters flew through withering antiaircraft fire in support of the beleaguered defenders, but by March 1 the entire northern flank was collapsing under the weight of three enemy divisions.

While the NVA rushed more and more troops into battle, the armored column stalled along Route 9 waiting for orders from higher command. On March 6, behind B–52 raids that reduced the Laotian town to rubble, helicopter-borne ARVN troops seized Tchepone

but almost immediately began a general withdrawal toward the South Vietnamese border. Pursued by enemy forces now totaling 34,000 men, the withdrawal quickly became a disorganized retreat and finally disintegrated into a total rout as panicked soldiers abandoned equipment and fought each other to reach evacuation helicopters. Despite thousands of sorties by American fighter-bombers and B-52s, some units were almost entirely annihilated. Thousands more South Vietnamese soldiers were saved only by American helicopter crews who braved intense fire to rescue them.

Although many South Vietnamese troops performed well in individual battles during the course of the operation, President Thieu's announcement that Lam Son 719 was "the biggest victory ever" struck many in Vietnam and the United States as ludicrous. The ARVN had destroyed several enemy stockpiles and to some extent interrupted the Communist logistical buildup. But the delay at best amounted to no more than a few months. Against this had to be placed the 9,000 South Vietnamese soldiers killed, wounded, or captured—nearly 50 percent of the 20,000-man force ultimately committed to the invasion.

Plagued by faulty planning and poor leadership at every command level, the elite troops of the ARVN had taken a terrible beating. Were it not for U.S. air support, the outcome could well have been catastrophic. As the last American ground combat units prepared to leave the country, and the Communists resumed their preparations for a new offensive, it appeared that American air power might be the only sure defense that South Vietnam still possessed. One year later that weapon would again be called upon to prevent disaster.

On March 30, 1972, two months after the departure of the last major American ground contingent, 40,000 North Vietnamese troops backed by tanks and mobile armor units smashed across the DMZ heading for the provincial capital of Quang Tri City. Within two weeks the NVA had opened two more fronts in a stunning Easter offensive that everywhere sent ARVN units reeling backward in disarray. By mid-April all that stood between the Communists and victory were pockets of South Vietnamese resistance and a greatly diminished American military presence.

Unwilling to delay the withdrawal of the remaining U.S. ground troops, President Nixon instead pledged air and naval support to halt the enemy advance. The promise of help was more difficult to keep than ever before. Compelled to draw down their numbers over the previous twelve months, the air force had fewer than 90 combat aircraft left in South Vietnam at the time of the Communist assault, the navy only two carriers with 170 airplanes on station in the Gulf of Tonkin. Even with the addition of air force B–52s and F–4 Phantoms diverted to Da Nang and Bien Hoa from Thailand, neither the American nor the South Vietnamese air force had enough firepower to stabilize the disintegrating ARVN lines. Within six weeks, however, the call for reinforcements brought U.S. strength in Southeast Asia up to twenty American cruisers and destroyers, a half-dozen aircraft carriers, 70,000 air force personnel, and nearly 1,000 U.S. warplanes.

American pilots found the skies over South Vietnam far more dangerous than ever, thanks to new Communist air defenses, including large-caliber guns, surface-to-air missile (SAM) sites, and the small, shoulder-fired SA–7 SAMs that were particularly deadly to helicopters. But they also discovered a heavily mechanized North Vietnamese Army highly vulnerable to air attack. At Quang Tri, An Loc, and Kontum, American B–52s, fighter-bombers, and AC–47 gunships blasted enemy concentrations and cut enemy supply lines while American transports delivered thousands of tons of equipment to battered South Vietnamese defenders. By the end of June the aerial onslaught had stalled the Communist offensive amid the smoking wreckage of thousands of North Vietnamese tanks, trucks, and self-propelled artillery pieces.

Long before that—less than sixty hours after the start of the invasion—American aircraft were hitting Communist staging areas north of the DMZ. Then on May 8, as soldiers and refugees fled from Quang Tri City under a merciless Communist artillery barrage, President Nixon authorized the resumption of full-scale bombing against North Vietnam. The operation was code named Linebacker. It would be different from previous air assaults against the North in three key ways: the employment of new weapons, the inclusion of new targets, and the absence of tight civilian oversight.

Because Washington felt it could now discount the prospect of Chinese or Soviet intervention, Nixon left target selection and tactical control in the hands of his field commanders, providing them with a long-awaited flexibility they utilized to the fullest. Beginning on May 10, Linebacker missions struck fuel dumps, warehouses, railroad marshaling yards, rolling stock, trucks, petroleum pipelines, and power plants all across North Vietnam—from SAM sites along the DMZ to MiG air bases within ten miles of the center of Hanoi to railroad bridges near the Chinese border. The president also gave navy leaders something they had long sought—permission to mine North Vietnam's harbors and blockade the coast. Using airdropped magnetic-acoustic mines, the navy seeded coastal approaches and major river estuaries so effectively that no ship of any size either entered or left a North Vietnamese port for the rest of the war.

The air raids were enormously successful, thanks to a new family of laser-guided and electro-optically guided "smart" bombs that offered unprecedented accuracy and to such improved electronic countermeasures equipment as radar-detection and jamming devices. These technological developments made it possible to destroy more targets with fewer sorties and less bomb tonnage, and at a lower rate of aircraft losses, than had been experienced during the earlier Rolling Thunder campaign. In fact, the damage inflicted by American bombers from April to October 1972 exceeded all that had been accomplished between 1965 and 1968: North Vietnam's transportation system was crippled, the shipment of goods through Haiphong and other ports virtually eliminated, and the flow of war materiel to southern battlefields cut by as much as 50 percent.

The massive damage and staggering casualties endured by Vietnamese on both sides during the summer of 1972 marked a new level of violence in what already had been a costly war. But the bloodletting finally prodded negotiators 6,000 miles away toward an agreement that would bring the fighting to at least a temporary halt.

Formal talks between the United States and North Vietnam had begun in Paris in May 1968 and immediately became deadlocked. When Lyndon Johnson turned over the presidency to his successor eight months later, all that had been determined was the shape of the conference table. Richard Nixon told the American people he had a "secret plan" to end the war, but three-and-a-half more years of public and secret meetings did nothing to break the stalemate in Paris. The talks continued to founder on two key issues: Washington's insistence that NVA troops withdraw from the South and Hanoi's refusal to accept any provisional South Vietnamese government involving Nguyen Van Thieu.

By the summer of 1972, however, Washington's desire for détente with China and the Soviet Union gave both sides reason for compromise. Hanoi's fears of diplomatic isolation, the fearful pounding North Vietnam had undergone from the latest round of U.S. bombing,

Henry Kissinger and North Vietnamese diplomat Le Duc Tho leave a heavily charged negotiating session in Neuilly, France.

and the prospect of complete American withdrawal inclined the Communist leadership to take what they could get at the negotiating table and wait for the Americans to leave. Eager to remove the chief obstacle to his larger foreign policy designs and anxious to put Vietnam behind him before the upcoming presidential election, Nixon was willing to meet them halfway.

Even before the talks resumed, national security adviser Henry Kissinger gave Hanoi private assurances that the United States was willing to permit North Vietnamese troops to remain in the South after a cease-fire. Now Kissinger hedged Washington's commitment to Thieu by accepting an electoral commission—made up of neutralists, Vietcong, and members of the Saigon government—that would supervise a political settlement for South Vietnam. In return, the North dropped its insistence upon the departure of Thieu as a precondition for any cease-fire so long as the National Liberation Front was granted political status in the South.

On this basis negotiations between Kissinger and North Vietnam's Le Duc Tho moved into high gear. By early October a provisional cease-fire agreement had been reached. The tentative accord provided for the simultaneous withdrawal of U.S. troops and the return of American POWs, followed by a political settlement worked out through a tripartite National Council of Reconciliation and Concord. Infiltration of new NVA troops into the South would end, and Washington would extend postwar economic assistance to help North Vietnam rebuild its economic infrastructure. On October 22 President Nixon suspended all bombing north of the twentieth parallel. Four days later Henry Kissinger announced that "peace was at hand."

In fact, the painfully garnered accord was in grave jeopardy. Thieu, who had not been consulted during the negotiations, demanded wholesale changes that Hanoi would never accept. When the talks resumed in early November the U.S., at Thieu's insistence, proposed sixty-nine amendments to the agreement. The North Vietnamese responded with dozens of demands of their own. After weeks of increasingly heated exchanges, the two sides broke off talks on December 13. Caught between a truculent ally and a stubborn adversary, Richard Nixon determined to teach both a lesson.

To the South Vietnamese the president extended weapons, promises, and threats. First, he authorized the immediate delivery of more than $1 billion in military equipment and supplies, including enough aircraft to make South Vietnam's air force the fourth largest in the world. At the same time, Nixon gave Saigon "absolute assurances" that should North Vietnam violate any peace agreement signed with the United States, he would order "swift and severe retaliatory action." But the president also warned Thieu that if the Saigon government did not accept the cease-fire terms ultimately worked out between Washington and Hanoi, South Vietnam would be on its own.

Meanwhile, Nixon sent a different kind of ultimatum to the Communists, demanding that Hanoi return to the bargaining table within seventy-two hours. When no reply was forthcoming, the president summoned Admiral Thomas Moorer, the chairman of the Joint Chiefs of Staff, and told him to prepare a massive air attack against the North Vietnamese heartland. "I don't want any more of this crap about the fact that we couldn't hit this target or that one," Nixon told the admiral. "This is your chance to use military power to win this war. And if you don't, I'll hold you responsible." The resulting operation, called Linebacker II, was the most concentrated air offensive of the war.

On the night of December 18, 1972, 129 B–52 Stratofortresses took off from Andersen Air Force Base on Guam in the largest heavy bomber operation mounted by the United States Air Force since World War II. Their targets were heavily defended MiG airfields around Hanoi. As the first wave approached the North Vietnamese capital salvos of SA–2 surface-to-air missiles lit up the sky around them. So thickly did they fly among the American planes, said one pilot, that he could have read by the light of the rocket engines as the missiles rushed past. In all, the enemy fired more than 200 SAMs at the B–52s that night, forcing 1 aircraft back to base, damaging 2 more, and bringing down 3 of the giant bombers. But the rest of the heavily loaded aircraft hit their targets and returned safely to Guam.

Linebacker II continued day and night for almost two weeks, interrupted only by a thirty-six-hour Christmas truce. Day after day the giant bombers took to the North

Vietnamese skies supported by hundreds of fighters, fighter-bombers, tankers, radar-jamming EA–6s, F–105 Wild Weasels crammed with electronic countermeasures equipment, F–4 Phantoms laying down corridors of chaff to confuse enemy radar, and the newly deployed, supersonic F–111s the North Vietnamese called "whispering death." During twelve days of intensive bombing the American planes flew nearly 2,000 sorties and delivered 35,000 tons of bombs against transportation terminals, rail yards, warehouses, military barracks, oil and gas tank farms, factories, airfields, and power plants in the Hanoi-Haiphong corridor.

The scope of the air campaign and the concentration on targets in heavily populated areas led critics to charge Nixon with indiscriminate destruction and even genocide. To the contrary, most of the bombing was conducted with extraordinary precision, thanks to advanced onboard radar systems and laser-guided bombs. Some "spillage" from the target areas did result in residential damage and civilian deaths. The most notable case was the destruction of the Bach Mai Hospital outside a military airstrip in Hanoi. Accusations of terror bombing or deliberate attacks on civilian targets, however, were totally unfounded. Indeed, the number of civilian deaths—approximately 1,400 by Hanoi's own count, some of whom were killed by North Vietnamese missiles falling back to earth—was remarkably low considering the weight of bombs dropped and the experience of comparable bombing operations during World War II.

On December 26 Hanoi signaled to Washington its willingness to talk once the bombing stopped. Four days later Linebacker II came to an end. By then the Americans had exhausted their targets, and the North Vietnamese had run out of missiles.

The final American blow of a long and terrible war, Linebacker II cut North Vietnamese rail lines at more than 500 points, demolished nearly 400 pieces of rolling stock, heavily damaged ten airfields, shattered Hanoi's air defenses, and left some 1,600 separate military structures in ruins. In two short weeks 25 percent of North

A wing of the Bach Mai Hospital lies in ruins after being hit by an errant bomb dropped by a B–52 during Operation Linebacker II, the Christmas bombing of Hanoi.

Focus: The Easter Offensive

Noon, March 30, 1972. With a sharp crack and a thunderous explosion, a high-velocity 130MM howitzer shell crashed into the Ai Tu Combat Base just north of Quang Tri City. The first round was followed by a barrage of long-range Communist artillery shells that blanketed the thirty-kilometer-long South Vietnamese defensive line below the demilitarized zone. Behind the lethal rain of fire three North Vietnamese divisions—some 30,000 troops supported by more than 200 Soviet T54 tanks—poured across the border.

The Easter offensive had begun. Before it was over, North Vietnam would commit 200,000 men in fourteen divisions to the greatest military operation since the Chinese crossed the Yalu River into Korea twenty-one years earlier. With American combat troops almost completely withdrawn from the South, the Communists discarded a strategy of protracted war in hopes of crushing the South Vietnamese army and forcing a negotiated settlement on their own terms. They learned to their regret that the ARVN would fight back and that Washington was not yet prepared to abandon South Vietnam to defeat. During the first weeks of the invasion, however, Hanoi had reason to celebrate.

The green recruits of the 3d ARVN Division, deployed along the northern frontier precisely because no one expected an overt breach of the DMZ, buckled under the pressure of the mechanized enemy columns and raced for the protection of the Cua Viet River. At Dong Ha, South Vietnamese marines held off the invaders long enough for a pair of American army advisers to blow up a crucial bridge along Highway 1. But farther west near Camp Carroll, enemy tanks rumbled across the Cam Lo Bridge when the 56th ARVN Regiment surrendered en masse. Along with the firebase, which occupied a key strategic position in the South Vietnamese defense lines, Colonel Dinh also turned over to the NVA the largest concentration of artillery in the northern provinces, including four huge 175MM guns, the only weapons capable of responding to the enemy's long-range artillery.

As northern soldiers raced through the gap in the South Vietnamese lines, ARVN units on either side of Camp Carroll staggered eastward toward Highway 1. Using American-supplied light antitank weapons (LAWs) to good advantage, the 3d Division temporarily halted the NVA advance and stabilized a defensive line south of the Cua Viet River. But unfounded rumors of an enemy breakthrough precipitated a panic. On April 27, ARVN troops abandoned their fortifications and fled south through Quang Tri City, where they were joined by thousands of frightened refugees. Crammed together along Highway 1, the mass of soldiers, trucks, and civilians proved an irresistible target for Communist gunners who lashed the confused column with 130MM fire. Those troops who survived the carnage finally established a new defensive line south of the My Chanh River. Behind them lay twenty kilometers of smashed bodies, broken vehicles, and smoking debris.

While ARVN units in the northern part of the country reeled under the shock of the invasion, North Vietnamese troops opened two more fronts in their far-flung offensive. On April 5, the 5th NVA/VC Division, supported by tanks and armored personnel carriers, rolled out of its Cambodia base area and attacked the ARVN outpost at Loc Ninh. The outgunned and outnumbered garrison—2,000 men of the 9th ARVN Regiment and a South Vietnamese Ranger battalion, plus a handful of American advisers—held out for two days against five separate tank assaults. But by the morning of April 7 those defenders not dead or captured had fled south toward An Loc.

The political and commercial center of Binh Long Province, An Loc stood astride Highway 13 only ninety kilometers from Saigon. Fearing its loss would open the way for a drive on the nation's capital, President Thieu dispatched the 5th ARVN Division and ordered the city "held at all costs." Even as South Vietnamese troops moved into position, however, the Communist forces that overran Loc Ninh were joined by two more NVA divisions moving out of Cambodia. Together they surrounded An Loc, blocking further overland reinforcements, and began shelling the city with artillery captured during the 1971 ARVN invasion of Laos.

U.S. Army Cobra gunships and U.S. Air Force and Navy fighter-bombers pounded enemy positions. But North Vietnamese soldiers backed by artillery, tanks, and armored personnel carriers ground forward relentlessly, smashing into the city, seizing the airfield, and reducing the South Vietnamese perimeter to a square kilometer. On April 20, the senior U.S. adviser on the scene reported a desperate situation: "Supplies minimal, casualties continue to mount, medical supplies low. Wounded a major problem, mass burials for military and civilian, morale at low ebb." Most discouraging of all, "In spite of incurring heavy losses from U.S. air strikes, the enemy continues to persist."

With An Loc invested, three more Communist divisions struck the central highlands town of Dak To on April 12, opening the third phase of the North Vietnamese offensive. After capturing the high ground to the west, enemy units encircled the outlying military camps of Tan Canh and Dak To II held by two regiments of the 22d ARVN Division, the only South Vietnamese forces in the region. On April 24, NVA tanks blasted through minimal resistance to overrun both outposts. An armored column from Ben Het attempting to come to the rescue drove straight into an ambush and disintegrated under concentrated enemy fire that included Russian AT–3 radio-controlled Sagger antitank rockets. Scattered into small groups, the surviving ARVN soldiers limped down Highway 14 toward Kontum—only twenty-five miles away and now completely defenseless.

Inexplicably, the NVA waited three weeks to attack the province capital. "It was the dumbest possible thing they could have done," said U.S. Army Colonel Joseph Pizzi, "and I'm very grateful they did because there was nobody to stop them except a few people like me with pistols." Given the reprieve, the ARVN command moved the 23d Division and several Ranger groups into the city where they raced to construct trenches, dugouts, and other fortifications before the enemy's inevitable arrival. On May 16, when the Communists finally swung down Highway 14, they attacked right into the teeth of the ARVN defenses.

The tank-supported assault made an ideal target for B–52 bombers, which pounded the enemy column without mercy. For ten days the NVA attempted without success to smash through the ARVN lines, absorbing horrific casualties with each new assault. Then, in the early morning hours of May 27, Communist forces located a gap in the South Vietnamese defenses. Advancing behind a spearhead of armor, three enemy regiments fought their way into Kontum, when out of the smoke hanging over the city flew two U.S. helicopters carrying experimental airborne TOW missiles. By day's end the "tube-launched, optically tracked, wire-guided" rockets had destroyed ten enemy tanks. When the North Vietnamese attempted to withdraw, they were blasted by fighter-bombers and B–52s. Their fuel running out, their losses reaching critical proportions, the NVA had no option but to retreat.

Everywhere across the country the lethal impact of American air power, the mistakes of Communist commanders, and the stubborn courage of South Vietnamese soldiers were having the same effect. Nowhere was this more true than at An Loc, where government troops held out for ninety-five days under constant shelling and ground attacks. By the middle of June the enemy's offensive potential had been exhausted. Communist artillery bombardments continued to make life difficult at Kontum and An Loc, but decimated NVA armor and infantry units had already begun to withdraw toward the sanctuary of their bases in Cambodia and Laos. The North Vietnamese invasion had reached its high-water mark. Now it was Saigon's turn.

The loss of Quang Tri Province and the near collapse of the 3d ARVN Division had precipitated a change in personnel and approach on the northern front. Taking over command of I Corps on May 3, Lieutenant General Ngo Quang Truong wasted no time in proving his reputation as South Vietnam's best general officer. To restore discipline, Truong issued orders for the execution of deserts and looters. To regain the initiative, he sent South Vietnamese marines on raids behind NVA lines. And to recapture the territory lost in April, Truong gathered new troops and supplies for a major counter-offensive. By the last week of June, he was ready.

Marked by boldness and audacity unusual for South Vietnamese operations, Truong's attack began with diversionary feints west of Hue and north of the Cua Viet River. With the Communists preoccupied by these simultaneous assaults, the ARVN Airborne Division quietly crossed the My Chanh on the night of June 27 and fell upon unsuspecting North Vietnamese troops along the north side of the river. The stunned enemy soldiers tried to withdraw to new positions, only to discover four ARVN and marine battalions blocking their path. Within hours the NVA defensive line had completely unraveled as Communist officers accustomed to a primitive supply system and light arms struggled to protect the vulnerable logistical network of their new mechanized army. By the end of the first week of July, the South Vietnamese counterattack had rolled the NVA all the way back to the outskirts of Quang Tri City.

During the two months since they occupied it, the Communists had laced the city and its suburbs with a formidable network of bunkers, strongpoints, trenches, and observation posts. Any assault would have to cross pretargeted fields of artillery, mortar, and machine-gun fire. Even when these obstacles had been overcome, Truong's men would face enemy troops barricaded behind the thick stone walls of Quang Tri's central citadel, a miniature version of the fortress at Hue which the NVA had held for more than a month during the 1968 Tet offensive. Moreover, since the North Vietnamese still controlled two sides of the city, they were able to funnel supplies and reinforcements to defend their captured prize.

Truong gave the job of regaining Quang Tri to the Airborne Division. The paratroopers advanced one house at a time, enduring a continuous barrage of 130MM howitzer fire until they clawed their way to within 100 meters of the citadel. After U.S. aircraft carrying laser-guided bombs blasted a hole in the northeast wall, three airborne companies swarmed through the breach. Then, with victory at hand, an errant South

Vietnamese air strike dropped three 500-pound bombs on the troopers, killing forty-five and wounding twenty. The dazed survivors stumbled back through the gap in the wall, their dead comrades in their arms.

The disaster stalled the counteroffensive for more than a month. During the interval Truong replaced the battered Airborne Division with new units, realigned his own defenses, and finally asked for full U.S. air support. On September 9, behind a cascade of explosives from American fighter-bombers and B–52s, five battalions of marines began another assault. Finally, at noon on September 16, the bloodied victors raised the South Vietnamese flag over the walled fortress.

By then, observed Major John Howard, a U.S. Army adviser who had survived An Loc and witnessed the costly northern counterattack, the opposing armies were like "two fighters in the fourteenth or fifteenth round; they could hardly do anything but hold on to each other." With the recapture of Quang Tri City the Easter offensive came to an end, the existing battle lines transformed into de facto boundaries of occupation.

The offensive had killed 30,000 ARVN soldiers, reduced three province capitals to rubble, and gained for Hanoi a narrow strip of land along the northern and western borders of South Vietnam. The new territory helped safeguard Communist base areas in Laos and Cambodia, simplified the task of supplying troops in the South, and permitted political cadres to renew organizational work among the rural farmers. The price for these modest gains was an estimated 100,000 North Vietnamese dead. The staggering casualty figures were due in part to the failure of the Communist military command to concentrate its forces, the inexperience of field officers in coordinating infantry and armor, and an overreliance on shock assaults into heavily defended positions—all valuable lessons the Communists would put to good use in the future.

For all the NVA mistakes and all the tenacity displayed by the ARVN, what ultimately saved South Vietnam in the spring and summer of 1972 was the devastating weight of American air power. If that could be removed, concluded Hanoi, nothing would stand in the way of victory but time. In the final analysis, that was the most important lesson of all.

North Vietnamese soldiers advance over a bridge in South Vietnam's northernmost province, Quang Tri, as they move to capture the provincial capital during the early phases of their Easter 1972 offensive.

Above. *With their U.S. adviser, South Vietnamese Rangers in Dong Ha, Quang Tri Province, plot their next move in the face of the North Vietnamese onslaught. Minutes later, they were mortared by enemy troops and had to draw a hasty retreat.*

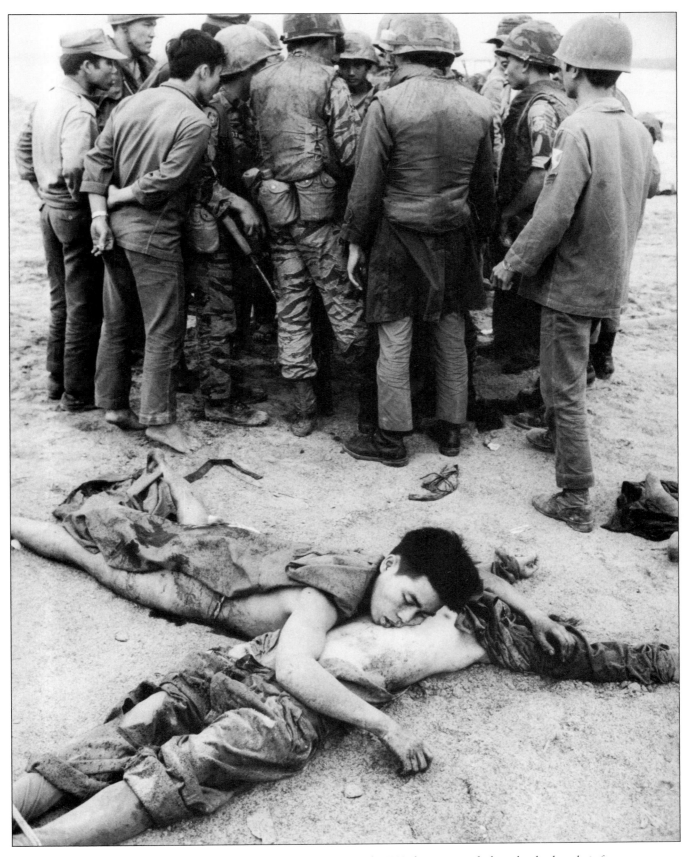

Along Route 1 north of Hue, ARVN troops regroup after a skirmish with NVA forces, two of whom lie dead at their feet.

Just south of An Loc, a key city encircled by the Communists as they opened the offensive's second front just 100 kilometers north of Saigon, the ARVN ammunition dump at Lai Khe goes up after being hit by an enemy round.

Above. *After depositing fresh reinforcements on April 29, a helicopter takes off from besieged An Loc as South Vietnamese troops, some of them wounded, try desperately to climb aboard.*

Left. *On their way to overrunning several of the key South Vietnamese central highlands outposts, North Vietnamese capture an ARVN firebase outside of Dak To.*

Focus: POW

During the course of the war some 700 U.S. military and civilian personnel were taken prisoner by the Communists. Among them were soldiers and Marines, development workers and missionaries captured in South Vietnam. But the vast majority were air force and navy pilots shot down over North Vietnam and Laos.

Wherever they were captured, most were sooner or later taken to one of a half-dozen prison camps scattered across North Vietnam. The most famous was Hoa Lo in downtown Hanoi, nicknamed the Hanoi Hilton. The POWs had names for the other camps, too— the Plantation, the Zoo, the Rockpile, Alcatraz—names that came closer to conveying what went on behind the prison wire. For both the camps and those who ran them were in deadly earnest. To the North Vietnamese, the POWs were not unfortunate victims of war but valuable pawns to be used without compunction for whatever advantage Hanoi could derive.

From the moment of their capture the Americans found themselves on center stage in a cynical propaganda campaign whose targets were both international and domestic public opinion. On the one hand, Hanoi denounced the POWs as heinous criminals. Handcuffed together, captured aviators were paraded through the streets of Hanoi before mobs of angry Vietnamese who screamed insults, threw rocks, and spat on the helpless men. Official U.S. protests were met with threats that as many as sixty American military personnel would be tried for unspecified "crimes against humanity." Faced

with widespread international protest, Hanoi abandoned its plans for war crimes trials, but the Democratic Republic of Vietnam (DRV) continued to whip up internal support for the war effort by constant condemnation of the American POWs.

At the same time, the North Vietnamese trumpeted the compassionate care they provided the prisoners. Staged photos released to the press showed apparently well-fed men housed in clean compounds, while such sympathetic journalists as Australian Wilfred Burchett assured the world that the POWs were receiving decent treatment. Hanoi invited American antiwar activists to meet with the prisoners and periodically released small groups of prisoners to U.S. antiwar groups. These media events not only displayed North Vietnam in a favorable light, they also gave considerable coverage to antiwar figures like Rennie Davis, who lauded the DRV for its enlightened care of the POWs.

Lieutenant Robert F. Frishman had another point of view. Released in September 1969, the navy flier held a news conference from his bed at Bethesda Naval Hospital in which the former POW unequivocally challenged Hanoi's claims of benevolence. "I don't think forced statements, living in a cage for three years, being put in straps, not being allowed to sleep or eat, removal of fingernails, being hung from the ceiling, having an infected arm almost lost without medical care, and being dragged along the ground with a broken leg are humane." Some journalists and antiwar activists criticized Frishman's grim portrayal as a serious misrepresentation of prison conditions in North Vietnam. In fact, he had told only part of a long tale of brutality, abuse, and mistreatment.

For much of the war the conditions of captivity for U.S. prisoners in Vietnam remained generally unknown to the American public. North Vietnam had ratified the Geneva convention regulating the treatment of POWs in 1957. But, since there was no formal declaration of war between the United States and the Democratic Republic of Vietnam, Hanoi maintained that captured Americans were not entitled to POW status. Nor would the North Vietnamese or Vietcong allow representatives from the International Red Cross to visit the camps. The handful of Americans who escaped or were released from Communist captivity were constrained from public description of their treatment by fears of retaliation against the remaining POWs. What glimpses Americans did get of North Vietnamese prisons were carefully selected by the Communists themselves and scarcely conveyed the reality of the prisoners' existence.

Those Americans captured by the Vietcong were held in jungle camps in South Vietnam or Cambodia under the most primitive conditions; the life of American POWs in North Vietnamese prisons was only relatively better. Most prisoners spent years confined by themselves, or sometimes with another prisoner, in narrow cells that provided little more than a concrete bed and a bucket in the way of amenities. Fed twice a day with watery soup and a slice of moldy bread or a bowl of rice, the POWs only occasionally were allowed from their cells for exercise or the use of common showers. Medical care was minimal, mail privileges nonexistent. During the Christmas season of 1966, 457 packages sent to the POWs by their families were returned bearing the message: "Refused by the Postal Authorities of Vietnam."

The months and years of isolation were difficult enough. But worse than that, worse than the inadequate food and squalid living conditions, was the fear and pain of torture—systematic and purposeful, physical and psychological—to which the majority of the prisoners were subjected. The pattern of abuse ranged from solitary confinement to vicious beatings with leather straps and rubber hoses. The POWs were denied sleep, tormented with ropes that forced their bodies into excruciating positions, or lacerated by steel manacles slowly tightened around their wrists. One prisoner was hung from a rafter by his broken arm. Another collapsed into unconsciousness after a beating that left his nose broken, his teeth cracked, and his buttocks a mass of bloody flesh. Colonel Fred V. Cherry, the senior black POW, was tortured for ninety-two days in a row when he refused to denounce his country. Commander Richard Stratton's interrogators stuffed the navy flier's mouth with urine-soaked sand, then burned his body with cigarettes. "You better believe I talked," Stratton later admitted.

That was the point of it all. The torture of American prisoners of war was more than the perverted pastime of sadistic guards. It was a policy dictated from the highest levels of the North Vietnamese government. As a result of the savage treatment they received, many prisoners signed statements or taped radio broadcasts condemning the war and asking for forgiveness. Stratton, paraded before the press in the spring of 1967, made a much publicized confession of guilt. The navy officer's gaunt features, striped prison garb, and dull, monotone voice shocked Americans who saw films of his appearance.

Others recognized in the exaggerated bow Stratton made before his captors a signal that his "confession" had been coerced. For despite their apparent helplessness, the American prisoners found courageous and ingenious ways of misleading their jailers and holding on to their own sanity. During interrogation the men tried to keep their stories simple, responding to pressure with information of only trivial importance. Some confused the North Vietnamese with fanciful tales of farms on aircraft carriers and antiwar fliers named Clark Kent or Casey Jones. At the same time, the prisoners created an elaborate system of clandestine communications using tap codes, hand signals—even coughing, hacking, and spitting noises—to break down their physical isolation from one another. By such means they were able to establish a secret organization they called the 4th Allied POW Wing that provided the structure and discipline necessary to maintain morale and continue resistance.

As the war went on, support from back home also became more vigorous. Hoping to gain North Vietnamese cooperation and fearful of endangering the prisoners further, the Johnson administration refrained from publicizing abusive treatment of the POWs. Since this restraint produced nothing, President Nixon adopted a much tougher policy. Beginning in 1969 U.S. officials made formal complaints to the United Nations while publicly pressing Hanoi to cease its brutality and exchange prisoners of war. Meanwhile, POW wives and other family members mobilized for action, dispatching representatives to demand information from the Communist delegation to the Paris peace talks and establishing the National League of Families of American Prisoners and Missing in Southeast Asia. The mounting pressure on Hanoi produced some improvement in living conditions at the prisons, including the initiation of limited mail privileges.

Ironically, the greatest change occurred as the result of a spectacularly unsuccessful rescue mission. On November 20, 1970, a select group of air force and Special Forces volunteers hit the Son Tay Prison twenty-three miles from Hanoi. Within minutes the commandos knocked out the guard towers, broke into the cells, and escaped in their helicopters, leaving up to 200 dead NVA behind. The Americans suffered only 2 minor injuries. The daring raid had gone like clockwork, with one single exception: The prisoners at Son Tay had been moved out four months earlier.

While recriminations flew thick and fast in Washington, the startled North Vietnamese evacuated all their outlying camps and brought the POWs into Hanoi. The consolidation had a profound impact on the prisoners' lives. Placed in large, open rooms housing twenty to fifty men each, the POWs were able to meet, talk, and organize as never before. Although senior officers remained in isolation, they were now able to exert more effective command and provide the younger men with much greater support. "The raid may have failed in its primary objectives," one POW later wrote, "but it boosted our morale sky-high!"

It would be two more years, however, before the American POWs again had cause for celebration. And once more it would be the result of dramatic U.S. military action. On the night of December 18, 1972, in an attempt to force the North Vietnamese to complete negotiations on a peace agreement with the United States, President Nixon sent 126 B-52 bombers against Hanoi. Even as cracks appeared in the walls of their cells and dust swirled around them, the POWs rejoiced. Colonel Jon A. Reynolds, a long-time prisoner, immediately noted the effect of the bombing raid on the prison guards. "There was no joking, no laughing, no acts of defiance or reprisal. They simply headed for their shelters and pulled the lids over their heads. For the first time, the United States meant business. We knew it, the guards knew it, and it seems clear that the leaders of North Vietnam knew it."

Within a month Henry Kissinger and North Vietnam's Le Duc Tho had initialed a cease-fire agreement. The document provided for the repatriation of 591 American POWs in four increments over a period of sixty days, their release tied to the withdrawal of the remaining U.S. combat forces in South Vietnam. On February 12, 1973, the first group of prisoners was brought to Hanoi's Gia Lam Airport and marched up to an imaginary line serving as a boundary between the U.S. and North Vietnam. Waiting to receive them were American military personnel. As his name was called each man walked across the line to freedom. Minor problems and delays affected each of the subsequent releases, but on March 29, only twenty-four hours behind schedule, the last of the 591 American POWs left Hanoi.

The Pentagon had been planning Operation Homecoming for years. As they were released, the former POWs were flown to Clark Air Force Base in the Philippines. Greeted by cheering crowds and specially selected escort officers, they were given medical examinations, outfitted with new uniforms, brought up to date on personal family news as well as recent world events, and provided with information on accrued salary, promotions, and decorations. In between, the men gobbled down hamburgers and banana splits and received gifts from schoolchildren at the base. Once certified fit to travel, each man was flown to the military hospital closest to his home and reunited with his family.

Although the military officially regarded the status of prisoner as neither honorable nor dishonorable but rather as an accident of war, the American people welcomed home the former POWs as heroes. In personal homecomings all across the United States the men were surrounded by joyous neighbors, feted with parades and special ceremonies, and showered with gifts. In the months that followed, the former captives found much had changed during their imprisonment, and not all of it would be easy to get used to. For some the transition to "normal" life would be long and difficult. But to the American people, the return of the POWs marked at last, more certainly than any other event, the end of the Vietnam War.

Captain Charles Boyd, a captured U.S. Air Force pilot, is paraded before Vietnamese villagers as part of an anti-American propaganda campaign in 1966. North Vietnam frequently tried to use the POWs to strengthen support for the war at home and to undermine the U.S. position abroad.

A view inside the compound of Hoa Lo Prison, better known as the Hanoi Hilton, a few days after North Vietnam released the last American prisoners held there, March 18, 1973.

Apprentice Seaman Douglas Hegdahl (left) and Lieutenant Commander Richard Stratton (right) sweep the prison yard at the Hanoi Hilton. Such chores provided the prisoners some relief from the boredom of captivity.

Navy Lieutenant Paul Galanti sits inside a barren prison cell and awaits his next meager meal, usually nothing more than watery soup and bread.

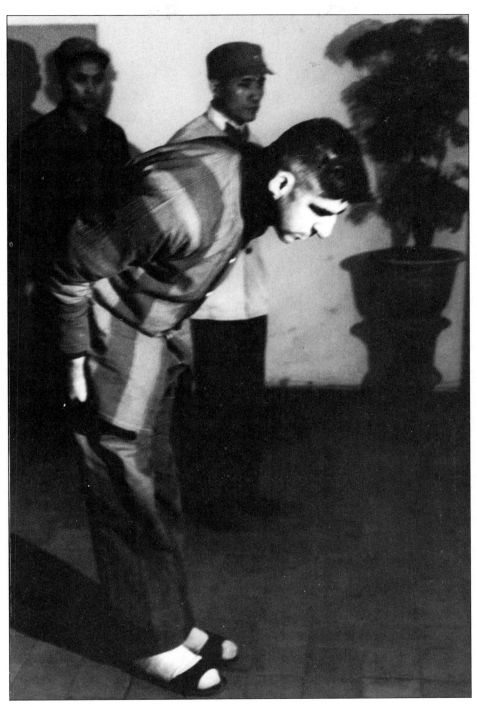

Lieutenant Commander Stratton bows at a press conference in North Vietnam in March 1967. Stratton's vacant expression and submissive demeanor at this meeting led many to believe the North Vietnamese were employing mental and physical pressure to break their prisoners.

Above. *Free at last. Returning prisoner Captain Galand Kramer of the U.S. Air Force holds up a handmade sign after arriving at Clark Air Base in the Philippines, February 12, 1973.*

Right. *Captain James Stockdale, the highest-ranking naval officer held as a prisoner of war in North Vietnam, is reunited with his wife, Sybil, and three of his sons at Miramar Naval Air Station near San Diego, February 15, 1973.*

Witness: Everett Alvarez

On August 5, 1964, during American retaliatory raids on North Vietnam after the Gulf of Tonkin incident, an A–4 Skyhawk from the carrier *Constellation* was shot down over Hon Gai, and its pilot, Lieutenant (j.g.) Everett Alvarez, Jr., ejected into the water. He was the first pilot taken prisoner by North Vietnam. Alvarez would spend more than eight years in captivity, one of the longest terms as a prisoner of war in American history.

As I floated in the water, all sorts of things ran through my mind. I thought, My poor wife. What's she going to do? My poor mother. What's she going to do? How's she going to feel? I also had visions of them capturing me, hanging me by my feet, and skinning me alive. I even remembered that I was going to miss roast beef night on the ship. All this went through my mind as I was trying to swim, dragging my seat pan. Finally, after about thirty minutes, I felt something graze my elbow. I looked behind me and saw a fishing boat with guns sticking over the side and smoke drifting from the barrels. They could have hit me if they wanted to—they were that close. I was captured.

I was taken to a nearby prison, then to a farmhouse. In the first couple of days they didn't try to harass or abuse me. I was sleeping most of the time because I was hurting. I got so stiff that I could hardly walk, and I had hurt my back during ejection. Years later, after I was released, the doctors found evidence of a hairline fracture from the ejection that had eventually healed.

A week later, when they put me in a jeep to go somewhere, I thought I was going home. I mean, the United States was a world power. They were going to fix things up really fast. But then I saw a road sign that said "Hanoi" and we went into Hoa Lo Prison. I didn't think I was going to be there very long, until a week passed, and I thought, Well, I guess I will. They told me they were going to try me for war crimes. But there was no state of war or declaration of war. Not only that, as far as I knew there weren't any other prisoners. We came in and struck and hadn't come back. I thought, What the hell do I do now?

I went through some interrogation, but nothing too difficult. I talked to them but didn't tell them anything. They thought I was showing a "good attitude." They wanted to know things like the layout of a carrier and how a plane took off, but I was telling them such things as how I was in charge of the popcorn machine on the ship and how I made popcorn. They quit after about six weeks.

They let me receive and write letters until the bombing started again, in February 1965. Then they came back with equipment from planes that were shot down that they wanted me to explain to them. I refused to do that, so they said I had a bad attitude, cut off my mail, and stuck me in a very small cell. Then I found out they had captured a second American, Bob Shumaker. Then I thought, Well, this is it. We're really in a war. Before that I debated what my tactics should be and what I was expected to do. But after the bombing it was very clear: From now on we don't help our captors or answer questions.

From then on I got very meager rations, which I wolfed down, and I lost quite a lot of weight. For a few years I was down by about 50 pounds to between 100 and 105 pounds.

As more men came in, we worked to maintain communications. Messages were dropped at certain places, such as where you would clean out your latrine can. Words were scratched at the bottom of bowls. We also used a tap code and hand code, especially for the men who didn't have roommates. We always managed to keep the lines open. That was very important. The senior officers were able to pass along orders to all the pris-

oners, and we sent all kinds of information back and forth, mostly just anecdotes and sea stories.

I think everyone always shared the sense that it was their responsibility to contribute to keeping the others up. When a person's morale went down you'd do your best to keep him up, and when you were down they pumped you up. Especially when we had roommates. You had to develop a real sense of consideration; you were living in very close, cramped quarters. Twenty-four hours a day, every day, you'd sleep together, exercise together, eat together, and if your roommate was sick or had diarrhea, my God, the stench would be terrible. I remember Bob Shumaker taught his cell-mate, Smitty Harris, how to play the piano by using a "keyboard" written on contraband rice paper. Things like that kept us going.

The North Vietnamese were always trying to use us for propaganda. They would show us movies of the antiwar movement in the United States, like Berkeley and the march on Washington, and ask us if we would also protest. Hell, no, we'd say. They got many of us to sign "confessions" stating that we were war criminals who had attacked innocent civilians and things like that, but we agreed only after days of torture. They'd tie your arms together at the shoulders and lift you off the ground or beat you with a rubber strip. That was tough. There was fear, and not only that, there was punishment. They were very brutal at times. There was no lying back. I mean, they actually killed guys. Others got sick from the diet or the treatment. In late 1969, the last time I was really physically abused, I got sick with jaundice and hepatitis.

From 1970 to 1973 we began to see a gradual improvement in our diet and treatment. By the summer of 1972 they were bringing in wagonloads of canned meat and canned fish, even bread, to fatten us up. We could get a lot more exercise and recreation. We got playing cards, packages, and letters from home and got more up-to-date on what had happened in the years since we had been shot down. We were getting the royal treatment— I guess in preparation for eventual release.

During the whole time we never thought that our government would forget us or just drop us. When we were put together at the Hanoi Hilton in late 1970, we found out it was because there had been a raid by American forces on the Son Tay camp. That showed they hadn't forgotten and were still concerned. Then by the 1972 elections in the United States we could tell that the Vietnamese were hurting. When the bombing started after the election, we were cheering for joy. We knew it wouldn't stop. The bombing got to the point where the Vietnamese wouldn't even bother to man their guns anymore. Those people were tired. We knew it was close to the end.

A few weeks later, in January 1973, they marched us all out into the yard and read us the peace agreement. We all just sat and listened. Nobody cheered. It was so long overdue. We just went back and finished our bridge games. It was sort of anticlimactic. I was emotionally drained by that time. I still wasn't sure that this was it, the end of the war.

But on February 12, Lincoln's birthday, the first group of forty prisoners, the ones there the longest, got on buses and went to the airport. We sat on the bus at the field, still wondering if it would fall through when, sure enough, an American C–141 landed. A colonel came up and said, "Just a few more minutes, guys, hang on." Then we just stepped over the line and into the hands of the Americans. It wasn't until we had taken off and the wheels were in the well that I felt elated and everyone went crazy.

Life has its way of taking its turns and, you know, I'm very lucky to be alive. We had to face each day one at a time. We had to be positive. We couldn't give up. We also learned the value of having each other. You gain individual strength through the chain; each link contributes to the strength of the chain, and through group unity each individual that I was there with gathered his own strength. We had won. We had maintained our strength.

8
THE FALL OF
SOUTH VIETNAM

To the disappointment of many but to the surprise of no one, the Paris accords did not bring peace to Vietnam. Even as the mutually proclaimed cease-fire went into effect at 8:00 A.M. on January 28, 1973, fighting between ARVN and Communist forces continued to rage across the length and breadth of South Vietnam. Hoping to gain control of as much territory as possible before the International Commission of Control and Supervision overseeing the cease-fire certified their claims, both sides took to the offensive in what came to be known as "the war of flags." In the days leading up to the cease-fire, South Vietnamese forces hastily established forward outposts and resettled refugees in Communist-dominated areas, while Communist cadres slipped into countless villages and hamlets to proclaim their "liberation." When counterattacks followed, Hanoi and Saigon both charged that their "legitimate" claims had been "violated" by the enemy.

Efforts to affix blame for the failure of the peace agreement proved pointless, since neither party had abandoned its long-range goals and each seemed willing to observe the accords only to the extent that suited its interests. For his part, President Thieu acted from the outset as if the accords did not exist. Still wedded to the "four no's" he had first proclaimed in 1969—no negotiating with the enemy, no Communist activity in South Vietnam, no surrender of territory, no coalition government—he systematically undercut any possibility of a political solution by denying any legitimacy whatsoever to the Provisional Revolutionary Government set up by the National Liberation Front, by cracking down on all domestic political opponents, and by refusing to cooperate with the ICCS and Joint Military Commission. Nor did he make any effort to curtail offensive operations. Even though the GVN controlled approximately 80 percent of the land and 90 percent of the people at the time of the cease-fire, Thieu immediately ordered his military forces to attack NVA military bases and PRG-held villages in the delta, the coastal lowlands, and the environs of Saigon. As a result, during the first three months of "peace" ARVN

In April 1975 with South Vietnam falling to the NVA, residents of the delta head for Saigon.

lost more than 6,000 men, among the highest quarterly totals of the war.

In adopting his belligerent stance, Thieu drew encouragement from the promises he had received of continuing U.S. support. Though Henry Kissinger seems to have sought nothing more than a "decent interval" between the signing of the Paris pact and a final settlement in Vietnam, Richard Nixon remained as determined as ever not to be the first American president to lose a war. In addition to supplying the South Vietnamese with vast stores of war materiel in the months preceding the cease-fire, Nixon secretly assured Thieu that the United States would continue to provide "full economic and military aid" and would "respond with full force" if the North Vietnamese violated the agreements. In an April 1973 meeting with Thieu at the Western White House in San Clemente, California, Nixon reiterated his pledge. "You can count on us," he told the Vietnamese leader.

For a variety of reasons, the Communists approached the "postwar war" much more cautiously than did their South Vietnamese adversaries. Still suffering the effects of the bloody campaigns of 1972, forced to accept cutbacks in Russian and Chinese aid, and eager to ensure the complete withdrawal of all U.S. forces, the North Vietnamese leadership decided to avoid any major military action and focus its energies on economic reconstruction, military regrouping, and political organization. During the first year of the cease-fire Communist military forces in the South were ordered to assume a primarily defensive posture while the PRG concentrated on consolidating the newly gained territories under its control. To assist in the creation of this Third Vietnam, as it came to be called, as many as 5,000 political cadres headed south to establish local administrative offices, set up new schools, and organize collective farms among the peasantry.

Although the United States formally protested the continued infiltration of North Vietnamese troops into South Vietnam, President Nixon could do little to stop it. Already reeling from the political shock of the un-

An NVA soldier stares across the Thach Han River separating North Vietnam from South Vietnam after the cease-fire agreement on January 28, 1973.

folding Watergate scandal, Nixon found his ability to take unilateral military action sharply limited by the assertive 93d Congress. As soon as all American troops and POWs were safely home, liberal and conservative legislators alike moved swiftly to halt any further U.S. military operations "in or over or from the shores of South Vietnam, Laos, or Cambodia." Several months later, in November 1973, Congress raised the "Indochina Prohibition" to the level of principle by passing the War Powers Act, which required the president to inform the legislative branch within forty-eight hours of the deployment of U.S. troops abroad and obligated him to withdraw them within sixty days in the absence of explicit Congressional approval.

Despite these clear signals of flagging American support, President Thieu refused to scale back either his political ambitions or his military offensives. After talks aimed at political settlement formally broke off in late 1973, South Vietnamese forces stepped up ground and air attacks on NVA base camps and launched a new series of land-grabbing operations in PRG strongholds along the eastern seaboard, in Tay Ninh Province north of Saigon, and in the Mekong Delta. "We will not allow the Communists to enjoy stable security in their staging areas from which they will harass us," Thieu told officers of the delta command in early January 1974, as he proclaimed the advent of the "Third Indochina War." Taken by surprise, the NVA and PRG suffered heavy losses during the early stages of the campaign. In the late spring, however, the Communists went on the counteroffensive and scored success after success, mauling ARVN units in the Iron Triangle, recapturing much of the territory they had lost, and seizing additional lands previously under the control of the GVN.

The willingness of the Communists to resume full-fledged, open warfare reflected a major shift in strategy. Yielding to the hawks within the Hanoi Politburo, notably Defense Minister General Vo Nguyen Giap and NVA chief of staff General Van Tien Dung, the Communist party central committee had passed a compromise resolution in October 1973 reaffirming the priority of reconstruction in the North but also authorizing a return to "revolutionary violence" in the South. Armed forces were henceforth to strike back at the GVN when-

ever possible and to initiate strategic raids that would bleed ARVN units, allow further expansion of NVA base areas and supply corridors, and undermine support for the Thieu regime. Rather than an all-out offensive, the new campaign would take the form of a "protracted and complex" struggle, General Dung observed, between "anti-nibbling forces and the nibblers."

For the Saigon government, the escalation of the fighting could hardly have come at a worse time. By mid-1974 the South Vietnamese economy was teetering on the brink of total collapse, partly as a result of the American withdrawal and partly as a result of President Thieu's aggressive policies. Loss of the $400 million that the United States annually spent in Vietnam, a cutback in American military aid from $2.3 billion in 1973 to about $1 billion in 1974, a series of poor rice harvests, and a sharp rise in worldwide oil prices had combined to produce massive unemployment, soaring inflation, and a marked increase in corruption at every level of society. The economic crisis had an especially profound impact on Saigon's 1-million-man army, causing chronic shortages of vital military necessities, sapping morale, and promoting further corruption. The payment of bribes for air and artillery support became commonplace, and desertion reached epidemic proportions. Compounding the government's problems, the Buddhist opposition began agitating during the late summer for peace and accommodation with the PRG, while the Catholics, Thieu's principal base of support, launched a nationwide anticorruption campaign aimed at the president himself.

As the situation steadily deteriorated, officials at the U.S. Defense Attaché's Office (DAO) in Saigon pleaded with Washington to find some way to provide an additional $500 million in military aid. Secretary of State Kissinger echoed their entreaties, warning that the failure of the United States to uphold its "moral obligation" to the South Vietnamese would have "a corrosive effect on our interests beyond Indochina." But Congress, reflecting the mood of a war-weary nation, refused to be swayed. Faced with the threat of runaway inflation at home, angered by reports of rampant corruption in South Vietnam, and tired of underwriting what one legislator described as a "self-perpetuating dictatorship," many legislators agreed with Senator Edward Kennedy that the time had come to terminate America's "endless support for an endless war." Some even believed that a reduction in aid would enhance the prospects for peace by forcing President Thieu to negotiate a political settlement of the conflict. As a result, in September 1974 Congress voted to cut military aid to South Vietnam for fiscal 1975 to $700 million, half of which would be consumed in shipping costs alone.

A month before, the Watergate scandal had finally ended in President Nixon's forced resignation. That and the vote reducing aid together had a devastating impact on the South Vietnamese, intensifying Thieu's political and economic problems and encouraging what one historian has called "a psychology of accommodation and retreat that sometimes approached despair." Unaccountably, however, neither Thieu nor the members of his Joint General Staff made any effort to adjust to their country's radically altered strategic situation. Though ARVN outposts continued to fall to the enemy with alarming regularity, no attempt was made to concentrate scattered South Vietnamese forces along more defensible lines. Nor were any contingency plans drawn up in anticipation of a major North Vietnamese offensive. "Our leaders continued to believe in U.S. air intervention even after the U.S. Congress had expressly forbidden it," one high-ranking ARVN general later wrote. "They deluded themselves into thinking that perhaps this simply meant that U.S. intervention would take a longer time to come because of the complex procedures involved."

While the leaders of the GVN waited and hoped, their North Vietnamese counterparts carefully reassessed the shifting military balance in the South. At a joint meeting of the Politburo and the central military committee in early October 1974, the hawks once again pressed their case for all-out war, arguing that the growing vulnerability of ARVN availed "new opportunities" only waiting to be grasped. By that point the North Vietnamese had already infiltrated ten full divisions into the South—some 200,000 troops—backed by 700 tanks and 450 long-range artillery pieces as well as twenty antiaircraft regiments armed with sophisticated SA–7

Strela surface-to-air missiles. Another seven reserve divisions had been mobilized in the North, several taking up positions just across the DMZ. Vast quantities of weapons, ammunition, and supplies had been stockpiled, new training and hospital facilities built, and the logistical network under construction since early 1973 all but completed. "It was a picture to be proud of," North Vietnamese chief of staff General Van Tien Dung later recalled. "In that region of our Fatherland were more than 20,000 kilometers of strategic roads running north and south, with campaign roads running east and west—strong ropes inching gradually, day by day, around the neck, arms, and legs of a demon, awaiting the order to jerk tight and bring the creature's life to an end."

Before that order could be given, however, the North Vietnamese first had to consider the likelihood of American intervention. Though even Dung agreed that caution was in order, the consensus of the conference was summed up by Le Duan, Communist party first secretary-general. "Now that the United States has pulled out of the South," he declared, "it will be hard to jump back in. And no matter how they may intervene, they cannot rescue the Saigon administration from its disastrous collapse." What finally emerged from the October deliberations was a document known as the Resolution for 1975, a two-year plan to "liberate" the South not through negotiations, but by force of arms. During the first year of the campaign, Communist forces would move out of their jungle base camps and systematically eliminate exposed ARVN outposts, further extend supply corridors, and force ARVN to retreat to urban areas. Large-scale attacks against the cities and major ARVN garrisons were to be launched in the following year, 1976, culminating in a "General Offensive, General Uprising" that would topple the Saigon regime or, at the very least, force acceptance of a coalition government.

As outlined by General Dung, the centerpiece of the 1975 offensive would be a thrust into the vast, lightly defended region that the Vietnamese called Tan Nguyen, known by the Americans as the central highlands. In early December, however, Dung was forced to modify his plans after Lieutenant General Tran Van Tra, the

With portions of South Vietnam along the Cambodian border already having fallen to the North Vietnamese, South Vietnamese troops try to hold positions west of Saigon on March 12.

commander of Communist forces in the low-lands–Mekong Delta region, and Pham Hung, the chief political officer of COSVN, the Central Office for South Vietnam, convinced the Politburo to begin the campaign with a major assault on Phuoc Long Province northeast of Saigon. Not only would the liberation of Phuoc Long make a mockery of Thieu's "no territorial concession" policy, the two men argued, it would also tie down ARVN's mobile reserves and thus prepare the way for a bold strike against the capital in 1976.

As it turned out, the attack on Phuoc Long proved even more successful than Tra had anticipated. Beginning on December 13, the 7th and newly formed 3d NVA Divisions quickly captured a series of key outposts, surrounded the garrison town of Don Luan, and severed the main road leading through the province. During the next two weeks the remaining ARVN garrisons were also cut off and the province capital of Phuoc Binh brought under siege. As the Communists bombarded the town with long-range 130MM artillery shells, two companies of highly trained Rangers were dispatched to bolster ARVN's defenses. But it was hardly enough. Outgunned and outnumbered nearly four to one, the defenders of Phuoc Binh finally succumbed on January 6, 1975.

Emboldened by the ease with which Phuoc Long had been liberated, the Hanoi Politburo immediately directed the NVA General Staff to revise its plans for Campaign 275, the previously planned drive into the central highlands. Scrapping the conservative objectives initially outlined by General Dung, which called for a series of attacks on exposed outposts, new orders were now drawn up for a surprise attack on Ban Me Thuot, capital of Darlac Province and headquarters of the 23d ARVN Division. "Never have we had military and political conditions so perfect or a strategic advantage so great as we have now," Le Duan told Dung, as he dispatched the general south to take personal charge of the highlands offensive.

In Saigon, meanwhile, the South Vietnamese Joint General Staff scrambled to cope with the unfolding military crisis. Uncertain where the enemy might strike next and lacking the manpower to defend every front, the ARVN commanders began fleshing out plans to shorten their defense lines and at the same time reconstitute a national mobile reserve capable of rapid deployment. As in the past, however, President Thieu refused even to consider a strategic withdrawal since it violated his policy of "no retreat." Instead he continued to cling to the hope that somehow, in some way, the Americans would eventually come to his rescue. His faith derived in part from the secret assurances given by the past president, in part from his calculation of U.S. geopolitical interests, and in part from his ignorance of the American political system. In South Vietnam Nguyen Van Thieu *was* the government; he seems never fully to have comprehended that in the United States, the president was not.

When news of the fall of Phuoc Long reached Washington in early January 1975, Richard Nixon's successor, Gerald Ford, had been in office only five months. Already burdened by a host of domestic problems ranging from rising inflation and widespread unemployment to a CIA wiretapping scandal, further preoccupied by the threat of renewed war between Egypt and Israel in the Middle East, he was hardly inclined to risk his political capital by taking forceful military action in Southeast Asia. Even if he had been willing to do so, the Indochina Prohibition of 1973 and the War Powers Act of 1974 sharply limited his options. As interpreted by Congress, Ford could not even send a U.S. naval task force to the coast of Vietnam without legislative approval, much less unleash thundering fleets of B–52s. He therefore decided that the only alternative was to seek a supplemental appropriation of $300 million in military aid for South Vietnam and an additional $222 million for Cambodia, where Khmer Rouge forces were rapidly closing in on the capital city of Phnom Penh.

At Ford's urging, in late February a special Congressional delegation traveled to South Vietnam and Cambodia for an on-the-spot appraisal of the deteriorating military situation. Though skeptical at the outset, all but one of the legislators—Congresswoman Bella Abzug of New York—returned to Washington on March 2 favoring some additional military and humanitarian aid to both countries. But their recommendations had little effect. Most members of Congress, and with them the majority of Americans, thought giving South Vietnam more aid would be throwing good money after bad.

While the president's supplemental-aid request languished on Capitol Hill, the North Vietnamese Army resumed the offensive. In accordance with the Politburo's latest directive, early on the morning of March 10 the 320th, 316th, and 10th NVA Divisions surged out of the jungle and attacked the ARVN garrison at Ban Me Thuot. Employing a tactic General Dung called the "blossoming lotus," a single regiment of infantrymen and sappers spearheaded the assault, striking quickly at the government command centers inside the town and then turning outward, "like a flower bud slowly opening the petals." In the meantime, columns of tanks and armored personnel carriers closed in from the north and south behind a shield of long-range artillery, trapping the ARVN defenders between the claws of an ever tightening pincer. Although the South Vietnamese troops fought bravely, at times savagely, to hold their ground, within two days only a few pockets of organized resistance remained. By March 15, the battle for the Darlac Province capital was over.

The fall of Ban Me Thuot finally convinced President Thieu that he would have to start trading land for time. In order to prevent the North Vietnamese from marching to the sea and cutting the country in two, he decided to withdraw his remaining highland forces from Kontum and Pleiku to the coastal town of Tuy Hoa and from there to mount a counterattack on Ban Me Thuot. Since the main road leading to the coast, Route 19, had already been cut by the NVA, retreating forces were to descend along interprovincial Route 7B, an old logging road that snaked its way from the outskirts of Pleiku through Phu Bon Province. Though the road had rarely been used in recent years and parts of it were known to be heavily mined, it had the advantage of passing through territory that the enemy had largely ignored in the past. With careful planning and any luck, the force would be gone before the North Vietnamese realized what was happening.

Once the order was given, II Corps commander Major General Pham Van Phu immediately began planning the evacuation. Thinking only of speed, he decided that the withdrawal would begin within two days, on March 16,

with the 20th Combat Engineer Group leading the way. As the engineers repaired the road, built fords, and replaced bridges—a process that, in Phu's estimation, would take no more than two days in total—infantry, armor, and medical units would follow. Crack South Vietnamese Ranger groups would act as a rear guard, while the Territorial Forces at Pleiku remained behind to screen the movement of the column.

Even before the first convoy departed, however, serious problems arose. On March 15 Phu himself departed for Nha Trang, leaving contradictory orders as to who was in command and without alerting the Territorial Forces of their assigned role in the withdrawal. As a result, as soon as the regular units began moving out, many Regional- and Popular-Force troops gathered their families and joined the mass exodus. So did thousands of other civilians. As the military convoys headed south kicking up clouds of red dust, unbroken lines of refugees on foot paralleled the path of the army on each side of the road.

As the South Vietnamese had hoped, General Dung and his staff were initially fooled by ARVN's strategic retreat. But after receiving both Western news reports of civilians fleeing the highlands and radio intercepts of flights from Pleiku to the coast, the North Vietnamese general became convinced that the enemy was on the move. Seizing the opportunity to destroy a major ARVN command, Dung immediately ordered the 320th NVA Division to drive northeast, attack the flank of the column, and stall the retreat long enough to allow the 968th Regiment to close in from the rear. Other forces along the coast were to cut 7B in advance of the withdrawing South Vietnamese as they headed toward their refuge at Tuy Hoa.

Darkness was falling on the evening of March 18 when the lead elements of the NVA 320th caught up with the II Corps column at Cheo Reo (Hau Bon), where engineers had been frantically working for two days to construct a pontoon bridge across the Ea Pa

On March 21, 1975, a one-legged ARVN veteran leads a group of refugees from Ban Me Thuot, taken by the NVA on March 12, into the outskirts of the coastal town of Nha Trang after a 125-kilometer march.

River. Just as they completed their work, a shower of heavy artillery shells, mortar rounds, and rockets rained down on the throngs of soldiers and refugees who had converged on the riverbank, waiting to cross. At the same time, other Communist units began hitting the tail end of the column, which still stretched back to the outskirts of Pleiku.

Nevertheless, the next day the column pushed on, as helicopters darted in to evacuate the sick and wounded and VNAF aircraft bombed the advancing NVA troops. The convoy continued to flow through Cheo Reo until March 21, when the North Vietnamese finally broke through the Ranger rear guard and seized the town. On orders from General Phu, the trapped Rangers abandoned their heavy weapons and fled into the jungle. Elsewhere along the column panic dissolved into chaos as roving bands of leaderless soldiers fought with civilians over dwindling supplies of food and water. One priest later reported seeing people so weak and exhausted they could "barely climb onto helicopters" and children dying of starvation.

By the time the lead elements of what had come to be called the Convoy of Tears fought through the last NVA roadblocks and reached Tuy Hoa on March 25, the losses were staggering. Of an estimated 180,000 civilian refugees who began the journey, only one-third were accounted for. Of 7,000 Rangers, only 900 eventually made it to the newly established II Corps headquarters at Nha Trang, while about one-quarter of 20,000 logistics and support troops completed the withdrawal. All told, JGS chairman General Cao Van Vien later reported, "Seventy-five percent of II Corps combat strength, to include the 23d Infantry Division as well as Ranger, armor artillery, engineer, and signal units, had been tragically expended."

The morale-shattering defeat in the central highlands was soon followed by an equally disastrous collapse of ARVN forces in the northern provinces. There, too, a decision to pull back to more defensible positions pre-

The Convoy of Tears—the column of soldiers and civilians retreating to the coast from the hard-pressed highland city of Pleiku along disused Route 7B—presses through smoke and debris left by NVA shellfire.

cipitated a mass panic among the civilian population after President Thieu ordered the redeployment of the elite ARVN Airborne Division to Saigon and the withdrawal of other units to enclaves along the coast. Further complicating matters, Thieu repeatedly failed to clarify his commands, at first indicating that the city of Hue should be abandoned and then demanding that it be held "at all costs." In the meantime, the NVA 324B and 325C Divisions rapidly closed on the retreating army, cut Route 1 to the north and south of Hue, and isolated the city from all overland access. Realizing that he could not possibly hold out against the enemy's superior force, I Corps commander General Truong ordered his troops on March 24 to head for the shore, where a flotilla of South Vietnamese naval vessels was to carry them south to Da Nang.

The hastily planned evacuation soon turned into a rout, as soldiers scrambled to locate their families and then dissolved into the civilian throngs streaming toward the coast. Behind them the NVA, with their own troops now entering Hue, trained their artillery guns on the ten-mile stretch of road leading to the port town of Tan My, the principal embarkation point, inflicting heavy casualties and feeding panic among those waiting to be evacuated. When the promised naval fleet at last appeared, a combination of low tides, rough seas, and increasingly accurate enemy shellfire prevented the ships from reaching the shore. Dozens of soldiers and civilian refugees drowned as they attempted to swim to the 100 or so junks, river craft, and barges that the South Vietnamese navy had brought from Da Nang. In the end, most of one regiment of the 1st ARVN Division and a single boatload of South Vietnamese marines were successfully evacuated to Da Nang, along with 7,700 people on Vinh Loc Island. Thousands of others were left on the beach to await the arrival of the conquerors of Hue.

Although President Thieu still entertained hopes of holding the line at Da Nang, it soon became apparent that any attempt to resist the advancing North Vietnamese Army would be futile. As tens of thousands of terrified refugees poured into the city during the last days of March, doubling the population to some 2 million, any semblance of order or discipline evaporated. By March 27 crowds of Vietnamese occupied every inch of

ground in the downtown area, bringing traffic to a virtual standstill. Along the streets armed soldiers, no longer under any control, wandered aimlessly, while at the main airport frenzied mobs converged on every aircraft shuttling in and out of the city.

Amid the mounting anarchy South Vietnamese and American authorities frantically pressed ahead with plans to evacuate as many people as possible to Cam Ranh Bay and Saigon. Nonessential U.S. consular personnel, senior GVN officials, and third-country nationals were among the first to leave, flying out in aircraft provided by Air Vietnam, World Airways, Air America, and the Vietnamese air force. But as the backlog of passengers grew and the crowds at the airfield became increasingly unruly, the airlift had to be suspended and some other means of escape found. At the suggestion of an American DAO official, it was decided that a small fleet of tugs and barges assigned to move military supplies would instead be used to transport people. In the meantime, several large cargo ships were dispatched from Saigon to assist in the evacuation.

As rumors of the impending sealift spread through the city, thousands of civilians and renegade soldiers rushed the docks, overwhelmed a cordon of ARVN security guards, and tried to board the waiting boats and barges. Many civilians drowned or were trampled to death in the crush. Others were shot by South Vietnamese soldiers determined to make room for themselves. Still others waded into the sea, hoping to be picked up by one of the boats already making their way out to sea. "Vietnamese mothers saved their children by throwing them to British girls, Aussies—everybody grabbing babies," recalled one American.

The North Vietnamese 2d Army Corps waited until Easter morning, March 30, before entering Da Nang. By that point much of the madness that had gripped the city had already burnt itself out, even though only 50,000 civilians and 16,000 soldiers had managed to escape. Resigned to their fate, those who remained offered no resistance as the Communists raised their flag over South Vietnam's second-largest city, where ten years before the first contingent of American combat troops had splashed ashore.

The following day, March 31, a flash telegram arrived

at General Dung's command post near Ban Me Thuot, informing him that the Politburo had reached a "historic decision." Abandoning the two-year plan outlined the preceding fall, the North Vietnamese leadership had decided to seize the "once-in-a-thousand-years opportunity" that lay before them and "liberate Saigon before the rainy season." All available units were to be committed at once to the southern front, while Dung himself was to proceed to the regional military base camp at Loc Ninh. There he would be joined by COSVN political chief Pham Hung and General Tran Van Tra to begin preparations for the "final decisive battle" of the Vietnam War.

Le Duc Tho joined Dung and his comrades in the South to apprise them in detail of the Politburo's latest resolutions and to monitor the final phase of what had been designated the Ho Chi Minh Campaign. Dung was

to serve as supreme commander and Hung as chief political officer, with Generals Tra and Le Duc Anh, a northerner, their deputies. The offensive against Saigon was to be launched no later than the last week of April. "From then on," General Tra later wrote, "we were racing against the clock."

In the meantime, the North Vietnamese Army continued its seemingly inexorable southward advance. Along coastal Route 1 and the newly paved roads of the central highlands, long convoys of trucks, armored personnel carriers, tanks, and artillery pieces ran bumper to bumper, day and night, throughout the first week of April. As the NVA juggernaut rolled forward, the principal population centers of II Corps fell in rapid succession. On April 1 the coastal city of Nha Trang, the northernmost point on ARVN's latest defense line, fell without a fight after II Corps commander General Phu

Nha Trang offered no safe haven for highland refugees; they arrived to find the people of the coastal town fleeing south to Saigon. Here, the pilot of the last aircraft out of Nha Trang uses his fists to keep more people off the already overloaded plane, April 1.

panicked and fled to Saigon. Two days later the huge installation at Cam Ranh Bay was similarly abandoned as the 10th NVA Division closed in.

In Saigon, news of the latest territorial losses raised tensions to the brink of panic, sparking a run on the banks as well as widespread calls for President Thieu's resignation. In characteristic fashion, the South Vietnamese leader lashed back by censoring opposition newspapers, arresting alleged "plotters," and authorizing local police to "shoot and kill on the spot" anyone who violated a 9:00 P.M. curfew. Yet aside from promising to form a new "fighting cabinet," he made no effort to rally the nation behind him or to provide any real leadership to the government or armed forces. Plans to reorganize and re-equip the troops that had straggled back to the South were in disarray, while inside the GVN bureaucracy, one American reporter noted, "officials either stopped working altogether or kept mindlessly issuing instructions that could not be carried out." "The President had all the power in his hands and could easily impose his policy," recalled Bui Diem, former South Vietnamese ambassador to the U.S., "but somehow there was no sense of purpose or direction among the high officials of the government," nor "strangely enough . . . any sense of urgency about the situation."

Convinced that an independent, if "truncated," South Vietnam might still be salvaged from the wreckage of the current military campaign, U.S. ambassador Graham Martin and other American officials eventually persuaded Thieu to organize a new defense line centered around the garrison town of Xuan Loc, thirty-five miles northeast of the capital along strategically vital Route 1. At the same time, however, Martin authorized U.S. defense attaché General Homer Smith to update contingency plans for a full-scale U.S. evacuation in the event that ARVN failed to hold the line. Smith promptly ordered his staff to set up an evacuation processing center adjacent to Tan Son Nhut Air Base, to draw up lists of nonessential U.S. personnel and "high-risk" Vietnamese, and to identify and locate any

Bodies of refugees trampled in the rush to escape lie on the Nha Trang dock on April 1, as a crowded barge headed for Saigon approaches.

321

other Americans still living in Saigon. Yet Ambassador Martin wanted to proceed slowly, since he feared that any visible sign of a U.S. pullout might precipitate the same kind of mass panic that had engulfed Da Nang and Nha Trang. As a result, out of a total American population of more than 6,000, only 1,285 left the country during the first two weeks of April.

By that point twelve Communist Main-Force divisions were bearing down on the South Vietnamese capital from three directions—from the northwest in the area surrounding Tay Ninh, from the south along Route 4 leading from the delta, and from the east along Route 1. Only at Xuan Loc did General Dung's army meet with more than token resistance. There the 18th ARVN Division dug in for what would prove to be a desperate last stand. Though heavily outnumbered and outgunned, the South Vietnamese troops launched counterattack after counterattack, stalling the North Vietnamese advance for nearly a week. Yet once fresh NVA forces began to arrive from the coast on April 15, it became clear that the defenders of Xuan Loc could not hold out for long. "It's like running a twenty-mile race with one contestant going the distance while the other runs a four-man relay," one Western military analyst lamented. "There's simply no way ARVN can win."

As the North Vietnamese Army tightened its noose around Saigon, Ambassador Martin came under increasing pressure to accelerate the pace of the U.S. withdrawal. On April 19, two days after the Senate Armed Services Committee formally rejected President Ford's

In the midst of the 18th ARVN Division's heroic last stand at Xuan Loc seventy-five kilometers northeast of Saigon, helicopters land to drop off supplies and pick up civilians on April 20.

aid request, Admiral Noel Gayler, the U.S. commander-in-chief, Pacific, was dispatched to inform Martin that Washington wanted the American presence reduced to no more than 1,100 as soon as possible. To facilitate the departure of Vietnamese nationals, U.S. and GVN authorities agreed to relax their respective immigration and emigration rules, while Martin and Gayler devised a scheme that broadly expanded the definition of "dependent." In the days that followed, the number of evacuees leaving the Tan Son Nhut airfield on outbound C–130 and C–141 cargo planes grew dramatically from an average of 200 to more than 3,000 per day. In addition, DAO officials organized a series of ultrasecret "black flights" to insure that especially "sensitive" Vietnamese, many of them former U.S. intelligence operatives, could get out of the country without the knowledge of the GVN.

The American decision to begin a full-scale evacuation came as no surprise to President Thieu. Having finally realized that there would be no eleventh-hour U.S. rescue, he knew that the end was drawing near. The government he ruled no longer supported him, his once loyal generals were threatening to depose him, and his army was collapsing on every front. On April 18, a group of leading political moderates and opposition figures had informed him that they would publicly demand his resignation in six days if he did not step down. Two days later, Ambassador Martin carried a similar message to Independence Palace. Emphasizing that he was speaking "only as an individual," and not as a representative of the United States government, Martin told Thieu that "almost all of his generals" considered the military situation hopeless and that most Vietnamese believed his departure would facilitate a negotiated settlement with the Communists. Though Martin personally thought it would make little difference, many GVN officials "felt it might buy time, which was now the essential commodity for South Vietnam."

The next day, April 21, Thieu announced his resignation in a ninety-minute televised address to the National Assembly. Often rambling and at times choked with tears, the South Vietnamese leader devoted most of his speech to a bitter attack on the United States, recounting President Nixon's "solemn pledge" to "re-spond with full force . . . if North Vietnam renewed its aggression" and comparing the recent Congressional aid debate to "fish market bargaining . . . over the bodies of our soldiers.

"The United States has not respected its promises," Thieu declared. "It is inhumane. It is not trustworthy. It is irresponsible." Only after he had concluded his tirade did Thieu unveil his decision to yield his tattered authority to Vice President Tran Van Huong. "I depart today," he announced. "I am resigning, but I am not deserting."

In the wake of Thieu's resignation it was widely hoped that the aged and enfeebled Huong would immediately transfer power to a coalition government headed by self-styled "neutralist" General Duong Van Minh, thus paving the way for a negotiated settlement. If there were ever a time when such a bargain might have been acceptable to the Communists, however, it had long since passed. By April 26, when Huong finally agreed to put the question of Minh's accession before the National Assembly, General Dung and his staff had already put the finishing touches on their plan for the last offensive of the Ho Chi Minh Campaign. The formal "resolution for attack" had been approved and signed. At precisely 5:00 P.M. on April 27, the "final decisive battle" of the Vietnam War—the "liberation" of Saigon—would begin.

Following page. *Their city surrounded and under rocket attack by the Communists, residents of Saigon clear rubble and search for survivors of the latest volley of fire on April 27.*

Focus: The Fall of Saigon

During the predawn hours of April 27, 1975, four heavy rockets slammed into the South Vietnamese capital, signaling the onset of the Communists' final offensive. As fires from the blasts raged out of control, 130,000 NVA soldiers went on the attack, pressing in toward the capital on five fronts.

Though the South Vietnamese forces defending the city fought "stubbornly," NVA chief of staff General Dung later wrote, his own troops "attacked like a hurricane" and made rapid progress. To the east, the 4th North Vietnamese Army Corps closed in on Bien Hoa Air Base behind a wall of long-range artillery fire, while the 2d Army Corps cut off coastal Route 15 and surrounded the port town of Vung Tau. To the south, a combined VC/NVA tactical force pushed up from the delta and permanently severed Route 4 nineteen miles from the city's edge. And to the north and northwest, the 3d Army Corps blocked Route 1 at several points between Saigon and Tay Ninh and encircled the 25th ARVN Division at Cu Chi.

As news of the latest Communist advances reached Washington, President Gerald Ford and his senior advisers quickly determined that the time had come for a total U.S. pullout. While some administration officials advocated the immediate implementation of Option IV, a worst-case emergency plan to remove all remaining Americans by helicopter to an offshore U.S. fleet, Ambassador Graham Martin assured the White House that such "extraordinary measures" were not yet required. Since no more than 1,000 Americans remained in Saigon and the Tan Son Nhut airfield seemed in no imminent danger, Martin was confident that he "could get a maximum number of Vietnamese and Americans out by the thirtieth" by means of the ongoing fixed-wing airlift. Deferring to their "man on the scene," the president and his men agreed to delay. That day more than 7,500 evacuees left Saigon on outbound cargo planes destined for the Philippines or Guam, the largest single daily exodus since the airlift began. Only 219 of those departing, however, were Americans.

Among the new leaders of the South Vietnamese government, the accelerated pace of the U.S. withdrawal went virtually unnoticed. Throughout the afternoon and early evening of the twenty-seventh, the 125 members of the National Assembly engaged in a meaningless constitutional debate over the prospective transfer of power from President Tran Van Huong to General Duong Van Minh. Not until 8:15 P.M. did the legislature finally agree to elevate Minh to the presidency to "carry out the mission of seeking ways and means to restore peace to South Vietnam." Minh, in turn, postponed his inauguration until the following evening so that he might have time to interview candidates for his new cabinet.

Loud thunderclaps mingled with the boom of distant artillery fire as Minh rose to deliver his acceptance speech at 5:30 P.M. on April 28. Still convinced that the Communists would negotiate with him, he called for an immediate cease-fire and a resumption of formal talks in accordance with the 1973 Paris agreement. Further pledging to free all political prisoners, lift restrictions on the press, and form a coalition government acceptable to all parties, Minh concluded with an appeal to those attempting to flee abroad to "remain here to join us and all those with good will to join in the building of a new South for our future generations."

As if to underscore the futility of Minh's eleventh-hour plea, no sooner had he finished his address than the Communists launched their first and only air strike of the war. Led by a former South Vietnamese pilot who had defected to the enemy earlier in the month, a group of five captured A–37 Dragonfly jets streaked over Tan Son Nhut Air Base and bombed a line of Vietnamese air force planes parked along the main runway. Though several aircraft were destroyed and others badly damaged, the runway itself did not come under attack until early the next morning, when an intense barrage of 130MM artillery shells crashed into the sprawling air base. Pandemonium broke out as ARVN soldiers swarmed onto the tarmac and VNAF pilots fired up their aircraft in a desperate attempt to get out of the country.

By midmorning on April 29 it was clear that the fixed-wing airlift could no longer continue. Jettisoned fuel tanks, abandoned trucks, and other pieces of discarded equipment littered the runways, while rampaging Vietnamese troops still chased any aircraft that moved. Realizing he had no choice but to go to Option IV, Ambassador Martin telephoned the White House. At 10:51 A.M. Saigon time, President Ford gave the execute order for Operation Frequent Wind, code name for the emergency pullout. A short time later, operators at the American radio station in Saigon began playing a tape of Bing Crosby's "White Christmas," a prearranged signal that the final evacuation had begun.

As conceived by U.S. officials, the worst-case extraction plan called for all remaining Americans and certain select Vietnamese to be shuttled by bus to the Defense Attaché's Office (DAO) compound at Tan Son Nhut, where they would board huge CH–53 helicopters dispatched from the offshore U.S. fleet. From the very outset, however, the operation ran into unanticipated delays, as large crowds of Saigonese converged on the designated assembly points throughout the city. "At every stop Vietnamese beat on the doors and windows pleading to be taken inside," recalled journalist Keyes Beech of the *Chicago Daily News.* "Every time we opened the door we had to beat and kick them back." Unable to bulldoze their way through the growing throngs, many drivers abandoned hope of reaching Tan Son Nhut and dropped off their passengers at the U.S. Embassy compound. As a result, by the time the first wave of helicopters arrived at the airfield, between 2,000 and 3,000 people slated for evacuation were still inside the city.

Despite rapidly deteriorating weather conditions, the evacuation from the DAO compound proceeded like clockwork. Beginning at 3:00 in the afternoon, an average of thirty-six helicopters per hour landed at Tan Son Nhut, boarded up more than 50 passengers each, and whisked them away to the armada of ships anchored off the coast. By 8:00 P.M. more than 6,000 people, 5,000 of them Vietnamese, had been safely extracted. Only a Marine security force remained, plus an undetermined number of American and Vietnamese civilians still awaiting evacuation from the U.S. Embassy.

With the operation now more than five hours old and visibility steadily diminishing in the deepening twilight, Secretary of Defense James Schlesinger strongly urged the president to suspend the operation until morning. But Ambassador Martin balked. Making it clear that he "damn well didn't want to spend another night here," he cabled the White House that "I need thirty CH–53s and I need them now." Secretary of State Kissinger then called and asked the ambassador how many people still remained in the compound. Unaware that the administration intended to use his estimate to calculate the number of helicopters required, Martin gave him a figure off the top of his head. "Seven hundred twenty-six," he said. As a result, when the last contingent of helicopters finally arrived to clear the embassy compound, more than 400 people were left behind.

Several hours later, at 10:24 A.M. on April 30, 1975, President Duong Van Minh went on national radio and called on his soldiers "to remain calm, to stop fighting, and to stay put." Throughout the environs of Saigon, the last vestiges of resistance wilted and the Army of the Republic of Vietnam began to disappear as thousands of soldiers discarded their weapons and uniforms and awaited the arrival of their conquerors. At midday, a convoy of tanks and trucks rumbled down Hong Thap Tu Street and turned left onto Thong Nhut Boulevard to face the presidential palace. Without slowing down, the lead tank crashed through the high, steel front gate and coughed to a halt inside the spacious courtyard. Other tanks followed, forming a huge semicircle before the main entrance. As one of the crewmen raced up the steps and unfurled a huge gold-starred liberation flag, the ranking North Vietnamese officer entered the palace and confronted President Minh. "You have nothing to fear," the officer declared. "Between Vietnamese, there are no victors and no vanquished. Only the Americans have been beaten. If you are patriots, consider this a moment of joy. The war for our country is over."

With the fall of Saigon imminent—sixteen NVA divisions surround the capital—Vietnamese citizens plead with a Marine guard (above) to let them into the U.S. Embassy while others (right) crowd toward the compound's outer walls, hoping to enter the American sanctuary, April 1975.

A few hours after South Vietnam's unconditional surrender, a Communist tank
flying the NLF flag smashes through the
gates of the presidential palace in Saigon,
April 30.

330

A South Vietnamese police colonel lies dead at the foot of Saigon's war memorial statue on April 30. Unable to accept the defeat of his country, he had walked up to the statue, saluted, and shot himself.

Evacuees board an Air America helicopter in downtown Saigon on April 29. In the nineteen hours before the collapse of the capital, U.S. helicopters evacuated more than 7,000 U.S. personnel and selected South Vietnamese citizens to ships of the Seventh Fleet waiting offshore.

Focus: Coming Home

With the fall of Saigon the people of the United States began a headlong rush into the post-Vietnam era. Some Americans had not even waited that long. Five days before the last Marine helicopter lifted off the roof of the U.S. Embassy, President Gerald Ford announced that the evacuation of Saigon "closes a chapter in the American experience." By and large his countrymen seemed to agree. Wearied of the bitter conflict and appalled at its conclusion, the American people began a period of national denial. "Today, it is almost as though the war had never happened," wrote newspaper columnist Joseph Harsch in late 1975. "Americans have somehow blocked it out of their consciousness."

Ironically, many of those who served in Vietnam acquiesced in this conspiracy of silence—not out of shame but out of bitter experience with the indifference and hostility of their countrymen. Unlike servicemen in World War II who came home with their units to formal ceremonies of welcome, most Vietnam veterans returned by themselves to the emptiness of an airport waiting lounge. Transported back to the United States with no time for readjustment, they were left to their own devices in a nation increasingly uncomfortable with their presence.

The veterans discovered that both ends of the political spectrum had rejected them. To those who backed the war they were losers. To those who protested the war they were either fools or criminals. "When I arrived in L.A. the first people I saw who were my own age gave me a look of such overwhelming contempt I felt as if they had slapped me in the face," recalled a former 1st Cav platoon leader. Others recoiled from movies and television shows that depicted Vietnam veterans as psychotic killers or freaked-out drug abusers.

In fact, the vast majority of veterans readjusted well to civilian life. Some became successful businessmen, professional athletes, actors, and elected officials (including within a decade of the war's end two governors and three U.S. senators). Most simply settled down like others of their generation. "We're just ordinary guys," said one veteran. "We live ordinary lives; we have wives and kids and ordinary jobs. We're OK. But you never hear about us. You only hear about the guys who are messed up." In a country unwilling to face its own responsibility for the past, the "taint" of Vietnam persisted. It became easier for some men to avoid the insults and disdain by simply hiding the fact that they had been in Vietnam. Said one New York City native, "When I go out for jobs, I don't put down that I was a vet. People think you're a time bomb or an addict."

Those fears, however compounded by guilt or ignorance, also reflected the very real problems of a minority of Vietnam veterans. In most cases these afflictions tormented only the individual; occasionally, the pain and anger turned outward in violence toward others. In either case, veterans initially found little help from the government in whose name they had served.

Nearly 100,000 Americans left Vietnam with acute physical disabilities, ranging from amputated limbs to shattered spines to blindness. Thousands more returned to the United States addicted to drugs or alcohol. A 1971 Harris survey indicated that 26 percent of Vietnam veterans took drugs, including at least 7 percent who were addicted to heroin or cocaine. Seven years later the Veterans Administration reported that alcoholics or problem drinkers accounted for 31 percent of the VA hospital population.

Less well recognized was a collection of infirmities—chronic skin rashes, respiratory problems, impaired hearing and vision, violent headaches, loss of sex drive, and cancer—resulting from exposure to a chemical defoliant called Agent Orange. Widely used in Vietnam to deny cover to the enemy and to clear friendly perimeters, the herbicide not only produced a multitude of problems for its original victims but also was suspected of causing higher rates of stillbirths and birth defects among their children.

Even more insidious were the hidden, psychological wounds that some veterans suffered. These disorders took the form of extreme restlessness, depression, sleep disturbance, and paranoia. Such problems were particularly acute for combat veterans, many of whom wrestled for years to suppress a nameless anger they were barely able to contain. "No matter how much I was able to keep a lid on it," said one former infantryman, "I was always aware that just beneath the surface there was this rage, this tremendous, almost uncontrollable volatility that I somehow had to absorb." Others became victims of Post-Traumatic Stress Disorder (PTSD), in which the individual actually re-experienced traumatic incidents—often as recurring nightmares, sometimes in the form of psychotic hallucinations.

The terror, guilt, and rage that frequently accompanied such episodes contributed to a suicide rate among veterans substantially higher than that for nonveterans of their generation. Psychological disorders and substance abuse also played a large role in the disturbing number of violent crimes committed by men who had experienced heavy combat and in occasional outbursts of unprovoked violence that claimed the lives of family members and total strangers.

Unfortunately, the Veterans Administration had neither the facilities, resources, nor understanding to cope with the manifold problems encountered by Vietnam vets. In response to complaints that its hospitals and clinics were overcrowded, unsanitary, and understaffed, the VA blamed Congress for insufficient funds. But VA officials could not escape responsibility for a lack of communication with the veteran population and an unwillingness to confront the unconventional ailments of a new generation of servicemen. Despite additional funds, new programs, and a concerted effort to increase the number of Vietnam veterans employed by the agency, many vets complained that the bureaucracy remained unresponsive and insensitive. The VA refused to accept PTSD as a diagnosis meriting treatment until 1981 and continued to insist there was no proof that exposure to Agent Orange could cause serious illness or death.

Seemingly rejected by the larger society, unable to find the help they needed from the government, Vietnam veterans broke through their self-imposed isolation and banded together in their own defense. The first self-help efforts began in the mid-1970s with discussion groups and vocational training programs in California and a successful employment referral service in Detroit. Then, in 1978, a disabled ex-Marine named Robert Muller founded the Vietnam Veterans of America, the most visible of several national Vietnam veterans organizations. The VVA initiated a vigorous lobbying campaign in Washington, finding an ally in President Jimmy Carter, who upgraded veterans' services across the board and appointed a former Vietnam combat officer, Max Cleland, as director of the Veterans Administration. The VVA went on to take up the cause of the MIAs, fight for official recognition of PTSD, support victims of Agent Orange, help form the Vietnam Veterans in Congress caucus, and shepherd two job-training acts through Capitol Hill. Perhaps the VVA's greatest accomplishment was Operation Outreach, a Congressionally funded, independent counseling program for Vietnam veterans. By 1983 its 137 centers had assisted more than 200,000 veterans.

The legislation, the rehabilitation programs, were all vitally necessary. But still lacking was any larger national recognition for the men and women who served in Vietnam and for the sacrifices of those who had not returned. Once again, the veterans had to look to themselves for the answer. In 1979, the same year that Robert Muller began the VVA, a former army infantryman named Jan Scruggs started raising money to build a Vietnam veterans memorial in Washington, D.C. Over the next three years Scruggs and many others labored to make his dream a reality. In the process, they ignited passions that had once divided the nation. But this time the storm acted as a catharsis: On Veterans Day 1982, the dedication of the memorial became a celebration of national reconciliation. "We waited fifteen years to get here, man," said one former soldier, still wearing the patch of the 101st Airborne Division on his faded green fatigues. "But it's not too late. I'm just proud to be here. We made it. It's like coming home."

From atop his father's shoulders, Gary
Wright III from northern Virginia peers at
the inscription on the Vietnam Veterans
Memorial of his grandfather's name, Gary
Wright, Sr., a colonel in Vietnam listed
as missing in action.

Above. *A couple mourns for a loved one lost in Vietnam.*

Left. *Two visitors examine a name on the memorial during the dedication of the nearby Frederick Hart statue in November 1984. Hart's traditional figure of three American soldiers was placed near the wall to accommodate those veterans who felt the original memorial was an inappropriate commemoration for those who fought in Indochina.*

Three Vietnam veterans share their emotions before the memorial. Thousands of people file past its polished granite walls each day, making it one of the more frequently visited monuments in Washington, D.C.

SELECTED
BIBLIOGRAPHY

Note: In the course of researching the Vietnam War, the authors have consulted unpublished documents, archival sources, first-person accounts, and interviews too numerous to list here. What follows is a selected list of their sources.

Amter, Joseph A. *Vietnam Verdict*. Continuum, 1982.

Anderton, David A. *The History of the U.S. Air Force*. Crescent Bks., 1981.

Arlen, Michael J. *The Living Room War*. Viking Press, 1969.

Bain, Chester A. *Vietnam: The Roots of Conflict*. Prentice-Hall. 1967.

Baskir, Lawrence M., and William A. Strauss. *Chance and Circumstance*, Alfred A. Knopf. 1978.

BDM Corporation. *A Study of the Strategic Lessons Learned in Vietnam*. Vols. 1–8. National Technical Information Service, 1980.

Berger, Carl, ed. *The United States Air Force in Southeast Asia, 1961–1973*. Office of Air Force History, 1977.

Bowman, John S., ed. *The Vietnam War Almanac*. World Almanac Publications/Bison Bks., 1985.

Braestrup, Peter. *Big Story: How the American Press and Television Reported and Interpreted the Crisis of Tet 1968 in Vietnam and Washington*. Westview Press, 1977.

Burchett, Wilfred G. *Vietnam: The Inside Story of the Guerrilla War*. International Publishers, 1965.

Butler, David. *The Fall of Saigon: Scenes from the Sudden End of a Long War*. Simon & Schuster, 1985.

Caputo, Philip. *A Rumor of War*. Ballantine Bks., 1977.

Casey, Michael, et al. *The Army at War*. Boston Publishing Co., 1987.

_____ . *Flags into Battle*. Boston Publishing Co., 1987.

Charlton, Michael, and Anthony Moncrieff. *Many Reasons Why: The American Involvement in Vietnam*. Hill & Wang, 1978.

Cooper, Chester L. *The Lost Crusade: America in Vietnam*. Fawcett Publications, 1972.

Dawson, Alan. *55 Days: The Fall of South Vietnam*. Prentice-Hall, 1977.

Dougan, Clark, and David Fulghum. *The Fall of the South*. Boston Publishing Co., 1986.

Dougan, Clark, and Stephen Weiss. *Nineteen Sixty-Eight*. Boston Publishing Co., 1983.

Doyle, Edward, and Samuel Lipsman. *America Takes Over*. Boston Publishing Co., 1982.

_____ . *Setting the Stage*. Boston Publishing Co., 1981.

Doyle, Edward, Samuel Lipsman, and Terrence Maitland. *The North*. Boston Publishing Co., 1986.

Doyle, Edward, Samuel Lipsman, and Stephen Weiss. *Passing the Torch*. Boston Publishing Co., 1981.

Doyle, Edward, and Stephen Weiss. *A Collision of Cultures*. Boston Publishing Co., 1984.

Draper, Theodore. *Abuse of Power*. Viking Press, 1967.

Drendel, Lou. *The Air War in Vietnam*. Arco Publishing Co., 1968.

Ehrhart, W.D. *Vietnam–Perkasie: A Combat Marine Memoir*. McFarland & Co., 1983.

Emerson, Gloria. *Winners & Losers*. Harcourt Brace Jovanovich, 1976.

Fallaci, Oriana. *Interview with History*. Translated by John Shepley. Liveright, 1976.

Fallows, James. "What Did You Do in the Class War,

Daddy?" *Washington Monthly*, October 1975.

FitzGerald, Frances. *Fire in the Lake: The Vietnamese and the Americans in Vietnam*. Vintage Bks., 1973.

Fowler, Will. *The Vietnam Story*. Chartwell Bks., 1983.

Frook, John. "Here's a New Crop—From Civilians to Sad Sacks." *Life*, August 20, 1965.

Fulghum, David, and Terrence Maitland. *South Vietnam on Trial*. Boston Publishing Co., 1984.

Gallup, George H. *The Gallup Poll: Public Opinion, 1935–1971*. Random, 1972.

Gallup Organization. *Gallup Opinion Index*. Gallup, June 1965–January 1981.

Gitlin, Todd. *The Whole World is Watching*. Univ. of California Press, 1980.

Glasser, Ronald J., M.D. *365 Days*. George Braziller, 1980.

Gravel, Sen. Mike, ed. *The Pentagon Papers*. Vols. I–IV. Beacon Press, 1971.

Halberstam, David. *The Best and the Brightest*. Random House, 1972.

———. *The Making of a Quagmire*. Random House, 1964.

———. *The Powers That Be*. Alfred A. Knopf, 1979.

———. *The Unfinished Odyssey of Robert F. Kennedy*. Random House, 1968.

Herr, Michael. *Dispatches*. Alfred A. Knopf, 1977.

Herring, George C. *America's Longest War: The United States and Vietnam, 1950–1975*. John Wiley & Sons, 1979.

Herrington, Stuart A. *Peace with Honor: An American Reports on Vietnam 1973–1975*. Presidio Press, 1983.

———. *Silence Was a Weapon: The Vietnam War in the Villages*. Presidio Press, 1982.

Hersh, Seymour. *My Lai 4: A Report on the Massacre and Its Aftermath*. Vintage Bks., 1970.

Hodgson, Godfrey. *America in Our Time: From World War II to Nixon*. Doubleday, 1976.

Hoopes, Townsend. *The Limits of Intervention*. Revised edition. David McKay Co., 1973.

Hosmer, Stephen T. *Viet Cong Repression and Its Implications for the Future*. Heath, 1970.

Hosmer, Stephen T. et al., eds. *The Fall of South Vietnam: Statements by Vietnamese Military and Civilian Leaders*. Crane, Russak, & Co., 1980.

Isaacs, Arnold R. *Without Honor: Defeat in Vietnam and Cambodia*. Johns Hopkins Univ. Press, 1983.

Isaacs, Arnold R., and Gordon Hardy. *Pawns of War*. Boston Publishing Co., 1987.

Jennings, Patrick. *Battles of the Vietnam War*. Exeter Bks., 1985.

Johnson, Lyndon Baines. Presidential Papers of Lyndon Baines Johnson (unpublished). White House Central File, National Security File, White House Aides File, Meeting Notes File, Declassified and Sanitized Documents, Oral History Interviews. Lyndon Baines Johnson Library, Austin, Texas.

———. *The Vantage Point*. Holt, Rinehart, & Winston, 1971.

Kahin, George McTurnan, and John W. Lewis. *The United States in Vietnam*. Dell Publishing Co., 1969.

Karnow, Stanley. *Vietnam: A History*. Penguin Bks., 1983.

Kearns, Doris. *Lyndon Johnson and the American Dream*. Harper & Row, 1976.

Kissinger, Henry A. *White House Years*. Little, Brown, 1979.

———. *Years of Upheaval*. Little, Brown, 1982.

Le Gro, Col. William E. *Vietnam from Cease-Fire to Capitulation*. U.S. Army Center of Military History, 1981.

Lewy, Guenter. *America in Vietnam*. Oxford Univ. Press, 1978.

Lifton, Robert J. *Home from the War*. Simon & Schuster, 1973.

Lipsman, Samuel, and Edward Doyle. *Fighting for Time*. Boston Publishing Co., 1983.

Lipsman, Samuel, and Stephen Weiss. *The False Peace*. Boston Publishing Co., 1985.

Maclear, Michael. *The Ten Thousand Day War: Vietnam, 1945–1975*. St. Martin's Press, 1981.

MacPherson, Myra. *Long Time Passing: Vietnam and the Haunted Generation*. Doubleday, 1984.

Maitland, Terrence, and Peter McInerney. *A Contagion of War*. Boston Publishing Co., 1983.

Maitland, Terrence, and Stephen Weiss. *Raising the Stakes*. Boston Publishing Co., 1982.

Manning, Robert, and Michael Janeway, eds. *Who We Are*. Atlantic–Little, Brown, 1969.

Matusow, Allen J. *The Unraveling of America: A History of Liberalism in the 1960s*. Harper & Row, 1984.

Millett, Allan R. *Semper Fidelis: The History of the United States Marine Corps*. Macmillan, 1980.

Morrocco, John. *Rain of Fire: Air War, 1969–1973*. Boston Publishing Co., 1985.

———. *Thunder from Above: Air War, 1941–1968*. Boston Publishing Co., 1984.

Moskin, J. Robert. *The U.S. Marine Corps Story*. Paddington Press, 1979.

Murphy, Jack. *History of the U.S. Marines*. Exeter Bks., 1984.

Nalty, Bernard C. "Seventy-Seven Days: The Siege of Khe Sanh," from *The Vietnam War*. Salamander, 1980.

National Advisory Commission on Civil Disorders. *Report of National Advisory Commission on Civil Disorders*. Bantam Bks., 1968.

Nixon, Richard. *RN: The Memoirs of Richard Nixon.* Grosset & Dunlap, 1978.

Oberdorfer, Don. *Tet!* Doubleday, 1971.

Palmer, Gen. Bruce, Jr. *The 25-Year War: America's Military Role in Vietnam.* Univ. Press of Kentucky, 1984.
Parrish, John A., M.D. *12, 20 & 5: A Doctor's Year in Vietnam.* Penguin Bks., 1972.
Pearson, Lt. Gen. Willard. *The War in the Northern Provinces 1966-1968.* Dept. of the Army, 1975.
Peatross, Brig. Gen. O.F., and Col. W.G. Johnson. "Operation Utah," *Marine Corps Gazette,* November 1966.
Pike, Douglas. *Viet Cong.* The M.I.T. Press, 1966.
Pimlott, John, ed. *Vietnam: The History and the Tactics.* Crescent Bks., 1982.
Pisor, Robert. *The End of the Line: The Siege of Khe Sanh.* Norton, 1982.
Polenberg, Richard. *One Nation Divisible.* Viking Press, 1970.
Pratt, John Clark. *Vietnam Voices.* Penguin Bks., 1984.
President's Commission on Campus Unrest. *Report of President's Commission on Campus Unrest.* GPO, 1970.

Race, Jeffrey. *War Comes to Long An: Revolutionary Conflict in a Vietnamese Province.* Univ. of California Press, 1972.
"Renaissance in the Ranks," *Time,* December 10, 1965.

Sale, Kirkpatrick. *SDS.* Vintage Bks., 1973.
Schandler, Herbert Y. *The Unmaking of a President: Lyndon Johnson and Vietnam.* Princeton Univ. Press, 1977.
Schlesinger, Arthur M., Jr. *A Thousand Days: John F. Kennedy in the White House.* Houghton Mifflin Co., 1965.
Searle, John R. *The Campus War.* New World Publishing Co., 1971.
Shaplen, Robert. *The Lost Revolution: The U.S. in Vietnam, 1946-1966.* Harper & Row, 1966.
Shawcross, William. *Sideshow: Kissinger, Nixon and the Destruction of Cambodia.* Simon & Schuster, 1979.
Shulimson, Jack. *U.S. Marines in Vietnam, An Expanding War: 1966.* U.S. Marine Corps, 1982.
Simmons, Brig. Gen. Edwin H. *The Marines in Vietnam, 1954-1973.* U.S. Marine Corps, 1974.
——. *The United States Marines, 1775-1975.* Viking Press, 1976.
Snepp, Frank. *Decent Interval.* Vintage Bks., 1977.
Stanton, Shelby L. *The Rise and Fall of an American Army: U.S. Ground Forces in Vietnam, 1965-1973.* Presidio Press, 1985.
——. *Vietnam Order of Battle.* U.S. News Bks., 1981.
Summers, Harry G., Jr. *Vietnam War Almanac.* Facts on File Publications, 1985.

Sweetman, Jack. "Command of the Sea: The U.S. Navy in Vietnam." Unpublished manuscript, 1987.
Szulc, Tad. *The Illusion of Peace: Foreign Policy in the Nixon Years.* Viking Press, 1978.

Tarr, Curtis W. *By the Numbers: The Reform of the Selective Service System, 1970-1972.* National Defense Univ., 1981.
Telfer, Maj. Gary L., Lieut. Col. Lane Rogers, and V. Keith Fleming, Jr. *U.S. Marines in Vietnam: Fighting the North Vietnamese, 1967.* U.S. Marine Corps, 1984.
Tran Van Tra, Sr. Gen. *Vietnam: History of the Bulwark B-2 Theatre.* Vol. 5, *Concluding the 30-Years War.* GPO, 1983.

Van Tien Dung, Sr. Gen. *Our Great Spring Victory.* Translated by John Spragens, Jr. Monthly Review Press, 1977.

Weiss, Stephen, et al. *A War Remembered.* Boston Publishing Co., 1986.
Welsh, Douglas. *The History of the Vietnam War.* Galahad Bks., 1981.
Westmoreland, Gen. William C. *A Soldier Reports.* Dell Publishing Co., 1980.
White, Theodore H. *The Making of the President 1968.* Atheneum, 1969.

PICTURE CREDITS

Cover
Larry Burrows—LIFE Magazine, © 1966 Time Inc.

The Roots of Involvement
p. 1, Larry Burrows—LIFE Magazine, © 1966 Time Inc. pp. 4-5, © Larry Burrows Collection. pp. 8-9, Larry Burrows—LIFE Magazine, © 1966 Time Inc. pp. 10, 14-15, Robert Capa—Magnum.

The Road to War
p. 16, Larry Burrows—LIFE Magazine, © 1964 Time Inc. p. 19, AP/Wide World. pp. 20-21, Larry Burrows—LIFE Magazine, © 1964 Time Inc. p. 25, AP/Wide World. pp. 26-27, Jerry Rose—LIFE Magazine, © 1964 Time Inc. p. 29, James Pickerell—Black Star. pp. 30-31, © Larry Burrows Collection. p. 33, Bill Eppridge—LIFE Magazine, © 1965 Time Inc.

Training
p. 37, Mark Kauffman—LIFE Magazine, © 1965 Time Inc. pp. 38, 39 top left, bottom left & right, Bob Gomel—LIFE Magazine, © 1965 Time Inc. p. 39 top right, Mark Kauffman—LIFE Maga-

zine, © 1965 Time Inc. p. 40, Richard Stack—Black Star. p. 41, U.S. Army. pp. 42–43, David Lomax—Camera Press Ltd.

ARVN and Its Advisers
pp. 49–51, © Larry Burrows Collection. pp. 52–55, Larry Burrows—LIFE Magazine, © 1963 Time Inc.

America Takes Over
p. 56, Co Rentmeester—LIFE Magazine, © 1965 Time Inc. p. 59, Bill Ray—LIFE Magazine, © 1965 Time Inc. pp. 60–61, Larry Burrows—LIFE Magazine, © 1966 Time Inc. p. 63, Bill Ray—LIFE Magazine, © 1965 Time Inc. p. 65, Paul Schutzer—LIFE Magazine, © 1965 Time Inc. p. 67, AP/Wide World. p. 68, Paul Schutzer—LIFE Magazine, © 1965 Time Inc. p. 70, Y.R. Okamoto, Courtesy LBJ Library. p. 73, Bunyo Ishikawa.

Masher/White Wing
p. 77, Henri Huet—AP/Wide World. pp. 78–79, Henri Huet—Hal Moore Collection. pp. 80–85, Henri Huet—AP/Wide World.

Prairie
pp. 88–89, Co Rentmeester—LIFE Magazine, © 1966 Time Inc. pp. 90–91, © Larry Burrows Collection. pp. 92–94, Larry Burrows—LIFE Magazine, © 1966 Time Inc. p. 95, © Larry Burrows Collection.

Stalemate
p. 98, Larry Burrows—LIFE Magazine, © 1967 Time Inc. p. 101, Mark Jury. pp. 102–103, Richard Swanson—LIFE Magazine, © Time Inc. p. 104, Co Rentmeester—LIFE Magazine, © 1967 Time Inc. p. 107, Catherine Leroy/Gamma-Liaison. p. 108, Larry Burrows—LIFE Magazine, © 1967 Time Inc. pp. 110–111, Larry Burrows—LIFE Magazine, © 1966 Time Inc. p. 112, Lee Lockwood. p. 115, Bunyo Ishikawa. p. 117, Dana Stone—UPI/Bettmann Newsphotos.

Con Thien
pp. 122–131, David Douglas Duncan.

Hill 875
pp. 136–137, Gilles Caron/Gamma-Liaison. pp. 138–139, U.S. Army. pp. 140–141, Bunyo Ishikawa.

The Tet Offensive
p. 142, U.S. Army. p. 145, Co Rentmeester—LIFE Magazine, © Time Inc. pp. 147–149, UPI/Bettmann Newsphotos. pp. 150–151, U.S. Air Force. p. 153, Eddie Adams—AP/Wide World. p. 155, UPI/Bettmann Newsphotos. p. 156, Ghislain Bellorget. p. 159, UPI/Bettmann Newsphotos. pp. 160–161, Philip Jones Griffiths—Magnum.

Hue
pp. 167–175, Don McCullin—Magnum.

Khe Sanh
p. 179, Robert Ellison—Black Star. pp. 180–181, Richard Swanson—Black Star. p. 182, Richard Swanson—LIFE Magazine, © 1968 Time Inc. pp. 183–186, Robert Ellison—Black Star. pp. 187–189, Larry Burrows—LIFE Magazine, © 1968 Time Inc.

The Home Front
p. 192, Bill Ray—LIFE Magazine, © 1966 Time Inc. pp. 194–195, Charles Harbutt—Archive. p. 197, Bernard Boston. pp. 198–199, Co Rentmeester—LIFE Magazine, © 1965 Time Inc. p. 200, William James Warren. pp. 202, 205, Burt Glinn—Magnum. pp. 206–207, Gerry Uphan—LIFE Magazine, © Time Inc. p. 209, Bill Eppridge—LIFE Magazine, © 1968 Time Inc.

Chicago
p. 215, UPI/Bettmann Newsphotos. pp. 216–217, Fred W. McDarrah. p. 218, UPI/Bettmann Newsphotos. p. 219, Roger Malloch—Magnum. pp. 220–223, Jeffrey Blankfort—Jeroboam. p. 224, Mark Godfrey—Archive. p. 225, Perry C. Riddle. pp. 226–227, Hiroji Kubota—Magnum.

Nixon's War
p. 228, Vernon Merritt—LIFE Magazine, © Time Inc. p. 231, Alfred Eisenstaedt—LIFE Magazine, © Time Inc. pp. 232–233, Larry Burrows—LIFE Magazine, © Time Inc. pp. 236–237, © Tim Page. pp. 238–239, UPI/Bettmann Newsphotos. pp. 240–241, Charles Phillips—LIFE Magazine, © 1969 Time Inc. p. 243, Mark Jury. p. 245, John Filo, Courtesy *Valley News Dispatch.* pp. 246–247, Mark Jury.

The Cambodian Incursion
pp. 250–251, Bunyo Ishikawa. pp. 252–257, © Larry Burrows Collection. pp. 258–259, Philip Jones Griffiths—Magnum.

The Long Good-bye
p. 262, UPI/Bettmann Newsphotos. pp. 264–265, David Burnett—LIFE Magazine, © 1971 Time Inc. p. 267, Ron Haeberle—LIFE Magazine, © 1969 Time Inc. pp. 268–269, UPI/Bettmann Newsphotos. p. 271, Akihiko Okamura. p. 272, Mark Godfrey—Archive. p. 274, Henri Bureau—SYGMA. p. 277, Roger Pic/Gamma-Liaison. p. 279, Christine Spengler/Gamma-Liaison.

The Easter Offensive
p. 283, Agence France Presse. pp. 284–285, © David Burnett 1983—Contact. pp. 286–287, Mark Godfrey—Archive. p. 288, Ngo Vinh Long Collection. p. 289, UPI/Bettmann Newsphotos. pp. 290–291, © David Burnett 1987—Contact. p. 292, Thomas Billhardt, Berlin, GDR. p. 293, Claude La Fontan/Gamma-Liaison.

POW
p. 297, Thomas Billhardt, Berlin, GDR. p. 298, Horst Faas—AP/Wide World. pp. 299–300, Thomas Billhardt, Berlin, GDR. p. 301, Lee Lockwood. pp. 302–303, AP/Wide World.

The End and Aftermath
p. 306, J.A. Pavlovsky—SYGMA. pp. 308–309, Bunyo Ishikawa. pp. 312, 315, AP/Wide World. pp. 316–317, Jean-Claude Francolon/Gamma-Liaison. p. 319, UPI/Bettmann Newsphotos. pp. 320–321, Jean-Claude Francolon/Gamma-Liaison. pp. 322, 324–325, Hiroji Kubota—Magnum.

The Fall of Saigon
p. 328, © Nik Wheeler. p. 329, Nik Wheeler—Black Star. pp. 330–331, Françoise Demulder/Gamma-Liaison. p. 332, J.A. Pavlovsky—SYGMA. p. 333, UPI/Bettmann Newsphotos.

Coming Home
pp. 338–339, Seny Norasingh. p. 340, © 1984 Patricia Fisher—Folio. p. 341, John Ficara—Woodfin Camp. pp. 342–343, Peter Marlow—Magnum.

INDEX